The Origins, History and Achievements of

THE CRANCH FAMILY

By And Cranch

They Came To Kingsbridge, Settled

and then

Spread Around The World

Family Crest

The drawing on the front cover is by the author's mother when a young girl. In her home were many inherited papers and relics. In a tin box was some wax candles and a stamp used to make the seal on important documents. She copied this seal. The stamp has yet to be found again

THE ORIGINS, HISTORY AND ACHIEVEMENTS OF THE CRANCH FAMILY

By And Cranch

This book was first published in Great Britain in paperback during December 2021.

The moral right of And Cranch is to be identified as the author of this work and has been asserted by him in accordance with the Copyright, Designs and Patents Act of 1988.

All rights are reserved, and no part of this book may be produced or utilized in any format, or by any means, electronic or mechanical, including photocopying, recording or by any information storage or retrieval system, without prior permission in writing from the publishers - Coast & Country/Ads2life. ads2life@btinternet.com

All rights reserved.

ISBN: 979-8777894816

Copyright © December 2021 And Cranch

Copyright holders and sources are acknowledged with thanks. We apologise in advance if any copyholders have not been duly acknowledged. We would be pleased to insert the appropriate acknowledgement in any future edition or sequel. Please contact us with any questions or concerns.

With Thanks to my Aunt Naomi

who was a wonderful source of gossip

And to Renee and John

who made it all possible

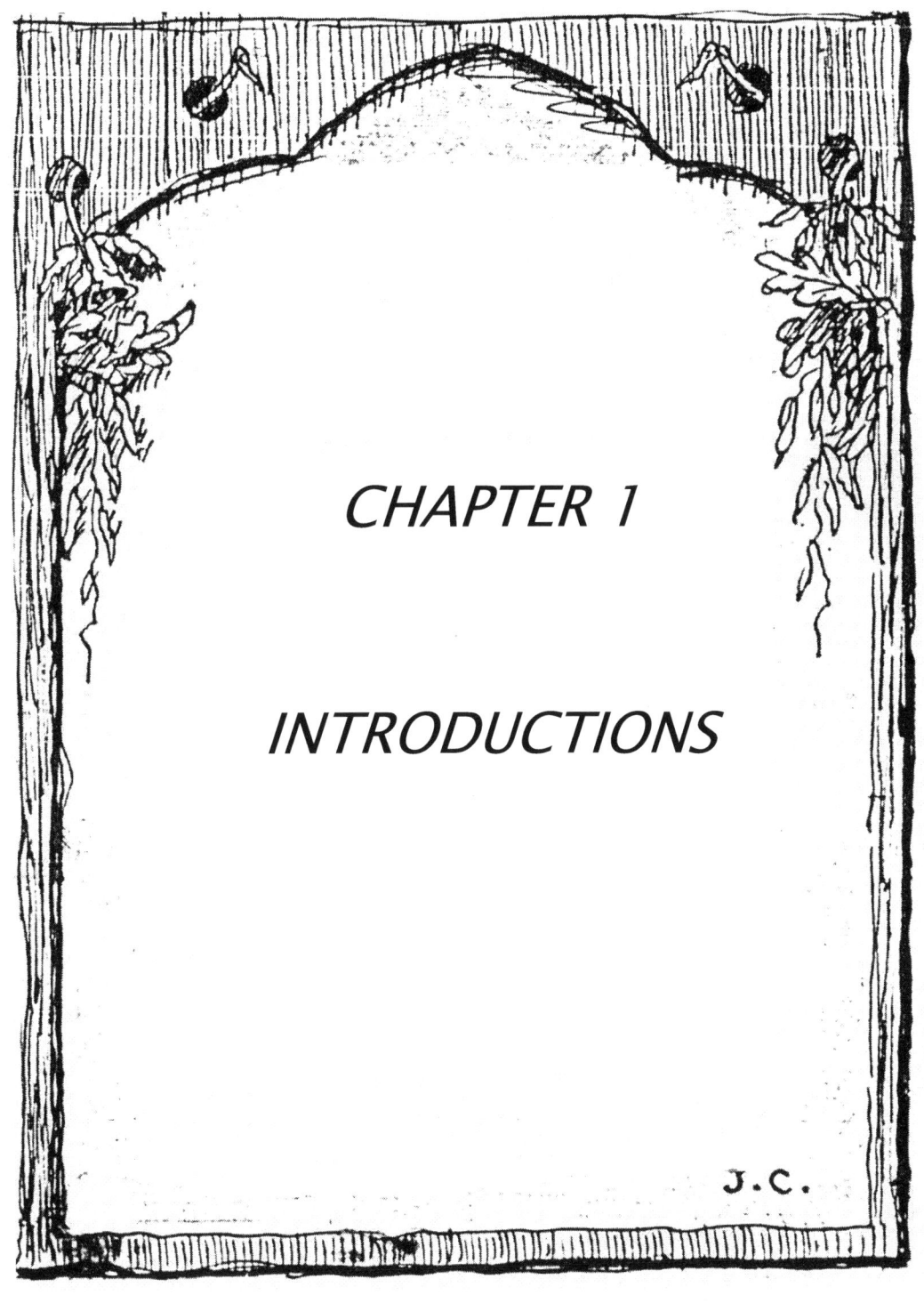

CHAPTER 1

INTRODUCTIONS

This frame and the sketches on all the Chapter lead-ins are from the notebooks of John Cranch the Painter.

PART ONE : INTRODUCTIONS

Chapter 1 Introductions

1.1 Contents of Book
Parts, chapters and their contents, charts within chapters.

1.2 Acknowledgements

1.3 Introducing the Cranch Family
Location, Family traits, Spellings of Cranch, Abbreviations, Family Trees and Charts, Superscripts, Contents of Chapters, Constraints, Why Publish?, Caution, The Cames.

1.4 The Charts – a Schematic

PART TWO : EARLY YEARS

Chapter 2 Early Kingsbridge

2.1 Early records
Parish Registers, Poll Tax, Subsidy Rolls, Hearth Tax, Conclusions, Yorkshire?

2.2 A Potted History of Kingsbridge
Shipping, Trade, Fish, Kingsbridge, West Alvington, Salcombe, Victor Ecclesiasticus 1534, Notable People

Chapter 3   The Woollen Trade

3.1 The Woollen trade in England in the Fourteenth Century
The Textile industry, Fulling, Social Change

3.2 The Woollen trade in Flanders in Thirteenth Century
Trade changes, migrations

3.3 The Woollen trade in Devon
Devon's Wool Trade, Devon Mills, The Clothier, References

3.4 The Woollen trade in Exeter in the 1600's
Exeter's Woollen Markets, Kersey, Serge, Merchants, Exports, Fulling and Mills

Chapter 4 The Cranch Family 1500-1700

4.1 Proposition on the Origins of the Cranch Family
Origins, Name

4.2 History of the Cranch Woollen Business
The Beginnings, Fulling, Shipping, Developments 1550-1650, Cloth trade after 1650, Farming after 1650, Cranches Farm

4.3 Earliest Known members of the Cranch family
Earliest members, The Two Trees, Crispin Connection

4.4 Chart - Andrew the Elder

4.5 Chart – Andrew the Younger

4.6 Chart - Early Richards

Chapter 5 Dissent

5.1 Civil War and Kingsbridge
Effects on Kingsbridge, Cranch sympathies, Turmoil

5.2 Dissent and Kingsbridge
Dissent and its consequences, Saltstone, Punishments, Rev Hicks, Declarations of Indulgence, Cranch Sympathies, References, Old painting

5.3 A Libellous Pamphlet
The 1821 Reprint, Explanations and Comment, the original A True and Faithful Narrative 1671

5.4 Continuing Protestantism (after 1700)
Cranch and Religion, a Satirical poem, G. Whitfield, Political Views

PART THREE : RICHARD TREE after about 1650
Chapter 6 Richard Tree after 1650
6.1   Introduction
6.2   Chart – Richard and Jone
6.3   Chart - Richard of Totnes
6.4   Chart - Richard and Anna of London
6.5   Chart – Richard and Mary of Shoreditch
6.6   Chart – Joseph, Thomas and John of Ireland
6.7   Family of Richard and Jone
Richard the Elder, the Reverend Richard, Joshua Reynolds, Richard's estate, John the Attorney, Richard the Vicar. Betsy, Mary
6.8   The family of Richard of Totnes
Richard (solicitor), Richard (dyer), James (weaver), grandson Richard
6.9   The family of Richard Charles Lovell Cranch
Richard CLC, Ellen Mary Bright, Charles L., George S., Archie L. and his daughters Patricia & Doreen, George brother of RCLC, Mary daughter of Richard and Anna
6.10 James and the Coat
An amusing story, Binnicknowle.

PART FOUR : TREE ANDREW after about 1720 - NATHANIEL [1]
Chapter 7 The Seven Children of John [2]
7.1   Introducing the Seven
7.2   Chart – John [3] of the Seven
7.3   Chart – Andrew [2] of the Seven
7.4   Chart – William of the Seven

Chapter 8 The Family of Nathaniel [1]
8.1   Chart – Nathaniel [1] of the Seven
8.2   Nathaniel[1] and His Descendants
Nathaniel[1], Salcombe Castle Key, Exeter contingent, His sons, Jackson the Organist, His Daughters, Roger Denbow C, grandchildren, Charlotte, Abigail's visit.

Chapter 9 John the Naturalist
9   John the Naturalist
Family Connections, Barrow's Account, Visit by British Museum, Appointment as Collector, Appointment to the Congo Expedition, The Congo Expedition, John's letter, Recognition, Newspaper Report, Notes and References, Monod's Booklet, a Recent Booklet.

Chapter 10 Jane Bowring Cranch
10.1 Jane Bowring Cranch
Family Connections, Property, Her Will, Bowring – Cranch Connections, Sir John Bowring, Collected and other Poems. Saltstone, Bolt Head, Poems in Newspapers
10.2 Chart – Bowring-Cranch Connections

PART FIVE : TREE ANDREW after about 1720 - JOSEPH [2]
Chapter 11 Family of Joseph [2]
11.1 Introduction
11.2 Chart – Joseph [2] of the Seven
11.3 Chart – Mary and the Wilcocks, Smith, Moginie families

Chapter 12 Richard and America

12.1 The First Cranches in America
Richard's Claim, Migrants after 1640, the Cranch Exodus in the 1700's, Mary, Joseph Palmer, Robert Garland C, Nathaniel [2], Joseph [4], Migrants after 1800s, T.S.Eliot

12.2 Richard
Portrait, Family Connections, America at that time, Outline of his Life, Family Life of Richard and Mary, Eulogies.

12.3 Chart – American Family of Richard

12.4 Chart – Mary Cranch, Pearse, Mead and Palmer families

12.5 The Bonds
William Bond, W.C Bond, Selina Cranch, Mary Roope Cranch, Cranch – Bond Connections, Mrs Brooks' Letter, Memorials

12.6 Chart – The Bonds of America

Chapter 13 John the Painter

13.1 An Introduction
Portrait, Outline of His Life, Self-Portrait, Character, Wit, Political Views, Travel and Friends, Later Years

13.2 Clerical work
John Knight, Simon Bunter and his Will, Travel to Spa, Letters, Adams' Visit to West Country, Publications, Lectures, Cromwell's Head.

13.3 The Artist and His Paintings
Assessment as a Painter, Man of Merit, Constable and the Edmonton circle, List of paintings, Notebooks, Salcombe Castle key and other Sketches.

13.4 Antiquities
"Expeditions", Antiquity Smith, Johes Cranch 1553, Mudie, Move to Bath, Bath and his Legacy

13.5 Obituaries
Gentlemen's Magazine, Bath Papers, his Will, Davidson's Biography, Tributes by Hawkins and others.

13.6 Uncommon genius
Some notes on the book

PART SIX : TREE ANDREW - JOSEPH [2] continued

Featuring **WILLIAM N CRANCH**,
his son **JOHN ROOPE CRANCH**
and **JOSEPH** [5] **and his Families**

Chapter 14 William N Cranch

14.1 Introduction
William N, his Pocket Book, Diary and Will, Mary's family (the Roopes), Aunt Sharland, Joseph [6] and his trip to Bath.

14.2 Chart - Lakeman Cranch, Curtis,

14.3 Norden
History of the Cranch family home, , Description by Hicks, The American Book, The Roopes at Norden, Mary [2] and Norden, Listing

Chapter 15 John Roope Cranch and South Brent

15.1 South Brent
Brent Village, Fair, , 3 Cranch families, The Primrose Line, Beating the Bounds Poem

15.2   John Roope Cranch
       John Roope C, His Family, Location, Obituary, Hannah, The Stidstons, Gravestones.
15.3   Chart – John Roope Cranch and A. William Cranch

Chapter 16   William Cranch Stidston Cranch
16.1   William Cranch Stidston Cranch
       His life, Vestry Meetings, Jubilee Day, Primrose Line, Tragic Death, his wife Mary.
16.2   John and His Family
       Sailor John, Vi and Leo, Josephine, London Bill
16.3   Richard and His Family
       Dick, Local Involvement, Australia, Death, Cissie, Hedley, Mary and her Will.
16.4   Mary
       Mary, Queensland
16.5   A. William
       Apprenticeship, Business, Interests, Family gatherings, Masonry and Church, Marriage, Hardship, The Great Fire, Death, Minnie
16.6   Ann
       Her Life, Will
16.7   A Pictorial Record

Chapter 17   Joseph [5] and his Families
17.1   Joseph [5]
       Joseph [5] and the Josephs of Kingsbridge
17.2   Chart – Joseph [5] and the Johns
17.3   Johns of Kingsbridge and South Brent.
       The Johns of Kingsbridge and South Brent, Cyril, William of Tavistock

PART SEVEN : MISCELLANEOUS
Chapter 18   Miscellany
M.1   Nathaniel of Exeter 1800
M 2   Cranch of New Zealand
M 3   Family Historians
       Family Historians, Aunt Ann's Notes, Further Notes, Lizzie Smith, Great Aunt Wilcocks, Wilcock Letters.

Ch. 1.2 Acknowledgements

Specific references are attributed in the relevant chapters.

The following General Sources and References (in no particular order) were used. Some sources have been used frequently, indicated by a **bold** abbreviation.

1. History of Kingsbridge and Salcombe by Anne Born 2002
2. The Family Genealogical Notebook, compiled ca 1872 by Nathaniel Cranch Peabody. Referred to hereafter as **Peabody**, this is a major source of information about the early Cranches. Some handwritten extracts are available at the Cookworthy Museum.
3. Cookworthy Museum, Kingsbridge
4. Parish Records: Births Marriages, Deaths, via various internet genealogical search engines
5. The Letters of Abigail Adams contained in two books: Dear Abigail and New Letters of Abigail
6. Exeter Dissenters Graveyard Trust
7. Devon Rural Archive at Modbury. (**DRA**)
8. Devon Heritage Centre (**DHC**). Many records still have Exeter City Library codes
9. Royal Albert Memorial Museum, Exeter (**RAMM**)
10. Family Archives (**F.A.**)
11. Salcombe, Kingsbridge and Neighbourhood by J. Fairweather
12. Kingsbridge and Salcombe, with the intermediate estuary historically and topographically depicted by A **Hawkins**, Esq. F.H. S. 1819
13. The Guide to Kingsbridge and neighbourhood (Devon & Exeter Library ref AD/KIN 02 WAY)
14. Massachusetts Historical Society, repository of most of the Adams, Cranch, Shaw and Peabody papers.
15. Boston Public Library
16. Devonshire Society of Arts and Sciences, Notes and Queries
17. Devonshire Association Transactions and Reports (**D.A.T.R.**)
18. Kingsbridge Estuary With Rambles In The Neighbourhood Compiled By S. P. **Fox**. 1864.

Sources used to establish the family trees
1. Peabody
2. The notebooks of John Cranch the Painter
3. Jane Bowring Cranch
4. A. W. Cranch (jun) and Mrs R.O. Cranch
5. Correspondence between Cranch family members.
6. Genealogical websites
7. Wills

Ch. 1.3 Introducing the Cranch Family

***Location, Family traits, Spellings of Cranch, Abbreviations,
Family Trees and Charts, Superscripts, Contents of Chapters,
Constraints, Why Publish?, Caution, The Cames.***

Location
The Cranch family were to be found in South Devon, particularly in the Kingsbridge area and hardly anywhere else.

Their name appears there in the earliest records (circa 1550- 1600) and with only a few in the London area

They were involved with the woollen trade and farming and many prospered. The family stayed in the area until the late 1700's, by which time members had migrated to other parts of southern Devon (Plymouth, Totnes, Exeter), London and to America.

They also diversified into other trades and professions. Many became solicitors. Some achieved national recognition.

By the late 1800's mortality and the exodus were such that one family historian [1] declared in a letter to her American cousins that she was "the only Cranch remaining in Kingsbridge". This was not strictly true. She was probably referring only to the branch she belonged to.

Cranches do still live in the South Hams, and in various parts of England. An important branch is in America. According to an American study [2] carried out in 1995, the number of residences occupied by a person with surname Cranch were estimated as about 120 in Great Britain, and another 120 elsewhere. A small number when compared with the more prevalent surnames.

Family traits
According to one source [3] probably referring to times before the mid-1700's:
> "The home of the Cranch family was in and around Kingsbridge. They were all given to books, with a marked artistic bent. ..."

Another writer [4] says;
> "The race of Cranch all had literary, artistic and poetic tendencies, they were always authors, poets, musicians and travellers in the family"

To this may be added "a sense of family", a trait which has been exhibited over the centuries. Another source [5] says that in the early 1700's "all the sons were brought up to trade". The trades and professions were not only those associated with woollen cloth manufacture but included saddlers, farmers, solicitors and ministers of religion. Another source says [6]:
> "Simple veracity and invariable fidelity to promises have ever distinguished the family we spring from".

To this may be added that one cannot help noticing how "painting" and "drawing" is frequently mentioned as a skill, hobby or indeed occupation of the family over the centuries.

If a few old pictures or photographs are any guide, one could detect the Germanic "Cranch nose" as an hereditary feature.

Ch. 1.3 Introducing the Cranch Family

Their beliefs very sympathetic to Dissent and the "freedom" cause. Most if not all were Protestants of various hues.

Spellings of Cranch
Often old records show considerable variation in how family names are spelt. Not so with Cranch. There are relatively few variations from Cranch. The few variations accepted for this history are Cranche, Craunch (as heard in the Devon dialect) Chranch and Crannch.

Variations such as Crinch or Crouch etc have been discounted as they are not supported by family knowledge, location or what may be termed "consistency". Cranich or Crannich is referred to in one instance. The sole early reference to a Crannich family has not been researched although they perhaps should be.

Some abbreviations used
Cranch surnames or the abbreviation C are not used except in cases of possible ambiguity (so John Cranch is just written as simply John, but John Roope Cranch is written as John Roope C.
- C   Cranch
- b,m,d   birth, marriage, death
- Kbg   Kingsbridge
- Marl   Marlborough, South Devon
- E.P.   East Portlemouth
- S.B.   South Brent

Many sources of information have also been abbreviated – see acknowledgements

Family Trees and Charts
Two distinct trees have been identified from the early times
The "Andrew" tree can be traced from Andrew the Elder 1560 – 1663.
A common theme for this tree is the use of the first names Andrew, or William or Joseph. Its branches include John Cranch the Painter, John Cranch the Naturalist, the Cranches of South Brent and the American Cranches. This author is in the Andrew tree.

The Richard tree can be traced from Richard born 1583 and has Richard and James as its most common first name. The tree includes the Rev. Richard of Modbury, Richard of Totnes (solicitor in 1700's) and thence the Richards of London (solicitors) and their descendants

These two trees run in parallel and were certainly known to each other. There are also a number of other Cranch members of unknown connections.

Both trees are represented in a series of Charts which attempt to trace their members from the earliest to the present. The actual charts are contained within the relevant chapters.

Names are contained in "boxes", linked to show their parentage and off-spring. Where either of these are unknown, no linkage is shown. The box will contain that person's dates of birth and death where known. Marriage date also or above the linkage to the person's spouse.

Ch. 1.3 Introducing the Cranch Family

For "births", up to about 1800 the dates are mostly those when a birth was registered (usually at baptism). This could be long after the actual day the child was born. After then the dates given are mostly actual dates of birth. In some cases both dates of birth and registering are available.

Continuation of non-Cranch families is generally not pursued unless the information was readily available or of relevant interest to the general history of the family

Superscripts
In the earlier chapters some names have superscripts e.g. John [1] to aid identification These are the ones originally used by a family historian (Peabody) even though that John may not actually be the first John Cranch. These suffixes have been kept to aid tracing the original source.
Otherwise a family member is identified by means such as his/her dates of birth and/or death, by initials, or by a label unique to the family in context (e.g. Eliza the Historian).

Contents of Chapters
There is no index. The book follows (roughly) a chronological order as do the charts. It is divided into several parts, each part corresponding to an approximate period of time. Chapters describe what is known about the family within that time. "Worthies" (significant members of the Cranch family) tend to have their own chapters.

Constraints
Many of the Cranch family fortunately made and kept family documents such as letters, wills or notes about birthdays. In many cases these notes are the only record surviving. Three main events have contributed to a lack of records:
- A WW2 bomb fell on the Congregational Church at Kingsbridge which destroyed its records and memorials.
- A WW2 bomb that created a fire in the Exeter Library which at that time housed the Devon Records. It is unknown what records were lost forever.
- Dissent – those dissenting from the established church may not have used it to register the births, marriages or deaths of their family, and the registers of the embryo non-conformist chapels may not have survived.

Why Publish?
Many members of the Cranch family and its offshoots have been fascinated by its name, location and origins. Many theories have been made. I had two main objectives:
1. to try to establish our origins once and for all
2. to describe the family and put our more notable members into a context that can be used as a reference.

The context requires a knowledge of times past. I have attempted to provide that context but by no means may I be considered to be a historian.
The contributions of other family historians are discussed at the end of the book.

A Caution
In view of the scale of this project, no guarantees are given as to absolute accuracy. It is not a work that can ever be said to be complete either.
Publication is being made now for several reasons. Quite apart from the world-wide pandemic, certain records in America are going to remain unobtainable for another

Ch. 1.3 Introducing the Cranch Family

two years, and access to other records in England is proving difficult. Further the mushrooming of the general population since the 1800's makes the task of tracing everyone who may be of interest huge.

It remains to be seen how to cater for the expected corrections and additions and events after about 1900.

The Cames
The families of Came and Cranch became associated through marriage in the 19th and 20th centuries. The earliest Parish registers show that the name of Came appears in proliferation in Somerset with only a few elsewhere including York. Is this a co-incidence? Perhaps the Came family has a back-ground similar to the Cranch family, choosing Somerset not Devon for their operations?

References in this chapter
- [1] *Jane Bowring Cranch correspondence*
- [2] *Burke's Peerage World of Cranches 1995*
- [3] *Memoirs of William Cranch Bond & George Phillips Bond 1897:*
- [4] *Obituary notice of death of Hannah Cranch Bond, Dorchester USA March 1870*
- [5] *Peabody*
- [6] *John the Painter in a letter to his nephew James Cranch Wilcocks 1802*

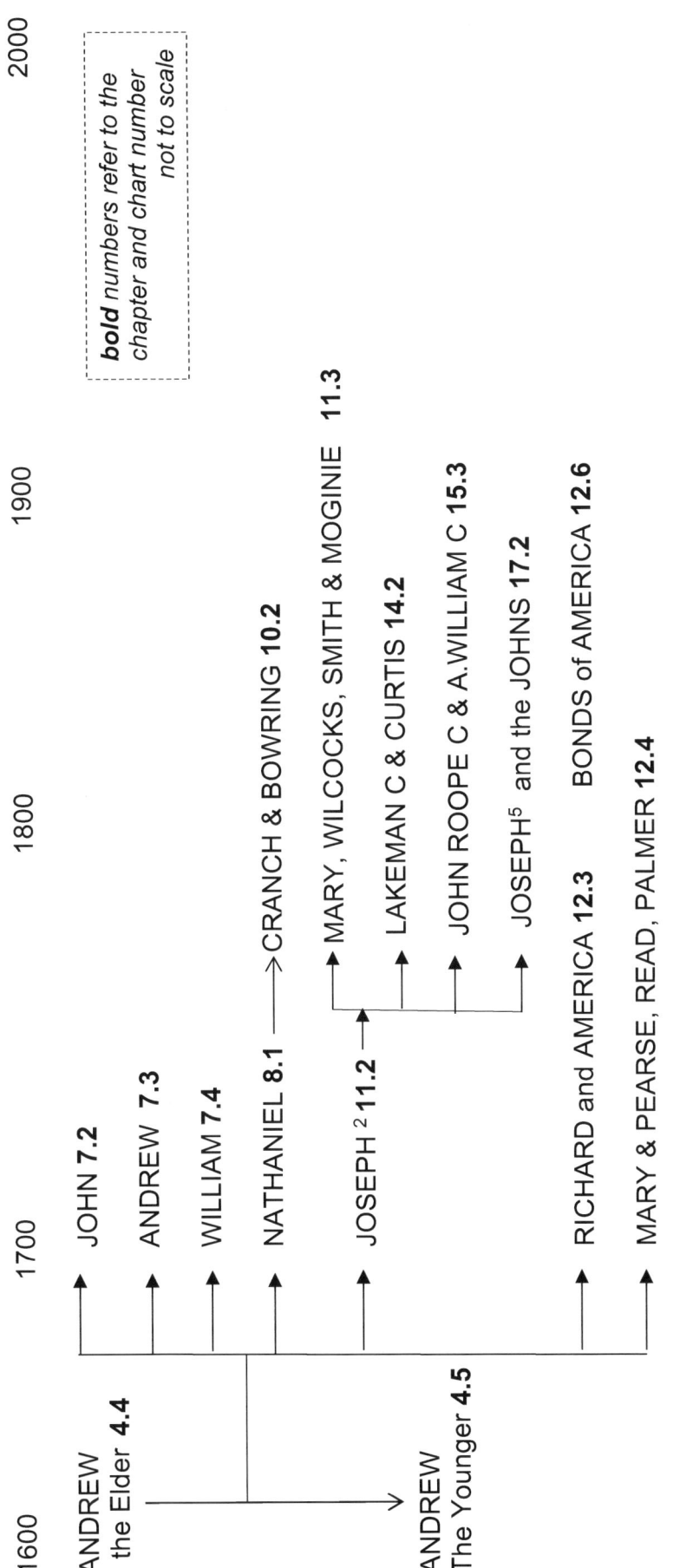

1.4 The Charts – a Schematic

CHAPTER 2
EARLY KINGSBRIDGE

Maria Bowring 1806

Ch 2.1 Early Records   *1*

Parish Registers, Poll Tax, Subsidy Rolls, Hearth Tax, Conclusions, Yorkshire?

Parish Registers
A listing of all references to Cranch in the earliest Parish registers from about 1550 to 1620 shows that the name of Cranch appears only in South Devon with a few in the London area:
- Marlborough, near Kingsbridge (many). It was the principal church of the area. Salcombe for instance had only a part-time sister chapel, so Marlborough held all the significant church activities
- Kingsbridge (some)
- South Huish (some)
- Kent (Cranbook, Wye, Canterbury) (3)
- Chelmsford Essex (1 family)

Valor Ecclesiasticus 1534 includes the East Portlemouth church in the Woodleigh Deanery. The records for East Portlemouth are lost, so no conclusion should be drawn about the apparent dominance of Marlborough. The Parish Book of Marlborough begins November 1558 with a reference to an earlier register (presumed lost)
The **Poll Tax** 1377 gives no mention of any Cranch in the Coleridge Hundred (i.e. the Kingsbridge area).

The Subsidy of 1581 (a tax on goods and land) shows.
- Andrew C   E. Portlemouth rated at   10/4   i.e ten shillings
- Andrew C jun   "   1/3   and four old
- Margery Craunch   Marlborough   3/-   pence
- Edward Chraunch   "   8/-
- Richard Chraunch   "   -/3

Thus there was a significant presence on the E. Portlemouth side of the river. Andrew senior was a rator, but had his business in the Marlborough diocese area as indicated in his will.
The **Subsidy Rolls** 1588/9 record no Cranch in Ashburton

A hundred years later, the **Hearth Tax** returns of 1674 shows that
- Andrew C   East Portlemouth   had   4 hearths
- Richard C   Stokenham   3
- Jone C   S.Huish   1 (exempt –poore)
- Roger C   Dartmouth   1
- Peter C   Stonehouse (Plymouth)   1 hearth
- Bes C   Ashburton   3 hearths

The significant early Cranch settlements would appear to have been on the East Portlemouth side of the river. There is no reference to a Cranch in (West) Alvington but the will of Andrew the Elder (died in 1624) gives him as owning or leasing property nearby at Batson (Salcombe).

There are also some unexplained anomalies: according to the Reperacon circa 1600 for E. Portlemouth church, no Cranch was charged rates. The Devon Protestation returns for E.Portlemouth show no Cranch registered.

Early Records

In 1879 the Duke of Cleveland demolished much of East Portlemouth and re-organised the farms there. A campaigner against this action described it as
"a community whose forebears had lived in the village since the Conquest"

East Portlemouth viewed from Salcombe   DRA.IB.000957

Conclusions
A conclusion is that the Cranch family arrived sometime between 1377 (poll tax data) and 1550 (first church records).

A popular conjecture is that the Cranch family arrived in the waves following William the Conqueror 1066 (or other notable events later). From the above information this seems unlikely, even though they may initially have settled in East Portlemouth.

There are no indications or traditions that the family were involved with fishing - a feature of port life in those times.

The Family Genealogical Notebook, compiled circa 1872 by Nathaniel Cranch Peabody, a descendant of a "worthy" who went to America, contains the following assertion:
> "The Cranch or Crantz family is believed to have come from the Netherlands in Queen Elizabeth's' time. Some of the family settled in Devonshire. Tradition places them in Yorkshire previously."

This provides an alternative explanation even if the date of arrival given by Peabody must be wrong (the Q.E.1 reign was 1558 -1603).

Yorkshire?
The assertion raises a number of questions. Why Yorkshire? When ? and Why? There is a clue in the wills of the early Cranches. They were associated with the woollen trade. This is explored in the next Chapter. First a brief outline of the Kingsbridge area in these earlier times.

Ch 2.2 A Potted History of Kingsbridge

Shipping, Trade, Fish, Kingsbridge, West Alvington, Salcombe, Valor Ecclesiasticus 1534, Notable People

Shipping

Trading ships visited S. Devon coastal ports from earliest times. In C12 the trade included wine from Normandy, limestone for church arcades. The main port was on the east side of the estuary - East Portlemouth.

It had significant trading, shipbuilding and fishing industries as well as farming, quarrying & smuggling. It was charged with raising warships and men for the King's battles. It supplied ships and men to the king in the 1300's, giving an indication of its size and importance.

In early times shipping in the South Devon area came under the customs control of Exeter and Dartmouth. Dartmouth itself then was one of the five most important ports of England.

Trade

Devon exported cloth which was the most esteemed in England from late 1500's for 200 years. There was a cottage industry of wool carders & spinners in every village. Batson was renowned for its cider orchards and exports

Dodbrook was famous for a "white ale" made from malt, hops, eggs & flour, fermented with a "grout" to a secret recipe.

Markets were established in Kingsbridge in 1219, Dodbrook 1257 (which is referred to in the Doomsday Book), Portlemouth 1280, and Salcombe had one once a year.

According to the Rev. W. Willis Price in his history of East Portlemouth Church
> "During the 14th century at a time when the rest of England was suffering severe depression , the South Hams found itself able to enlarge and in some cases substantially to re-build ..(churches) .....due to a revived tin industry and an expanding cloth trade."

Fish

There was a trade in dried fish in 1300's. In 1500's Salcombe was described as Fish Town. There were large scale pilchard fisheries all along S. Devon Coast right through to 1800's, when the pilchards largely disappeared. Similarly with dried salted other fish such as hake. Customs officials took large sums in duty in 1600's.

The opening up of the Newfoundland Banks for cod fishing in the 1500's through to the late 1700's was a significant step for Salcombe. It had 5 ships registered

Kingsbridge

The Abbot of Buckfastleigh carved out the new borough of Kingsbridge soon after 1220 from his manor of Churchstow   *(Hoskins 1954).*

The Manor of Kingsbridge was confiscated by Henry 8th in the late 1530s and
> " ..was held by the crown till 1558 when it was purchased by J & B Drake who sold it almost immediately to Sir William Petre" *Gentleman's Magazine 1799*

The Manor of Kingsbridge included rents from two mills; a vicarage at Churchstow, and a chapel at Kingsbridge   *(D & C Record Society Devon Monastic Lands)*

No regular mail came directly to Kingsbridge. Until the eighteenth century all letters were forwarded to the town and its vicinity three times a week by the Totnes postmaster. In 1798 the route was adopted of directing post from Ivybridge through Modbury to Kingsbridge. By 1805 a full service was established with the post office being in Fore Street just below the Quakers' meeting-house. Salcombe was then served on foot or by boat.

West Alvington
Originally Alfington (eventually becoming West Alvington) had a significant estate of **Bowringsleigh** (originally Leigh). It was built in 1303, bought by Bowring in 1332 and passed down via Webber and Gilbert until bought by Ilbert in 1696. The property was of over 1000 acres is still owned by his descendants.
In 1104 Roger de Nunant gave to Buckfast Abbey "for the love of God and his ancestors' souls" the right to make secure their mill of Norden. **Norden** in the tithe map of 1742 is referred to as a homestead, with gardens, orchard, and numerous parks, fields. A sizeable property.
In 1788 **Dodbrook** had some temporary barracks to house troops about to sail to America to fight in the War of Independence vs. The Rebels.

All references to the mills at Kingsbridge indicate they were for corn until 1798 when they were converted for the manufacture of woollen cloth with a large wool-combing shop built alongside.

Salcombe virtually did not exist. It had a chapel of ease built in 1399. Prior to that the people of Salcombe had to make their way 2 miles up a steep hill & along the ridge way to Marlborough church for worship. The chapel had no regular vicar or services, so baptisms & burials had still to be held at Marlborough. In 1844 a new church with a small cemetery was built.

By the late 1500's the excellent harbour of Salcombe had overtaken East Portlemouth in importance and activity and it declined rapidly. Thus Salcombe supplied the Armada Fleet in 1588. E. Portlemouth did not.
It had considerable trade in pilchards and a great variety of other commodities which continued for many years. Merchants and industrious people attained great wealth especially through overseas trade.
These ports (coming under the customs at Dartmouth) are known to have exported coarse cloth from Totnes, and woollen cloth from Ashburton.
They were able to function without severe government interference or control, but this created its own problems because
> "..in 1607 county justices complained to government that Salcombe harbour was infested with pirates who often landed armed parties to the great danger of the inhabitants"

The 1800's were the busiest times for Salcombe & Kingsbridge shipbuilding. Salcombe built special ships for the fruit cargos and the Salcombe yaw for crabbing.

Valor Ecclesiasticus 1534
This gives the values of benefices & details of local trade & industry.
Sir Philp Champernon owned land at Dodbrooke and a mill.
There were two main Deaneries : Totnes (Buckfastleigh,Kilbury,Brent,Churchstow, Kingsbridge) & Woodleigh (Ringmore,Portlemouth, South Pool, Churchstow with the chapel at Kingsbridge, Dodbrook etc). Salcombe not mentioned.
It refers to mills at Buckfast, Kilbury (which is just outside Buckfast on the river Dart), Brent (i.e. South Brent) and Kingsbridge.

Notable Kingsbridge People

Kingsbridge was a small town, and had a number of people who became known nationally as well as locally. They included over the years:

David Tolley	artist, worker in porcelain. In 1547 was theologian and teacher at Christ's Church, Oxford
William Cookworthy	physician and author
John Wolcot 1738 – 1819	satirist who wrote as Peter Pinder
Col. George Montague d 1815	naturalist
Charles Prideaux 1780 – 1860	naturalist, F.L.S.
Hugh Canning 1791 – 1865	conchologist
John Scoble 1799-1877	abolitionist, Canadian MP
Walter Stephens Lethbridge 1771-1830	miniature painter, painted John Wolcot's portrait
James Lackington	bookseller
Thomas Crispin	founder of the Kingsbridge Grammar school in 1670, cloth merchant
Sarah Prideaux Fox 1813 - 1885	great grand niece of Cookworthy. Her brother was George Fox who provided the photographs illustrating her book.

To this list may be added the following Cranches:
- John Cranch (referred to as John Cranch the painter): a book and many articles have been written about him
- John Cranch (the Naturalist): two pamphlets, articles
- Richard Cranch (emigrated, brother-in-law of John Adams the second President): a book could be written about him
- Jane Bowring Cranch, author of "Troublous Times", poet.
- Numerous Cranches who were prominent in their own time and locality, many were Feoffees

References:
1. *Anne Born 2002 "History of Kingsbridge & Salcombe" was the main source*
2. *Thomas Colehill's 1572 Register of Trading Ships*
3. *Salcombe's Register for Shipping (boat owners) 1867*
4. *Various Census returns*
5. *S.P.Fox 1864 "Kingsbridge Estuary with Rambles in the neighbourhood"*
6. *A. Hawkins 1819 "Kingsbridge and Salcombe with the Intermediate Estuary"*
7. *Fox, Harold, The Evolution of the Fishing Village: Landscape and Society along the South Devon Coast, 1086-1550*
8. *Devonshire Association Transactions and Reports: several papers, particularly R. Dymond 1877 Kingsbridge and Dodbrooke*
9. *Trading Vessels of Salcombe Haven 1820-1890, Exeter papers in Economic History No 4 (1971) by D.G. Murch*
10. *English Heritage Legacy*

CHAPTER 3
THE WOOLLEN TRADE

The Textile industry, Fulling, Social Change

The Textile Industry
The profitable part of the textile industry up to the early C14th was dominated by "mercers" who dealt in silk, linen, worsted cloth and such items as dress accessories, small luxuries and bedding. These were expensive materials favoured by royalty and nobles. The mercer was an important person in business and governance, especially in York, London and places where they established guilds.

Anyone dealing in other goods such as wool was not a mercer. Wool was wanted to make cloth that was needed by everyone. A great deal of this cloth was made abroad, Flanders particularly especially Bruges and Ghent. The best wool however came from English sheep, giving rise to wool merchants who supervised the export of the wool through country lanes, small ports, larger ports and then to ports such as Calais. Most merchants lived or had representatives there (Calais in the 1500's was under English control).

The textile people of Flanders manufactured cloth from the wool and would exchange their finished cloth for other goods. There was a considerable shipping trade conducted, even during the various wars. Most of the shipping was done in Flemish ships which created tensions between governments and gave rise from time to time to scuffles between the sailors of Middleburg, say, (a flourishing seaport in Zeeland) and those from Hull (the major port for York).

In the early C14 it was mostly wool that was exported. In 1353 wool Staple Centres were established (e.g. in York, Exeter) so that wool could only be exported from them and so be taxed. At this time the English textile industry was almost non-existent and Devon wool was not exported as it was mostly coarse and used locally.

But by the end of C14 nearly half of the wool exported was in cloth (mainly not dyed or finished). There were several reasons for this:
- The Black Death greatly reduced the population in rural areas. Agriculture went into sheep farming extensively as this needed less manpower. Cattle herds disappeared; cornfields fell out of cultivation, flocks of sheep everywhere. This in turn created a new system: manure for grass cultivation, sheep wool to be sold (at a good price), and a market for ewe milk, cheese and lambs
- The introduction of the Staple Tax and other taxations meant it became cheaper to export cloth made from wool than the wool itself.
- Technology changes - Fulling.

Fulling
The process of making woollens from short wool was: wool cleaned – carded to tease out the fibres- spun with a twist – fulled – tendered (dried on racks in open air while being stretched) - then dyed if need be – shipped.

Fulling was a messy and smelly job. Traditionally using stale urine (for the ammonia which acted as the scouring agent) in tubs pummelled by men's feet. The process shrunk the cloth, so had to be followed by stretching whilst drying.

During the C14 fulling mills were developed, basically by putting a cam on the shaft of a water mill wheel which alternately raised and lowered hammers similar to the action of the treading by human feet in a tub. This was a relatively easy change to carry out and reversible, as many mills centuries later reverted back to grinding corm.

These mills spread rapidly throughout the valleys of England and increasingly came under the control of the new "clothiers". The industry changed. York declined.

The West of England, East Anglia and the West Riding of Yorkshire became the new centres for wool cloth manufacturing. The Subsidy Tax of 1523 showed that Exeter was now equal to York.

West of England broadcloths were the best. Broadcloth originally referred to being made on a broad loom (as opposed to narrow as used in York), but then came to mean thick fettled fabric produced in mills.

During the first half C16 exports increased rapidly. 1565 was a particularly good year: cloth made up 78% of all England's exports, wool 6.3%, everything else 15.7%
The trend that had been developing since the fulling mill revolution of the C13 and C14 reached its climax in the middle of C16. The second half of the C16th saw no further expansion.

Almost all the undyed cloths went via London for export to Antwerp. London in 1547 handled 90% of this trade.

This large export trade required a complex organisation, including the ultimate buyer of the finished product, the finishers and dyers, the London agents and the West Country clothiers, who in turn handled the work of the weavers, spinners, fullers, staplers and probably farmers as well.

The great clothiers (Cloth Merchants) of the South West arranged for every stage of cloth manufacture. They bought the wool either direct or through staplers, organised its processing by spinners, weavers and fullers (some had their own mills), then arranged storage prior to shipping and customs.

The broadcloths tended to be produced East of Exeter. Kerseys and serges (narrow cloth) were otherwise the main product. Exports took place between Devon ports such as Dartmouth to Brittany and southern Europe in exchange for Breton linen, wine and other items.

Social change
The influence of the mercers (of York etc) with their guild system and the tight controls over workers declined. Rural activity increased where there was water for mills. By the mid C15 the exodus of people from York had already begun among the subsidiary branches of the textile industry i.e. by the cloth makers.

The C15 saw growth being selective and according to area partly due to the changed textile industry. It also gave rise to lease holding replacing the hiring of staff to run the estates (shortage of workers following the plague etc). Merchant's houses were notable for their size and comfort. Wealthy merchants, such as Crispin at Kingsbridge established Grammar schools.

Ch 3.1 The woollen Trade in England in Fourteenth Century

The Poll Tax riots and protests by such as John Wycliffe meant that by the end of C14 the established society was being challenged and led to the views held by protestant reformers with puritan bias becoming significant.

The mid C 16 was a turbulent period. Breach with Rome in 1530's (King Henry VIII), execution of Catholics, dissolution of monasteries, followed by Queen Mary's reversal and prosecution (burning) of Protestants

The following were consulted to gain background information on the textile industry and more specifically to any find references to Cranch in Yorkshire and the cloth industry:.
- *The York Mercers & Merchant adventurers 1336-1917 , M.Sellers, Surtees Society 1917*
- *The woollen Industry, E. Carus-Wilson, Cambridge Economic History ii (1952)*
- *Wool Merchants of the 15th Century, G.S.Thompson, 1966*
- *Mercery of London & sale of goods people 1130- 1578, Sutton 2016*
- *The Woollen Industry of S.W. England, K. Ponting 1971*

None of them mentioned a Cranch.

Ch. 3.2 The Woollen Trade in Flanders in the Thirteenth Century

Trade changes, migrations

The C14 woollen trade between England and the continent was mostly undertaken by:
- Staplers (people who graded staples – quantities of wool in its unmanufactured state)
- Merchant adventurers. The Mercer organisation at York was especially active in Flanders, with Brabant, Zeeland. Bruges, Ghent, Antwerp mentioned
- Hansas (German Hansards)

The traditional English wool export trade was undertaken by "denizens 55%, Hansards 21% and others i.e. largely not by the English. Flemish vessels traded between all the European ports – wool and the materials needed one way, goods the other. The cloth towns of Flanders (Ghent, Bruges, and Ypres) were dependent on English wool.

England sought alliances with The Low Countries in its efforts in the war against France, with mixed success, depending on which Count was wooed.
Flanders had an unsuccessful rebellion in 1328. A civil war in Flanders in 1379 with its origins in protestant reform had a disastrous effect on Flemish cloth production.

The outflow of English cloth, not wool, from mid C 14 resulted in the English cloth industry overtaking the Flemish cloth industry, with the accompanying development of trade routes and decline in Hansa influence.

The Flemings were becoming increasingly discontented with their situation and were enticed to carry on their trade in England. For example, in 1337 letters of protection and franchises were offered to all foreign cloth workers wishing to settle in England.

Flemish textile workers were arriving in York from about mid- C14 onwards and established a colony, but they do not appear to have contributed anything to the development of the cloth industry in the West Riding in this period.

Ponting quotes the following from *The Company of Drapers of London, by Mr Johnson*
"... after a very careful investigation of the conditions of the woollen industry in Yorkshire in the first half of the C14, it is impossible to avoid coming to the conclusion that a considerable immigration of textile workers from Zeeland and Brabant took place."

E.Carus-Wilson: Cambridge Economic History of Europe says:
Many came over relying solely on general offers of protection, leaving no trace in official records. The majority of settlers would appear to have been well-to-do artisans – weavers chiefly, also fullers and dyers – who brought with them their own journeymen and apprentices, but some were entrepreneurs, making woollen cloth and trading generally. Some found their way to the West of England and some to Yorkshire.

From this and the preceding pages we can draw some conclusions.

Ch 3.3 The Woollen Trade in Devon

Devon's wool trade, Devon Mills, The Clothier, References

The Woollen Trade in Devon
By 1400 at the latest, nearly the whole of the South Hams was cultivated, with sheep farming widely practised, especially after the Black Death, with close alliance between wool, the cloth industry and farming generally.

A C14th manuscript for Stokenham manor records that one of the tenant's duties was to carry "the lord's wool to the markets at Totnes and Dartmouth" The ubiquity in Devon of the names Fuller and Tucker (scourers and thickeners) emphasises the importance of the wool trade in South Devon.

In the 1400s the main cloth producers were in north Devon. Totnes grew to be a centre in the late 1400s with coarse cloth ("straits"). Then demand grew for kerseys and within 100 years Devon became the production centre of the UK for it.

Devonshire kerseys, serges and later 'draperies' were held to be the most esteemed in England and abroad throughout C16th and for 200 years after. Although Exeter was an important wool staple centre from the mid-1350's, it was not until 1538 that it opened its first woollen cloth market.

In C17 Exeter became the trade centre for serge, equalling East Anglia. All the cloths went to Exeter for final export and in many cases for finishing as well.
In the 1750's wool carders and spinners were recorded in all the villages, selling to the serge-makers in Dodbrooke and Kingsbridge.

Production initially was aided mechanically by using mills for fulling, then in C18 for spinning. In the C19th "Gig mills" were used to tease the wool.
However by then the local industry had declined as worsteds could now be made from long-fibred yarns and the centre of the trade moved away from the W. of E.

Devon Mills
Devon had an abundance of water. The Doomsday Survey recorded about 95 mills in Devon. The Mills Archive lists 38 mills on the Dart, 32 on the Avon and 12 in the Torquay area. Not dated so many of them may not have existed in C15. Some are actually described as being for cloth, such as Harberton Woollen mill, Totnes Fulling mill, Brent Leather Mill, Brent canvas mill, Buckfastleigh Tannery. Gages Fulling mill at Ashburton is claimed as being in operation in the 14th century.
In Exeter a lease document for the Earl of Devon in 1500 refers to two fulling mills there.

Before about 1500 there were three mills on the east of the estuary (E. Portlemouth area) and three on the Salcombe. All were probably using tidal power. Some may have been used for fulling but there is no record of it. The most known is Slades Mill (near Goodshelter, East Portlemouth). It was owned by the Dartmouth Corporation who constructed a quay there in 1600-1622.

The mill at Kingsbridge (owned by the Abbot of Buckfast) traditionally ground corn. He took the wool from his Churchstow manors to the mills at Buckfastleigh and Ashburton for processing. Ann Born claims:

> "In Kingsbridge the Abbot of Buckfast had mills, both for corn and wool, traditionally sited in Mill Street at the bottom of the town and rebuilt several times"

There is no record of there being mills for wool in Kingsbridge, but her comment that mills were rebuilt several times does not preclude there being a fulling mill there at some stage. By modern standards the mills were rickety affairs, unlikely to survive.

The Abbot's mill was believed to have been fed by streams coming down the Norton and Dodbrooke valleys supplemented by a salt water pool dammed back at high tide.

W.Davis in DATR 1918

In the late 1500s when the area about Norden was no longer owned by the Abbot, but by Lord Petre more mills were probably constructed, some of which became known as Towne Mills.

In 1798 the town mills at Kingsbridge were converted from grinding corn into a manufactory where large quantities of woollen cloth were made to meet a great demand for serge caused by the Napoleonic wars. In 1845 they reverted back to grinding corn. There was also in early C19 a mill in Duncombe Street Kingsbridge, for making serges, flushings, army cloths and blanketings. This was probably Washerbrook mill with Rack Park nearby, names which suggest a connection with the woollen industry.

The Clothier

This useful description of the life of a clothier is taken from
- *Report and Transactions of the Devonshire Association, July 1876* and
- *Sketch of Ashburton and the Woollen Trade* by P.F.S. Amery

The clothier was usually a man of some means, residing in his own house which made him a free man (exempt from import taxes). He bought his yarn in a market and had it spun by poor cottagers into chains to form the warp. One day a week the serge maker put on his long apron and met his weavers, who often hired their looms from him. He handed them the yarn (and some glue to size the chain before it was to be tied to a loom) and collected their finished work of the previous week. The serges were then fulled at a mill and despatched; if for the East India Company (E.I.Co), then to London for dying.

Only a small capital was needed as a clothier's level of business was limited by the number of weavers and spinners available and by competing clothiers. It did not take up a lot of his time. He had no workers to superintend as all the work was done in the houses of the poor. He set one day aside to tend his weavers, and on another attending a yarn market. This meant that as he prospered, he could invest his time and increasing capital in purchasing property and small farms which he could then improve by developing its neighbouring fields. Some clothiers had their own wool storage facilities and bought from local farmers.

Business fluctuated from year to year. A succession of good Government or E.I.Co. contracts would increase his balance in the hands of his London agent to a handsome sum. Some clothiers also acted as bankers. Once a quarter the E.I.Co. would meet clothiers at the Exeter serge market to arrange the next contracts. Devon executed nearly all the orders for China for which their serge was well suited.

Being mostly non-conformists the opportunity of a visit to London was seized as it meant they could also hear the discourses of eminent divines which were recalled for years afterwards.

The industry declined over the years and then changed considerably with the invention of the spinning jenny – it became a modern industrial manufacturing business. The mills had to be kept running demanding more wool and more weavers. The yarn markets ceased. The clothier was obliged to change in many ways from being a "small local trader" into a person who devoted his whole time and capital to his trade. Many clothiers could not or did not want to make changes to their business and so withdrew. In many cases the business was not taken on by the next generation.

Other References for this chapter

- *Anne Born's book.*
- *The Woollen Industry of S.W. England, K. Ponting 1971.*
  Although it refers to the South West as comprising Somerset, Wiltshire and Gloucester for the purposes of textile production, many of his observations can be extrapolated into Devon.
- *Devon Mills Archive website*
- *Discovering Watermills, John Vince 1984*
- *Peter Maunder who kindly assisted me with the above.*

Ch 3.4 The Woollen Trade in Exeter in the 1600s

Exeter's Woollen Markets, Kersey, Serge, Merchants, Exports, Fulling and Mills

Exeter's Woollen markets

The prosperity of Exeter 16th through to the 18th Century was due to its being the centre of the processing and exporting woollen cloth from Devon

The nature of the land in the south west lent itself well to sheep farming. The flocks were scattered across many small family run farms, combining sheep farming with general agriculture. The production of woollen cloth, initially kersey, and then serge, was also on a family basis - the carding and spinning undertaken by the wife, children and family servants of the household. The early cloths were quite coarse and known as "straits" and kept most people in work.

At its height it had at least three purpose-built cloth markets in the city. The first market was opened in 1538 for wool, yarn and kersey, followed by new markets in 1542 and 1555 and various others at times. The Guildhall in 1533 was used for foreigners (anyone who was not an Exeter merchant) to trade in linen and cloth. By 1640, St George's Hall, the New Inn and St John's were the markets used for buying and selling woollen products.

However over the years, the wool trade changed so that by 1805, Jenkins wrote:
> "the open street, before the Bear Inn, is weekly held….the Serge Market …. supposed to have been the largest in this kingdom, except that of Leeds, in Yorkshire….has ….greatly declined of late years".

Kersey

Kersey was introduced in the fifteenth century and by 1600, its production had made Devon one of England's leading textile areas. It was used to make clothing for servants and the poor. It was made from lower grade wool, using both long and short fibres. The kersey was woven in a twill structure, so a diagonal rib ran across the surface of the cloth, giving it a less coarse finish to the cloth and then dyed, mostly using local sources. An orange dye for example was obtained from the madder plant.

Serge

It was about 1615 that a finer cloth, known as serge, was introduced. It fast became the main product of Exeter's fulling mills, and by 1700, 1,200 weavers were employed across the county.

Serge is a cloth best suited to the wool that was available from Devon and Somerset. It was made from a combination of long fibre wool that traditionally produced worsted, and woollen yarn which is made from a shorter and softer fleece. The surface of serge was diagonally ribbed from its twill structure, giving a front and back. A form of serge was later developed that only used worsted wool for making suits.

The Woollen Merchants

After the Civil War the woollen merchants of Exeter controlled the whole process: they purchased the fleece at the local markets, sent it for carding and combing, and had it spun into yarn. The yarn was then woven into cloth before it was transported to Exeter on pack animals for finishing at the fulling mills.

The merchants were freemen who belonged to the Guild of the Fullers and Tuckers. Guild members in the 18th century were known as the *'Golden Tuckers'* because their wealth allowed them to clear the market of the most expensive items. They were also noted for their green baize aprons with red strings. The Guild in 1471 built Tuckers Hall in Fore Street. They were a powerful elite in the city and many of the members of the City Chamber (forerunner of the present-day City Council) were Guild members. Almost half of those admitted as freemen into the guilds in the 16th Century were engaged in one aspect or other of the cloth industry.

The Export Trade
Exeter produced cloth that was processed in the fulling mills of Exe Island from as early as the 13th Century. Much of this cloth was for the home market, with some exports. Much of the rest of England's wool exports were unfinished yarn to the Royal monopoly at Calais, where it was woven into cloth in France and the Low Countries. After the capture of Calais in 1558, the weaving industry expanded as skilled Calvinist serge weavers were driven out of the Low Countries by the Eighty Years War and settled in Exeter and Devon.

Exeter's woollen industry flourished and woollen products were exported to France, and Spain. After the Civil War, the Merchant Adventurer Company in London and the Exeter French Company lost control of the export trade and individual merchants started to export their own cloth and import other goods. *(see footnote)* In addition, a depression in trade after 1660 and after the French imposed fierce tariffs in 1667, the newly free merchants were forced to find new markets, especially in Holland. The exact export market would vary from year to year, dependent on which country England was at war with at the time, but the Dutch remained the main market until the end of the 18th century.

The export of woollen goods supported the ports of Topsham and Exeter, and allowed the merchants' ships to return with a variety of imports including wine from Bordeaux and the Canaries, canvas and linen from Normandy, and increasingly, tiles and bricks from Holland. The flocks of Devon sheep could not keep up with serge production, and fleece had to be imported from the surrounding counties and Wales, and eventually imports of raw wool from Ireland and Spain dominated the supply of raw material for weaving the cloth.

The Fulling Mills
The finishing of the cloth was centralised at Exeter - the abundance of water power in a small area allowed the mills to finish the cloth, ready for export. Before fulling the cloth was soaked in stale human urine, which contains ammonia and Fuller's earth to aid the process. This process would cleanse the wool of oils, dirt and other impurities and thicken the fibres by matting the surface texture. Every night, urine was collected from taverns, inns and houses by men from the *'piss cart'*. The wool was pummelled with large square wooden hammers, or fulling stocks, tripped by wooden cams, directly driven by the water wheel. Celia Fiennes gave a very thorough description of the process:

> *"The carryers... with their loaded horses, they bring them all just from the loom and so they are put into the fulling-mills, but first they will clean and scour their rooms with them - which by the way gives no pleasing perfume to a room, the oil and grease, and I should think it would rather foul a room than cleanse it because of the oil - but I perceive its otherwise esteemed by them, which will send to their acquaintances that are tuckers' the days the serges comes in for a roll to clean their house, this I was an eye witness of, then*

they lay them in soak in urine then they soap them and so put them into the fulling-mills and so work them in the mills dry till they are thick enough, then they turn water into them and so scour them; the mill does draw out and gather in the serges, its a pretty diversion to see it, a sort of huge notched timbers like great teeth, one would think it should injure the serges but it does not, the mills draws in with such a great violence that if one stands near it, and it catch a bit of your garments it would be ready to draw in the person even in a trice; when they are thus scoured they dry them in racks strained out, which are as thick set one by another as will permit the dresser to pass between, and huge large fields occupied this way almost all round the town which is to the river side; then when dry they burl them picking out all knots, then fold them with a paper between every fold and so set them on an iron plate and screw down the press on them, which has another iron plate on the top under which is a furnace of fire of coals, this is the hot press; then they fold them exceeding exact and then press them in a cold press;"

The serge was thoroughly washed in river water to prevent it shrinking, and then dyed in the dying houses, as Celia Fiennes explained:

"I saw the several vats they were a dying in, of black, yellow, blue, and green - which two last colours are dipped in the same vat, that which makes it differ is what they were dipped in before, which makes them either green or blue; they hang the serges on a great beam or great pole on the top of the vat and so keep turning it from one to another, as one turns it off into the vat the other rolls it out of it, so they do it backwards and forwards till its tinged deep enough of the colour; their furnace that keeps their dye pans boiling is all under that room, made of coal fires; there was in a room by it self a vat for the scarlet, that being a very chargeable dye no waste must be allowed in that; indeed I think they make as fine a colour as their Bow dyes are in London; these rollers I spoke off; two men do continually roll on and off the pieces of serges till dipped enough, the length of these pieces are or should hold out 26 yards."

The serge was hung on racks in large wooden drying sheds, and more usually, in dry weather, rack fields. The phrase, 'being on tenterhooks' comes from hanging the cloth on frames called tenters, using tenterhooks. The rackfields were also known as the tenterground. Much of Exe Island around the site of the old cattle market, where Colleton Crescent is situated, and parts of St Thomas were given over to rack fields.

References
- "Seventeenth-Century Exeter" by W B Stevens, Exeter Memories website
- "Exeter's Woollen Industry" by Celia Fiennes
- Izacke's Remarkable Antiquities of the City of Exeter
- Jenkin's Civil and Ecclesiastical History of the City of Exeter
- Exeter 1540-1640 by Wallace MacCaffrey,

Footnote
This observation relates to Exeter's growth after the Civil War – for reasons given elsewhere, areas other than Exter were able to flourish before then.

CHAPTER 4
THE CRANCH FAMILY
1500 – 1700

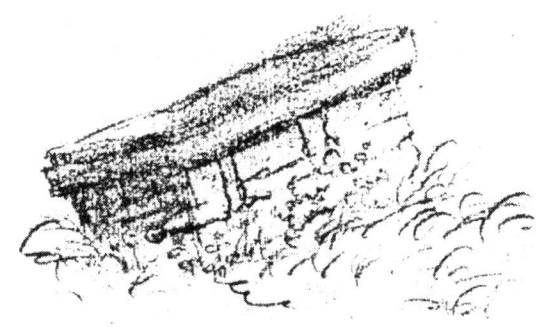

Ch. 4.1 Proposition on the Origins of the Cranch Family

Origins, Name

Origins

Piecing together the various themes emerging from the study of Kingsbridge, Yorkshire, Flanders and the woollen cloth trade, part of Peabody's statement may be reworded:

> *The Cranch family originated in Northern Europe, most probably Flanders. They were involved in the textile industry but were caught up in the various civil unrests in that area and decided to seek refuge in Yorkshire, probably in the late 15th or early 16th century*

In Yorkshire they found the closed shop of the York mercer guild no better than that they had left behind in Flanders. They were adverse to authoritarian controls, whether religious or commercial.

Through their business in Flanders, they would have known about wool from the south west and East Portlemouth as a significant port at that time. They would have known about Devon's abundant water, its mills and about the new fulling mills.

They decided to move to the Kingsbridge area to take advantage of Devon's wool, its mills, its ports and their knowledge of the cloth business and the European trade and its traders in Flanders and London especially. The date of the migration from Yorkshire to Devon would probably be sometime in the 1400s and not long after their move to Yorkshire - perhaps no more than a generation or two later.

As this was before Exeter became a pre-dominant and controlling centre, the Cranch family would have relative "freedom" to operate in the Kingsbridge area to establish their businesses.

They became wool producers (farmers) and cloth merchants (clothiers) with associated trades.

The Name?

The original name may have been Kranz, Krantz, Crantz, Cranach or any number of other variations. Those most frequently promoted in the past by family historians (perhaps with a romantic eye) were chosen because of their familiar and similar religious views and artistic talents and maybe a wish on the part of the family historian to be associated with some-one "famous". Two conjectured connections with notable people of protestant inclinations are *(Wikipedia):*
- **Lucas Cranach the Elder** c. 1472 – 1553 a German Renaissance painter
- **Albert Krantz** (or Crantz) c. 1450-1517 dean of Hamburg cathedral

No links have been established with either. They would appear to have risen to prominence after the Cranch family left for Yorkshire.

Ch 4.2 History of the Cranch Woollen business

The Beginnings, Fulling, Shipping, Developments 1550-1650, Cloth Trade after 1650, Farming after 1650, Cranches Farm

The Beginnings
The strongest evidence is for the cloth business to be first based in the East Portlemouth side of the Kingsbridge estuary. It had the port facilities from which the cloth could be despatched. Here the Andrew branch of family prospered. They were the main ones to be clothiers, although they may also have been wool farmers.

On the other side of the estuary the Richard branch became landowners and wool producers. They too prospered. The two operations of the Cranch businesses – wool production and cloth making - were complimentary and all part of the family business in the earliest times and since.

As was indicated in the previous chapter, in the 1500s the greatest demand and profit came from exporting the cloth, using the London markets and shipping via Dover. A London agent was required and this must have been at one time Johes Cranch. The London agents were men who prospered and Johes Cranch became sufficiently wealthy to commission a glass etching of himself in a London church dated 1553.   *(Chapter 13 John the Painter has more on this).*

Fulling
There is considerable uncertainty about how or where the family had their wool fulled. It is possible they may have relied on traditional labour-intensive methods but this is unlikely. They may have used those at Exeter initially thereby gaining knowledge of the local trade. They may have followed the practice of Buckfast Abbey and used the fulling mills in South Devon at that time – Ashburton probably, maybe South Brent or Totnes. They may have used one on the mills on the east of the estuary near East Portlemouth using tidal power then one on the Salcombe side. However, the family were not the only clothiers operating in the Kingsbridge area in the 1500s so there was demand for a fulling mill locally then if not later.

By about 1600 I am sure they must have been using a fulling mill attached to Norden.

Shipping
Sampling the customs entries for Dartmouth 1450 – 1600 shows no evidence of overseas trade by Cranch. However, there are entries in the coastal logs which show that ships used by Cranch were going to Dover, and therefore to the London markets where the woollen exports were controlled. For example, in 1565 there is an entry for a Joseph Cranch using the ship Clement of Salcombe, and there was a Nicolas "of Salcombe" trading to Dover in 1575 (believed to be owned by the Cranches).

Developments 1550 – 1650
The move to Salcombe: By the late 1500's the Cranch clothing business was using Salcombe as its main port. The spur for this change was the general (fairly rapid) change away from East Portlemouth by the shippers; the Dissolution in the late 1530s which freed up lands in the Salcombe / Kingsbridge area and the "freeing up" of trade controls after the Civil War 1643-5.

By the early 1600's they were wealthy. Andrew the Elder (died 1623) had business interests in the area around the west of Kingsbridge. He had leased or rented from the Courtenay estate property at Batson (Tor Hill, Horsecombe, Mount Knowle) which included many buildings, land and cellars. He also had property and land at Lower Towne in Kingsbridge leased from Lord Petre. It is fairly certain that this was the manor of Norden, plus at least one mill.

To justify the complete transfer of the business from East Portlemouth to the Kingsbridge / Salcombe / Batson area, the family surely had access to or owned their own fulling mill. The mill connected to Norden could have been converted or another in Lower Towne built for the purpose. The evidence is for the family to have had a long term association with Norden and the mill area of Kingsbridge.

However not all the family's interests "moved across the water". One Andrew Cranch still gave his residence as East Portlemouth in 1653 when bonding a yeoman.

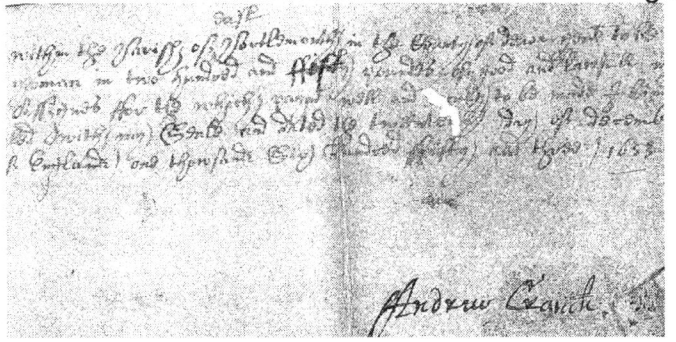

DHC 316M/0/EB/19

The Hearth Tax of 1674 also shows him as living there. Others by this time had moved to other parishes. (see Ch 2.1).

Ship ownership

The family's business had grown to the extent that having its own ship was a natural development – as well as being potentially profitable.

The Nicolas was a ship of about 30 or 35 tons (cargo capacity) owned by Andrew Cranch in 1619 when it was described as being 6 years old and again listed as his in 1626. However in 1604 the Nicolas was in a list with three others of ships for "tonnage for Dover Pier". There was also a Nicolas operating in 1575 from Salcombe. The interpretation is that the Cranches owned ships for quite some time, commonly called Nicolas.

In all probability members of the family were involved in crewing vessels owned or used by the family. In 1619 from the Marlborough area were the following (actual ages could be plus or minus 5) Mariners: William age 40, Richard 50, sailors: Andrew 30, William 18, John 25, Owen 40 Owen 30 (father and son?), cooper at sea: James 30

It was common for trading profits to be shared between the ship's owner, the ship's merchant trader, and the ship's crew. By lending money for a trade journey, the investor had shares in future profits which could be considerable, especially if it were for wine or fish. This also occurred with the Nicolas as there are references to shares being held by local people such as Roope and Follet who were in the woollen trade.

D & C Record S vol 33 (1990)
(The national Archives, Kew: E190 series and E122 series for Datmouth)
Early Stuart Mariners and Shipping quoting the Duke of Buckingham's survey 1619
and Sir James Bagg's survey 1626
Dartmouth corporation survey of ships 1619

Farming

In 1585 Richard Cranch and others as inhabitants of the town of Salcombe claimed to be exempt from the tolls and subsidies of Dartmouth as they were tenants of the Duchy of Devon and Cornwall.

The National Archives E 134/27

The Marlborough Parish records for deaths between 1563 and 1707 shows that there 13 Cranches from Bolberry (Bolburie and similar spellings) indicating an established presence in the district: farming, no doubt sheep and the initial processing of wool.

The Cloth Trade after 1650

Against the background of the Civil War and Dissent, plus events such as the great plague of 1666, the clothing trade in Kingsbridge diminished, but still engaged the family. The family business of Andrew the Elder was passed down successive generations.

Andrew [1] 1652 – 1728 was the great grandson of Andrew the Elder. His will describes him as Andrew Cranch of Kingsbridge, clothier. Peabody describes him as a farmer and freeholder. He leased in 1715 and 1717 for 99 years or three lives (son John, grandsons Andrew, Joseph) considerable lands associated with the manor of Norden. Much was surrendered in 1723 (upon his death) to the Petre Estate

(ref: Petre estate 123M/ copied by DCC in 1995).

His property was :
- Buttmeads meadows, part of Norton farm (inherited by daughter Elizabeth, grandson John)
- Halfpenny meadow, Norton Farm (grandsons Nathaniel , Joseph)
- Wester Norden 28 acres part of Norden Barton (grandsons John, Andrew & Joseph)
- Rack Park, Norton Farm (daughter Elizabeth, sons Nathaniel & Andrew?)

In 1712 Andrew was prosecuted along with about 20 others for not repairing his way in Sugar lane, Knowle. Sugar lane led towards Dodbrooke church from Mill Street. It was previously called Sigger lane or Sidger Lane

Andrew [1] was succeed by his son John[2] (born 1680). By 1714 he was married and carrying out his business in Shaugh (Prior), before returning to Kingsbridge. He had seven children "all brought up to trade" (Peabody).

This was a sign of the shifting fortunes of local clothiers. The centre of the clothing industry had moved to Exeter and the trade itself was diminishing through competition from upcountry. Not one of his sons took on his business as such. One son remained to be a fuller in Kingsbridge, another became a fuller in Exeter, two became sadlers, and the last one went to America before he competed his apprenticeship as a card maker.

And so the Cranch family business of being clothiers in Kingsbridge came to an end. The last members known to be associated with the woollen trade were:

Christopher (d. 1787)	Andrew tree	fuller, Exeter
Nathaniel (d.1793)	Andrew Tree	fuller Exeter
James (d 1836)	Richard tree	dyer Totnes
James (d 1745)	Richard tree	fancy weaving trimmer, London
Nathaniel (?)	? tree	fuller Exeter and London

Farming after 1650

Edward who died in 1651 was sufficiently prosperous to have a will. He farmed at Bolbury in what is still called **"Cranches Farm"**. He left the farm to his nephews, the Follets. The Follet family were still tenants in 1777 when the Survey of Lands owned by Viscount Courtenay shows that the farm was named as "Late Cranches" and had 83 acres with 51 acres pasture. In 1987 the shippon and linhay of Cranches Farm were listed. The shippon was given a date of "pre-1777"

Various Cranches continued to live and farm in the Marlborough peninsular. For example a Stephen Cranch and others were granted grazing rights in Salcombe, Bolburie and Marlborough districts down as far as Newton Ferris

Marlborough Parish records 16.May 1687

A Richard Cranch who died in 1702 is described as wool comber. He was wealthy with many properties in the region, retiring to live at Bigbury.

William, a son of Steven (Richard tree) of South Huish went to Ashburton as a young man. Since Gage's (fulling) Mill was there, he must have moved there in connection with the woollen trade. He married a local girl, but he and his wife must have died before the 1674 Hearth tax as their property was registered in his daughter Elizabeth's name.

His son William (1655-1717) at age 27 leased some land in 1682 (for drying cloth?) and was a clothier. In 1708 he is described as serge-maker in deeds referring to a Solomon Tozer.

Some of the descendants of the Richard tree continued to be associated with wool, but as with the Andrew tree, diversified into other trades and professions.

References
1. Andrew's will: Deed D.H.C 1011A/D/T33
2. Ref: Petre estate 123M/ copied by DCC in 1995).
3. The Ilbert estate papers also list transactions in the series 316M/TL: C9 in 1717 Petre's lease to Andrew's clothier, reserving timber rights in Rack Parks. C10 in 1739 Licence to alienate freely: Joseph C, saddler to Andrew, tucker, of Exeter. C11 in 1740 Andrew C to Joseph refers to moiety in C9 of West Pasture, part of Norton Farm. C13 in 1771 Reversion of Petre's lease to Andrew, clothier, of eastern part of West Pasture.

Earliest members, The Two Trees, Crispin Connection and Kingsbridge Grammar School.

Earliest recorded Cranches

To date no information is available about the members of the Cranch family before about 1550. The information that is available can be interpreted as indication that there was

- a Richard born about 1540, forerunner of the Richard tree
- a William born about 1530, forerunner of the Andrew tree
- a Walter born about 1540 with descendants
- a Jasper born about 1550 with descendants
- a Roger born about 1550 with descendants
- a Joseph born about 1500 the London agent with probable defendants

Projecting backwards from this it could be speculated that the first generation of Cranches in Kingsbridge were there about 1450 with two or more brothers.

The Two Trees

The earliest information has led to establishing two distinct family trees : the Andrew Tree and the Richard tree. They do not include all the known early Cranches.
No claim is made as to their accuracy. For the initial stages there is: difficulty in the interpretation of the will of Andrew (d 1623); a lack of information from East Portlemouth; insufficient information to enable the two trees to be linked together and insufficient information to be able to allocate all the earliest known Cranches.

So the first charts for the two tress contain an element of conjecture. Thereafter the subsequent charts have a degree of certainty, but again are not totally inclusive.

The first charts for the two trees follow. There are three. This is a brief outline of their immediate continuations. (The full schematic was given in Ch 1.4)

ANDREW the Elder **4.4** this leads to charts five generations later for the "seven"

JOHN	**7.2**
ANDREW	**7.3**
WILLIAM	**7.4**
NATHANIEL	**8.1**
JOSEPH [2]	**11.2**
RICHARD etc	**12.3**
MARY etc	**12.4**

ANDREW The Younger **4.5** grandson of the elder. No continuation

EARLY RICHARDS **4.6** which leads to charts for
  RICHARD & JONE **6.2**
  RICHARD of Totnes **6.3**

The Crispin Connection

The early Cranch family was connected to the Crispin family in a number of ways: shared protestant beliefs, shared trades and were related. The Crispins were yeoman from the South Huish area. Edward Cranch married a Crispin and was very much associated with the Crispin family. He witnessed his father-in-law's will and took the inventory for that as well as for his brother-in-laws John and William Crispin. However the relationship of Edward (or other Cranches) to Thomas Crispin has not been established definitely, but it most certainly would have been close.

The most notable Crispin in Kingsbridge was **Thomas Crispin**, born 1607 died 1688. At age 26 he went to Exeter and became a very successful and prominent fuller. He was a Calvinist. In 1670 he established the Kingsbridge Grammar School.
It is claimed that a Cranch was the first pupil. A John Cranch witnessed a codicil to the will of Duncombe, the first headmaster. John Crispin, yeoman of South Huish, was a trustee.
Carved into the woodwork in the schoolroom are two Cranch attenders: in window 6 H. E. Cranch (undated); in panel 2 Alfred Cranch 1763. Neither has been conclusively associated with either of the two Cranch trees.

The old school building now houses the Cookworthy Museum.

The Grammar School founded by Thomas Crispin in 1670
Cookworthy Museum

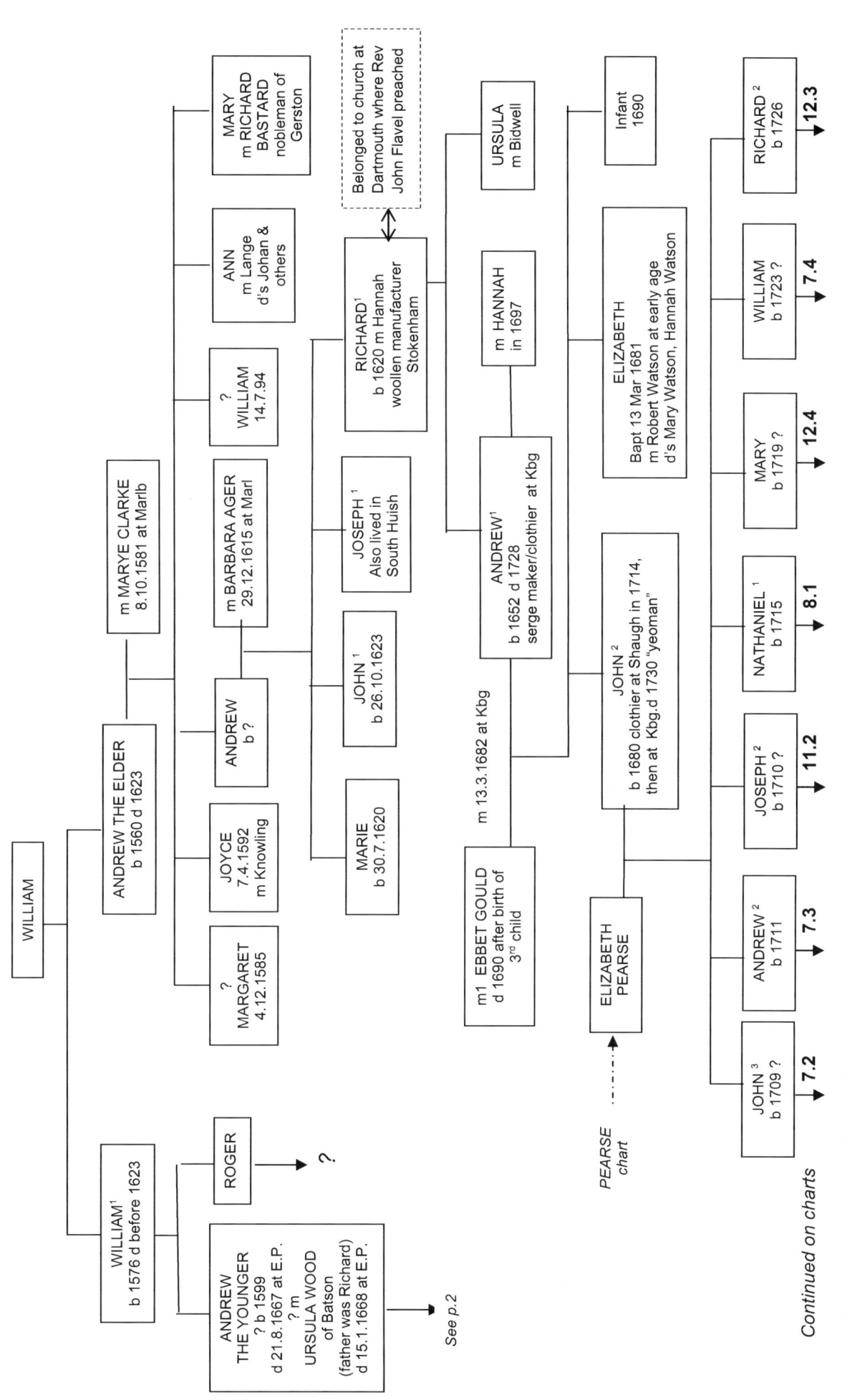

4.4 Chart   Andrew the Elder

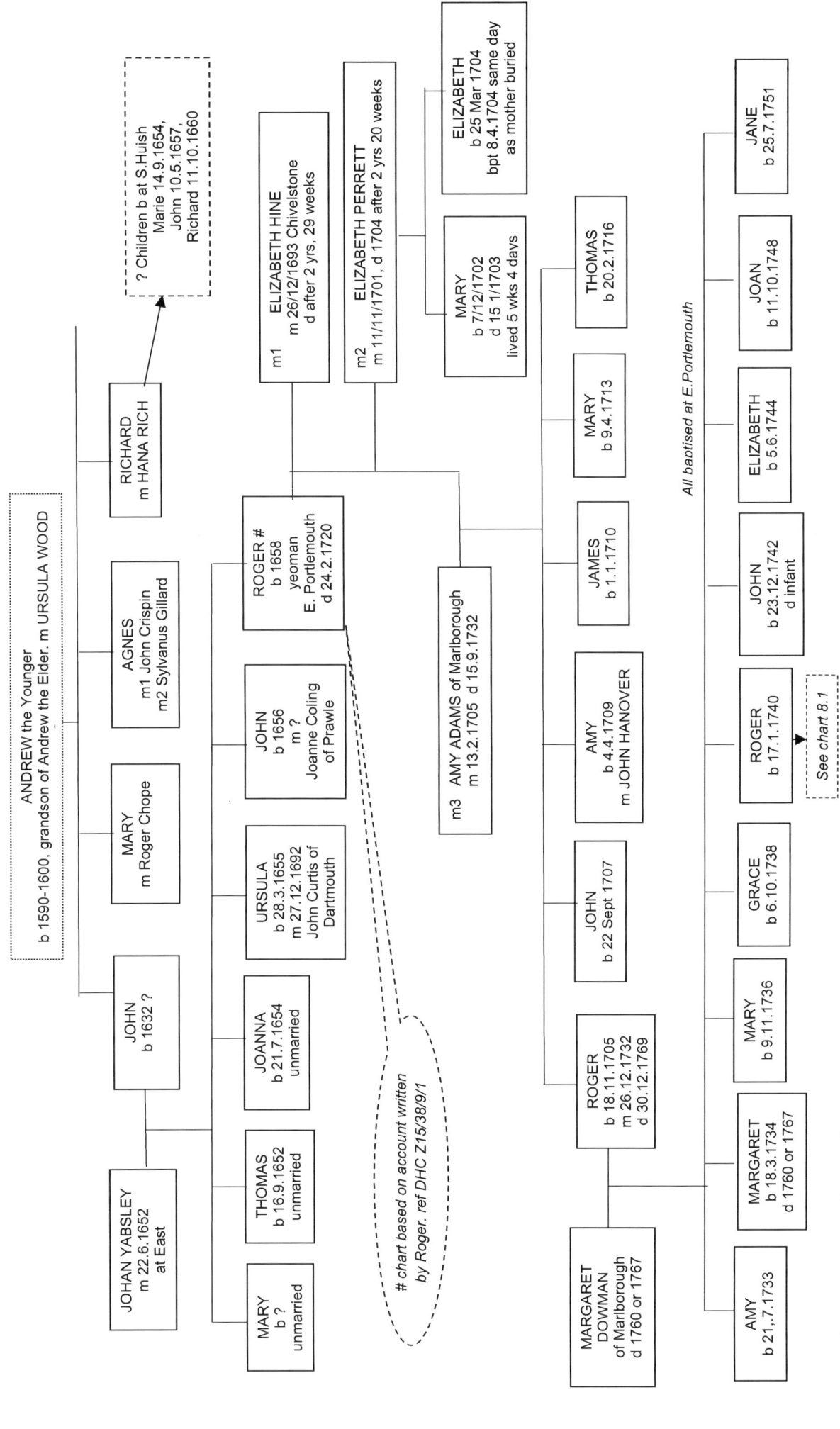

4.5 Chart   Andrew the Younger

11

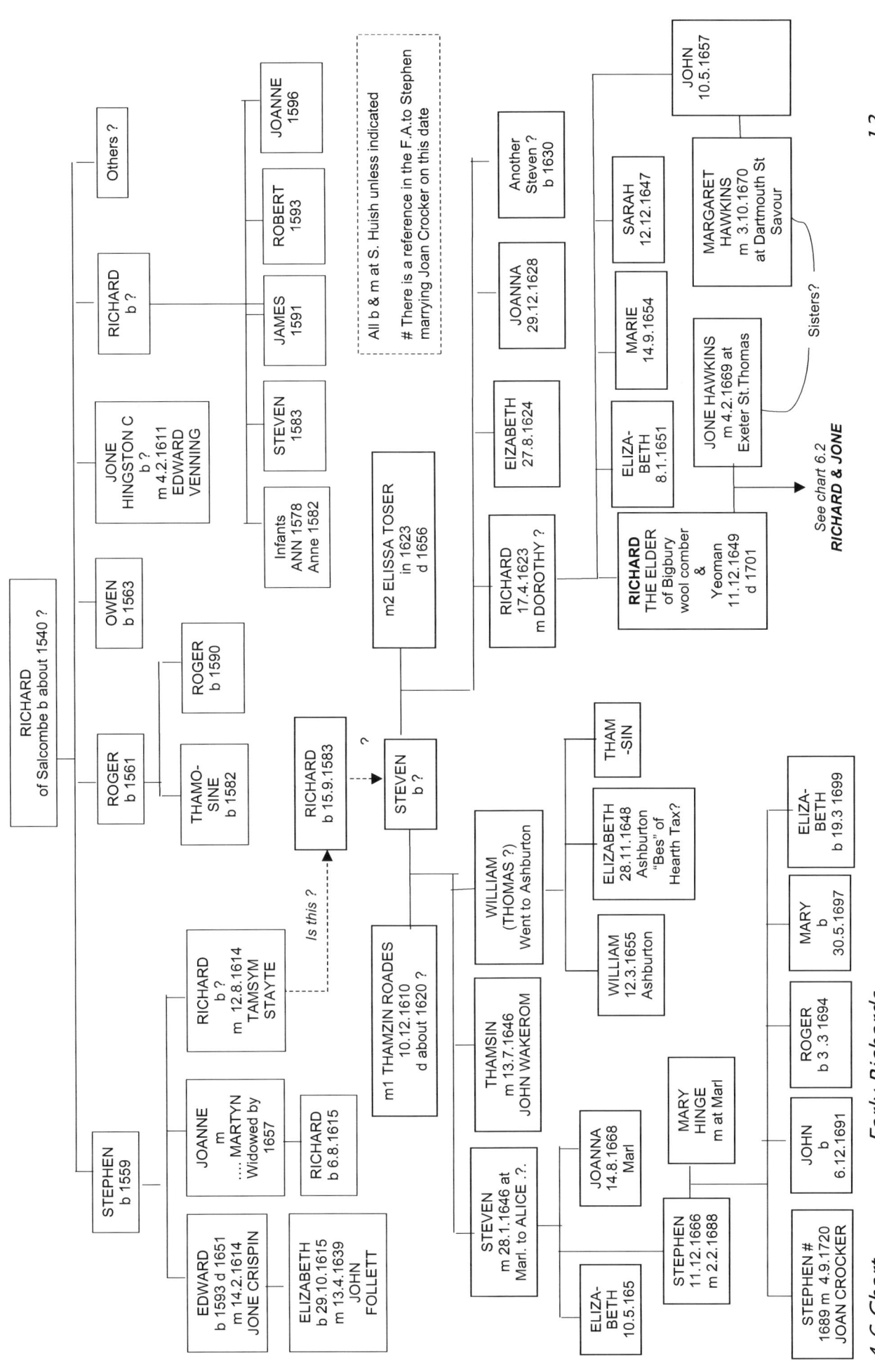

4.6 Chart Early Richards 13

CHAPTER 5

DISSENT

Ch 5.1 Civil War and Kingsbridge

Effects on Kingsbridge, Cranch sympathies, turmoil

Effects of The Civil War on Kingsbridge

"If a person writes about Kingsbridge and omits to notice the persecutions the Nonconformists underwent there, the most interesting and heart stirring period is omitted in the true history of this little town, ever since it has been discovered to have a history at all."

(A Nonconformist Memorial, Kingsbridge Gazette 4 Jan 1862)

Just prior to the civil war The Devon Protestation Returns 1641 required parishes to take the names of those who declared "their belief in the Protestant religion, allegiance to the King and support for the rights and privileges of Parliament". In South Huish, Richard Cranch and William Cranch registered; in Marlborough it was Andrew Cranch.

In the Civil War 1643-45 there were battles all around Kingsbridge: Fort Charles (Salcombe Castle), Modbury and the siege of Plymouth for instance. Cromwell's troops used Rickham Common in East Portlemouth as a campsite. The re-fortification and siege of Salcombe Castle nearby would have been witnessed by the Cranches. Later John the Painter reproduced in his notebooks the accounts and made a drawing of the key to the castle *(see ch 13)*.

The remains of Fort Charles DR.IB.000897A

Although it seems that no Cranches were active militarily, there is no doubt their sympathies lay with the Parliamentarians.

"In the account of the monies received by the Committee for the Defence of Plymouth against the King 1644" …..income is mostly from harbour dues, but as this was irregular, loans etc were sought from individuals……
"towards the continuation of the fight"

R.N Worth Calendar of Plymouth Municipal Records

One such individual was Jasper Cranch who made a loan of £50 on 4 October 1644

But that was not the only concern at the time. There was an outbreak of the plague locally in 1626. In 1666 there was "the great visitation of the plague", and all was not well:
> "not only did unusual and irregular taxation and borrowing harass the people of Devon but the strains of poor harvests, plague, inflation and unemployment added substantially to the distress caused by actions of arbitrary government. To the infringement of conscience and the slighting of principle occasioned by a zealous episcopacy must be added the fear of piracy, the dread of popery, the dearth due to overpopulation and the dislocation of internal and external trade "
>
> E.A Andriette , Devon and Exeter in the Civil War
> Writing about the period 1625 – 40 in
> Report and transactions of the Devonshire Association 1971

So if the Cranch family thought that by migrating to Kingsbridge they would escape conflict, they later found themselves in the midst of it again, with long term implications.

Turmoil
An indication of the turmoil at the time may be obtained from the following entry dated 22 April 1644 by the Minister of Marlborough, John Robinson in the Marlborough Parish Baptisms Register 1558:
> "From the 6th August 1643 those proceeding were baptised by me, which year with the present are years of blood and confusion, both in church and state not only in this kingdom but Ireland. The Judgements of God setting themselves in array that none know by reason of the present miseries what to expect but utter ruin. If God stop not the punishment this is for our sins luke-warm.... *(indecipherable words)* .... spiritual pride, contempt of God's messengers and open profanes. This I write that when God sends a blessed calm those who succeed me here might carefully admonish the lords of such of those horrid sins that all men follow their callings and seek to know what is fitting for their souls health to seek and pray for the peace of the Church and Commonwealth so they plunge themselves and their posterities into the like dreadful calamities. The Lord: look in mercy on us."

After the civil war, things began to settle down (relatively) under Oliver Cromwell's rule when the Church of England was established as a Protestant institution. Then came reactions and repercussions.

Ch 5.2 Dissent and Kingsbridge 3

Dissent and its consequences, Saltstone, Punishments, Rev Hicks, Declarations of Indulgence, Cranch Sympathies, References, old Painting.

Dissent
Dissent in this context refers to the struggle between Roman Catholicism and Protestantism begun in the 1500's. It reached its peak in the 1600's. The "Puritans" thought that the Reformation had not gone far enough in removing all the R.C doctrines and practices from the C. of E. They supported parliament and the Parliamentarians in their efforts to counteract Catholicism.

After the death of Cromwell, Catholicism returned officially as the national religion and reprisals against protestants resumed. The Act of Uniformity in 1662 caused almost 2, 000 Puritan ministers to be ejected from their "livings" for not conforming. The Conventicle Acts of 1664 etc punished anyone for attending a religious meeting held not according to *The Book of Common Prayer.* Ejected ministers were frequently fined and imprisoned. These dire times lasted until the 1689 Act of Toleration confirmed the status of the Church of England and dissenters were allowed to have licensed chapels.

This resulted in the Cranch entries in the Marlborough Parish registers dramatically diminishing after 1680. The registers of the chapels and other licenced places were in many cases poorly kept or indeed have been lost altogether. In the context of the tremendous changes that took place at this time, this would seem to be of minor importance, but it does frustrate the historian!

The consequences of dissent locally were explained in *The Nonconformist Memorial* referred to previously:
> "No fewer than six ministers, ….dwelt for a considerable period in Kingsbridge or its neighbourhood, viz the Rev John Quicke sometime vicar of this parish, Mr Birdwood, Mr Tooker (or Tucker), Mr Hicks, Mr Jellinger and Mr Hughes.
> Mr Birdwood rented land near the village of Batson….Mr Tucker lived at Norden [1], a little farm a scarce a third of a mile from the town, Mr Hicks, Mr Jellinger and Mr Hughes in the place itself......
> Mr Hughes was a person of very considerable eminence; he was buried in Kingsbridge Church and the worthy Mr Thomas Crispin ……friend and warm admirer of Mr Hughes (paid) ….the expenses of the funeral and …..erected a monument to his memory [2] John Quicke, ….(was) sent to prison once if not twice for his nonconformity "

The newspaper article includes this quote from Hawkins' book:
> "Near Kingsbridge there is an islet or rock, called Saltstone, above a hundred feet in length and more than fifty feet in breadth. …. being in view from the principle street. …it is extra-parochial, and perhaps doubtful to whom it belongs, lying nearly equi-distant from the parishes of Charlton, South Pool and Marlborough…… "

The article continues:
> Upon this hallowed rock the persecuted Nonconformists of the town and its adjacent villages ……………used to hold their religious meetings, and from the fact that of its being claimed by no particular parish, they felt there comparatively tranquil and secure, though occasionally exposed to much

rude insult from their enemies on shore. This islet with its picturesque surroundings and the group of worshippers who were wont of old to gather there would make as touching and lovely pictorial subject for an artist capable of treating it as it ought to be treated.

The Pilgrim Fathers who left for America held the same tenets as John Hicks and his companions ... and so did both Milton and Bunyan who narrowly escaped death. They were one with "those pious souls [3] who .... stood shelter-less upon Saltstone"

Notes
1. Norden – later occupied by Andrew (1650-1723)
2. In Kingsbridge (Dodbrook) church there is a marble tablet to the Rev George Hughes, vicar of St Andrews Plymouth who died 1667
3. Doubtless including members of the Cranch family

The Saltstone

This is a rock just off Warren Point in the Kingsbridge estuary. It is only covered during Spring Tides; at Neap Tides it is still exposed. As it is beyond the low water mark it was considered to be outside local parish boundaries and their legal jurisdiction. It thus became a meeting place for protestants during the "Troublous Times" free from the threat of harassment and prosecution . Getting there was another matter. Until about the 1950's a cross stood on the island. *(D. Murch 1990)*
The picture in Fairweather's book (1874) shows the cross still surviving to be a long pole with a cross piece.

Saltstone   Cookworthy

The rock has remined undeveloped, except by fishermen, occasional parties and as an object of speculation. It is now a nature reserve.

Other places where the early non-conformists in Kingsbridge used to meet undiscovered for worship were Garston (house and estate of Sir William Bastarde), Norden, Sorley Butts (now Sorley Green two miles from Loddiswell), Hill o' Linkum (Linckham Hill) and Ticket (Tacket) Wood so-called because entry was by ticket issued in advance to followers and so unlikely to escape detection. These are all places in or near land occupied by Cranch at that time.

Punishments

When found to contravene the conventicle Acts, punishment could be severe. The Rev George Hughes, ejected from Plymouth was imprisoned, his health suffered and he was permitted to pass his last days in Kingsbridge. In 1655 he was instrumental in forming the Assemblies of Ministers among the Dissenters to get the Ministers of several persuasions to co-operate rather than continually divide in religious debate.

The Rev. Tooker was ejected from Dittisham Parish Church. His family sought refuge at Norden. Master Beare arraigned him for praying with friends in his own home. He was fined £30 and all his goods sold. Well-wishers must have bought some of the goods back as an oak chair of his was later put in the Kingsbridge Congregational church when he succeeded the Rev Hicks. Jane Bowring Cranch *(see Ch 10)* had the chair restored and transferred to Loddiswell Congregational church in the late 1800's.

From the Order of Sessions (Exeter) 1673- 1689), Kingsbridge people recorded as being fined were: A.Budwell (chandler), J. Hingstone (fuller), Thomas Crispin (of Exeter, fuller), Mrs J Hinckson, A Brooking (widow and her daughter), N. Brooking (merchant), Thomas Crispin again (fuller at his house in Exeter), W. Phillips (of West Alvington).

In 1679 at the house of J Hopping Exeter 161 persons were fined including Ursula Cranch of Exeter. The occupations of the 161 people fined give support to the claim that the most active protestants were the middle classes of the period: butcher, merchant, silkworker, clothier, weaver, basket maker, wool comber, tobacconist, gardener, sailor joiner, tiler, fuller, cordwainer, ironmonger, goldsmith, brewer, grocer, linen draper, farmer, barrel bearer, comb maker.

By 1673 the Baptists seemed to have become a numerous and permanent religious body. The Baptist Burial Ground at Venn was
> "bequeathed to the church in 1673 by Arthur Langworthy of Hache so that the baptists would have somewhere quiet and private for their burials . It is situated on a hill overlooking the Aune valley with high walls surrounding three sides, The fourth wall is lower, permitting the view"
> *(Introduction in the grave register)*

At least one Cranch is buried there

Protests took many forms. In the Ashburton Parish Register on 11 August 1684 there is an entry for "repairing the church and for other pious uses thereto belonging". The vicar Mr John Bastard contributed £1/6/-, Elizabeth Cranch and William Cranch contributed 2/8d, William Cranch (for Blackler) paid 6d. Many parishioners opposed the rate, including William Cranch.

Rev Hicks
One of the more colourful radical firebrands of the time was the Rev John Hicks and we are indebted to Jane Bowring Cranch for writing her book **"Troublous Times"**. It is based on the diaries of Hicks circa 1670 which were given to a Mr Hawes for custody. It gives a good account of the activities of the dissenters and the persecutors and is essential reading for its local and family perspectives of that time.

It is clear the author was able to bring family knowledge to bear whilst writing the book. Many if not all of the assembling places were on Cranch land at Batson or nearby. The passage in the book involving the blacksmith thinly disguises that the blacksmith was a Cranch.

Ch 5.2 Dissent and Kingsbridge

In his Introduction to the book the Rev Charles Stanford says:
> "From family traditions, as well as from standard biographies, (the author) .... has collected many interesting notices of our Kingsbridge worthies .....every leading incident is a well authenticated fact ...."

In all the book lists 12 dissenting ejected ministers living in Kingsbridge at the time: Hammer, Flavel, Quicke, Lewis, Stuckley, Tooker, Makepeace, Hughes, Hicks, Jellinger, Howe, Habakkuk, Brande.

The book describes the antics of both the protesters in avoiding detection and the enforcers in trying to disperse the "illegal" gatherings and catching the main perpetrators. Judge Beare was a particularly active prosecutor. There is some irony in that 300 years later, a Cranch relative (protestant) lives in the manor of the infamous (catholic) Judge Beare.

In a bible was found the following, written by Robert Sparling 1681:
> "Mr Hicks preached at Charlton Chappell June the 24th 1681"

Charlton is just outside Kingsbridge. The bible was found by Loddiswell dustmen in a bin who offered it in exchange for a token gift such as a cake.
It is claimed that the account must be accurate as, although Hicks left the district in 1671, he was to some extent nomadic until he volunteered in 1685 to join Monmouth
(Information from Miss Michell).

Hicks also had some interesting things to say about emigration to America, (quoted later in the chapter on Richard and America). In the Fox book Hicks is described as being born in 1633 near Thirsk, Yorkshire and
> "..minister of Stoke Dameral, which living being in the gift of the Crown, he was obliged to quit at the Restoration of King Charles, when he removed to Saltash, whence he was ejected in 1662 and moved to Kingsbridge where he had a meeting"

A discussion about a libellous Pamphlet, attributed to Hicks, follows in Ch 5.3.

Declarations of Indulgence

An indication of the extent of local dissent may be gleaned from the number of applications for a Presbyterian Licenced Congregation made in 1672

- Dartmouth : by Richard Cranch (and others)
- Gittisham : house of Robert Michell (by John Hicks?)
- Exeter : house of Thomas Chrispin
- Newton Abbot : William Yeo (ejected from Woolborough)
- Kingsbridge : three from John Hicks (ejected from Saltash) : 1665 while still at Saltash, 1672 his Kingsbridge house, 1672 for his newly built meeting house
- West Alvington : a house at Auton by Edmund Tooker (ejected from Dittisham)
- Salcombe : three houses by Richard Smith (ejected from Whitstanton, Somerset), Mrs Elizabeth Isaack (Lincombe House), Joanne Baston (or Bastarde ?)
- Bigbury : house at Hexdown of James Burdwood (ejected from Dartmouth St Breock). A Conventicle gives him as residing in Dartmouth in 1665
- Plymouth ; three houses: Thomas Yeabsley, John Quicke (ejected from Brixton, Plymouth), George Hughes (ejecyted from Plymouth)
- West Allington : an application for a Quaker meeting place by William Hingston " a notorious Quaker".

Ch 5.2 Dissent and Kingsbridge

Cranch Sympathies

There is no doubt that the Cranch family were sympathetic at least to the causes of the Civil war and were very supportive of Dissent. They witnessed the events taking place on their land.!

This dissent was not a "passing phase" – the principles were continued by many of the family for generations and centuries to come.

In this context, Worth maintains that
> "the most puritan class was the middle class"

and that
> "Puritanism became identified with the principle of civil liberty in the Wars of the Commonwealth".

Puritans in Devon and the Exeter Assembly by R.N Worth, Reports and Transactions of the Devonshire Association (Plymouth) 1877

References
- *Americanus : Puritanism in E Devon and the New England Emigrants 1625-30 Devon and Cornwall Notes and Queries No 18 (1935)*
- *Reports and Transactions of the Devonshire Association No 32 (1900) by Jellinger*
- *Kingsbridge Nonconformists by Celia Strong. LHG Meeting 20 Feb 2013*
- *Non-Conformist Registers of Chapels (general Registry Office)*
- *Recusant Rolls 1592-1691   PRO E376, 377*
- *A Discourse delivered 24 June 1818 before the Annual Assembly of Dissenting Ministers at Exeter by James Manning in Sermons by Belsham and others 1823. It quotes Mr Flavel in 1692 as suggesting "the propriety of a union between Protestant dissenters of different denominations…" . Mr Flavel preached at Dartmouth and taught a John Cranch who became a dissenting Minister at Modbury, then Axminster*

Non-Conformist Service on Saltstone Rock 1672 from an old painting.

On a postcard, with above caption, origin of painting unknown.   *Cookworthy P0612*

A Reprinted Pamphlet and its Preface, Explanations, Comment, Title Page of the Original "True and Faithful Narrative".

A NARRATIVE

OF THE

PERSECUTIONS

AGAINST

DISSENTERS,

IN

KINGSBRIDGE,

And other Places in Devonshire,

UNDER THE REIGN OF CHARLES II;

Revised from an Old Work published in 1671.

Kingsbridge:

PRINTED AND PUBLISHED BY R. SOUTHWOOD.

1821.

Ch 5.3 A Libellous Pamphlet

The preface to this pamphlet:

"The matter contained in the following narrative is taken from an old publication, printed in the year 1671, which belonged to the late Mr. William Cranch; this, with another in the possession of Mr. William Lavers, late the property of Mr. Jeremiah Cranch, deceased, are the only two of the original copies now known to be extant. The name of the author or printer does not appear in any part of the work, both of which perhaps were omitted for very sufficient reasons; indeed the author would have gained but a small meed of praise as a scholar and grammarian, to say nothing of other necessary qualifications, if he had affixed his name to the title page. The general language of the work is very ambiguous, and by no means suited to the readers of the present day; and on this account we have undertaken the tedious task of revising it. Yet the facts and meaning of the original work, shall be carefully retained and related according to the author's own arrangement of the subject.

There has been a considerable degree of curiosity attached to this small pamphlet, by dissenters, on account of the information it gives of the state of religion in those times; but there can be a greater advantage derived from it, than merely knowing what was the order, or rather disorder of that day:—the reader will come at once to this reflection, that persecution cannot stifle or subdue truth, and that great privilege of our country, liberty of conscience. ....

It is evident those disturbers of the peace, did not act under any constitutional authority .... The author asserts in his preface that: "He will not charge it upon any of our legislators, that they have made unreasonable and unjustifiable laws ...."

In short he charges all the mischief to pride and ignorance ...... In allusion to the principles of the king (Chas. II) he says: ....our king is of that mild and compassionate temper, that if he did but read, and had a right information of such things as are contained in this narrative ....he would endeavour some speedy relief for the oppressed, and punish the wretched usurpers of his authority."

J. C. Kingsbridge, Nov. 22nd, 1820.

Explanations
The existence of this booklet is another indication of how closely the Cranch family were to dissent in Kingsbridge.

J.C is Joseph Cranch (1792 – 1874), the eldest son of the William Cranch referred to. Another son, John Roope Cranch is my direct ancestor. Jeremiah (d 1812) was a first cousin to J.C, and his eldest daughter married William Lavers. Whether a copy of the original 1671 pamphlet survives is not known.

Fox in her book claims that the original pamphlet was written by Hicks. How did she know this? Because she was told it by Jane Bowring Cranch, a close friend. No doubt Hicks was prone to long rambling speeches, so it is in keeping with his character that any text written by him would require "the tedious task of revising it".

Davidson copied out the 1821 version. Evidently not many were printed as he says:
"The following is a transcript if a very scarce tract in 8vo, lent me by Miss Jane B Cranch of Kingsbridge on the 19th Oct 1842"   *J.D. Secktor*

Ch 5.3 A Libellous Pamphlet

Hawkins comments that

"From this narrative it appears, that the Conventicle Acts …. occasioned much strife and persecution in Kingsbridge ; that George Reynel of Sherford, and John Beare of Bearscoombe ….. were two magistrates most rigid in carrying the law against conventicles into execution; while Matthew Hele, of Halwell, and William Bastard of Garston, two other justices of the peace, were mild and tolerant…. that one Hicks, a dissenting minister, was the particular object of the persecuting party… (who with)…eight others were tried at Exeter assizes for murder, but acquitted; and that the two tolerant magistrates, Hele and Bastard, were prosecuted for neglect of duly in not rigidly enforcing the law, and fined.
The invective which pervades this ….shows that the dissenters ….were harshly dealt with; and that …..liberal minded magistrates …were construed as …favouring conventiclers.
We may conclude that the "very sufficient reasons" stating that "The name of the author or printer does not appear in any part of the work….." are because of the libellous nature of the work and that the dissenters did not wish to give Beare any more cause to pursue and persecute them."

Comment: the last sentence probably also indicates why the print run of the original publication was very limited ! Its rambling and ambiguous language also clearly needed editing if it were to be more widely distributed (as the following illustrates)

The Original Pamphlet : A True and Faithful Narrative

Hawkins described the original pamphlet: about 40 pages crown 8vo, printed in 1671 possessed by the descendants of Jeremiah Cranch, which was called:

"A True and Faithful Narrative, of the Unjust and Illegal Sufferings, and Oppressions of many Christians (Injuriously and Injudiciously called Fanaticks, holding all the Fundamentals of the Christian Religion, Believing all the Articles of the Christian Faith ; and whose Lives and Conversations are as Consonant, and Agreeable to the Laws of God as theirs that Persecute them) under, and by several of his Majesty's Justices of Peace, and others, who are no officers, but Informers, in the county of Devon, since the Tenth of May, 1670, from a pretended Zeal, to put the Law against Conventicles in Execution. As Also, Of the most Malicious Prosecution of Nine Innocent Persons, to take away their Lives,under a False pretence of Murdering an Informer: And of the Trials that were betwixt Matthew Hele,of Halwel, in the Parish of (South) Pool, William Bastard,of Garston, in the Parish of West Alvington, Esquires, and Mr. Edmund Reynel, and John Bear, (called by a Nick-name Cockey Bear) Two Informers for pretended Neglects, of putting the Act against Conventicles in execution, and the hard Measure they met with from the Judge; with the Horrid Perjuries of Witnesses brought against them, at the Assizes held at Exon in the county of Devon, April 1671"

References
1. *J.D. is James Davidson (see chapter on John the painter)*
2. *His handwritten version is at DHC ref S 272.8 - KIN – HIC*
3. *An on-line copy is available via Google Books, but it does not have J.D's Sector [library] comment*
4. *Hawkins, Fox, J.B.Cranch – writers acknowledged elsewhere.*

Cranch and Religion, a Satirical poem, G. Whitfield, Political Views

Cranch and Religion

The Puritan / Nonconformist / Protestant influences continued in Kingsbridge and in the Cranch family. All became Protestants (if they were not already) in various guises: Independents (later Congregational), Baptists, Methodists, a few Quakers. Some remained with the (protestant) Church of England. The most frequent references are to Cranches with protestant and "liberal" views. Thus:

- Births, marriages and deaths being recorded at the meeting houses in the Kingsbridge area and Exeter
- in 1706 a meeting of the United Brethren of Devon and Cornwall was attended by Mr Cranch.
- John[3] (1709-1746), eldest of the seven children of Andrew[1], became a Dissenting Minister at Modbury, then Illmington. Taught by Rev. Flavel.
- The East Portlemouth parish register dated 16 December 1670 records that Mr John Cranch donated "towards the redemption of the English captives in Turkey"
- John the Naturalist (1785 – 1816) had the "gloomy view of Christianity taken by his church. His friends declare him to be a sincere Christian….."
- John the Painter sent John Adams a political tract in 1720 *(see Chapter 11)*
- Richard[2] who went to America is described as a Puritan as was his parents. The application of his beliefs is described in Chapter 12.

Other Cranches with references to religion;

- Richard (1719 – 1756 son of Richard of Bigbury) became the Rector of Dipford
- John the painter (1751-1821) expressed aversion to "popery" in his notebooks
- In the 17 and 1800's several Cranches were Feoffees (administrators of properties and funds donated to the church for charitable purposes). Known Feoffees in Kingsbridge: 1738 John, 1772 Joseph, 1817 William
- In the 18 and 1900's, three generations of the South Brent family were churchwardens (C. of E.)
- Anna Cranch. *The Western Times, 14 April 1881* reported this discovery:
    "The Society of Friends have recently sold their old and disused burial ground at the top of Duncombe Street to the Feoffees of the town lands here, who propose building on the site a public library and place for holding meetings … in excavating the ground, the workmen came across a tombstone on which was the following :
    > "Here lyeth the body of Anna Cranch, who departed this life
    > July 1746 aged 81"
    The Cranch family are very old parishioners … held parish offices in about 1600, their names appearing in the old Feoffee books of that date."
- In 1745 the inhabitants of the City and County of Exeter formed an Association in support of George II against "the young pretender" and the "wicked and unnatural rebellion begun in Scotland…….in favour of a Popish pretender". Andrew Cranch and Richard Cranch signed their names.

However it seems that not all the family took life so seriously. William (1754 – 1821), no doubt egged on by his brother John the Painter, penned this:

> Ten Commandments by our Omnipotent Minister
> Thou shalt not read
> Thou shalt not know what o'clock it is
> Thou shalt not put powder on thy pate

Thou shalt not look through thy window upon the sun
Thou shalt not ride to take in the air
Thou shalt not yoke dobbin to the plough
Thou shalt not cherish thy faithful dog
Thou shalt not associate with thy neighbour
Thou shalt not marry
But thou shalt put a hood coat upon thy back to defend and inforce these and any other my just commandments
To them we may add an Eleventh
Thou shalt not worship no other Minister but me for I am a jealous Minister and visit the sins of the father upon children even unto the fiftieth generation

George Whitfield 1714 – 1770

History has many proponents of the radical cause. One was George Whitfield. He was an English Anglican cleric, evangelist and one of the founders of Methodism, working closely with the Wesley brothers.

His style was to preach in the open, reaching out to people who normally did not attend church and eliciting their emotional response with a potent combination of drama, religious rhetoric, and imperial pride. Newspapers called him the 'marvel of the age'. His methods were controversial and he engaged in numerous debates and disputes with other clergymen.

He preached in the West Country:

- 26 July 1744 ....I have also made an elopement to Kingsbridge, where I preached to many thousands a few days ago. ....
- Plymouth 27 July 1744 ......people come daily to see me....Fresh news from Kingsbridge of souls being awakened ...
- Plymouth 16 Feb 1749 ....I rode 20 miles to Kingsbridge where to my great surprise, I found about a 1000 souls waiting till 8 in the evening to hear the word. ....I preached in the street. The moon shone. All was quiet & I hope some began to think of working out their salvation with fear and trembling. The next morning I preached again, four ministers attended. Our Lord was pleased to make it a very fine occasion. ....After sermon I had the pleasure of hearing that ....about 5 years ago many souls were awakened......

Sketches of Life & Labours of the Rev George Whitefield :

Of this occasion in 1749, Fox wrote:
> "Nathaniel Cranch lived in Mill Street (where Quay House now is) near where Whitfield was to preach. He lent his kitchen table for Whitfield to stand on. Nathaniel's eldest son *(Nathaniel then aged 7)* remembers the table being taken out for this purpose. The table returned to domestic use until unfit when it was put aside…. In 1853 Jane Bowring Cranch had it careful restored"

Jane Bowring Cranch's version is:
> "A godly man, who lived quite near the spot selected for the occasion lent a table for the preacher's use, Whitfield stood upon this homely household thing during the service. "

The "godly man" was her grandfather. The table was an English oak kitchen table. It was later donated to Loddiswell Congregational Church by Jane Bowring Cranch where it still is (with Tooker's chair).

Political Views

As implied above, the Dissenters came to be identified with radical political views, supporting the American revolution for instance and anti-slavery. However this is an over-simplification for as with any family there would be variation's. What is without doubt is that, as far as can be determined, all the Cranch family were "non-conformists". Some emigrated to America in the 1700's in pursuit of their beliefs.

References for this and preceding section
1. *Whitefield Preaching. A Tract. By Jane Bowring Cranch 1856 (British library). It also contains a poem and a sketch of the table.*
2. *Troublous Times or Leaves from the Notebook of the Rev Mr John Hicks, an ejected Nonconformist Minister `1670-71. Transcribed by Jane Bowring Cranch with an Introduction by the Rev. Charles Stanford. Jackson, Walford & Hodder, London 1862*
3. *A local explanation by a Unitarian Minister at Georges Meeting in Exeter:*
   Carpenter, Lant. A brief view of the Chief Grounds of Dissent from the Church of England by law established: A Discourse first delivered in Exeter, May 13th 1810, and repeated in Plymouth, April 5th, 1812. Second edition. T. Besley, Exeter, 1816,
4. *Fort Charles:, Salcombe: a Coastal Artillery Fort of Henry VIII , refortified in the Civil war by R. Parker, A . Passmore & M. Stoyle Proceedings of Devon Archaeological Society vol 63 2005*
5. *A short History of Dissent in Exeter (and further afield) c 1531-1854 by E .Legon, Exeter Dissenters Graveyard Trust.*
6. *Exeter Dissenters Graveyard Trust Memorials*
   11 Richard d 1793, his wife Jane d 1824, their d Maria Joanna d 1786 aged 3
   31 Jane (nee Hutchings) d.1787, wife of Christopher.
   Many for the Bowrings.
7. *A Narrative of the Persecutions against Dissenters in Kingsbridge in reign of Charles II originally published in 1671 (private Collection)*
8. *Puritanism in Devon and the Exeter assembly by R.N.Worth RTDA 9 (1877)*
9. *Friends of the Devonshire Association website F.O.D.A.org*

CHAPTER 6
RICHARD TREE AFTER 1650

Ch. 6.1 The Richard Tree After About 1650 Until Recent Times

Introduction

The chart 4.6 gave the memberships of the Richard tree known from the earliest records

This chapter is devoted to following the paths of the Richard tree from about 1700 onwards. To aid the tracking of members about whom we have some knowledge they have been given "labels". These labels were probably not in use when they lived.

Schematically
EARLY RICHARDS **4.6**

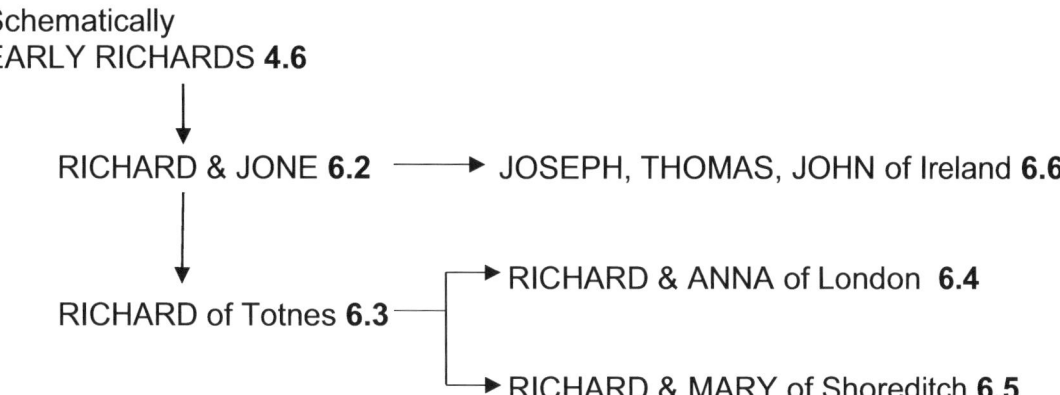

In chronical order :
- Chart 6.2 (approx. 1670 – 1720). The descendants of Richard and Jone. This takes off from the first chart 4.6 followed by:
- Chart 6.3 (approx. 1700-1800), Richard of Totnes, a solicitor followed by charts for two of his grandsons:
- Chart 6.4 (approx. 1800 – 1950) solicitor Richard and Anna of London
- Chart 6.5 (approx. 1800 – 1850) Richard and Mary of Shoreditch
- Chart 6.6 (approx 1800 – date) is for Joseph, Thomas and John of Ireland – descended from Joseph, a son of Richard of Totnes.

After these charts, there are notes on members in the charts, that is :

- Ch 6.7 describes the family of Richard and Jone
- Ch 6.8 describes the family of Richard of Totnes
- Ch 6.9 describes the family of Richard Charles Lovell Cranch and his brother George Cranch.
- Ch 6. 10 relates an amusing incident involving James, descended from Joseph (Richard of Tones's son)

Notes:
- *If it seems that just one chapter covers the Richard Tree whereas the rest of the book relates to members of the Andrew Tree shows bias - it is down simply to the availability of information.*
- *The tracing of the family of Joseph (son of Richard of Totnes) is far from complete but it is important in that it proves that members of the Richard Tree stayed locally – they did not all migrate to the London area.*

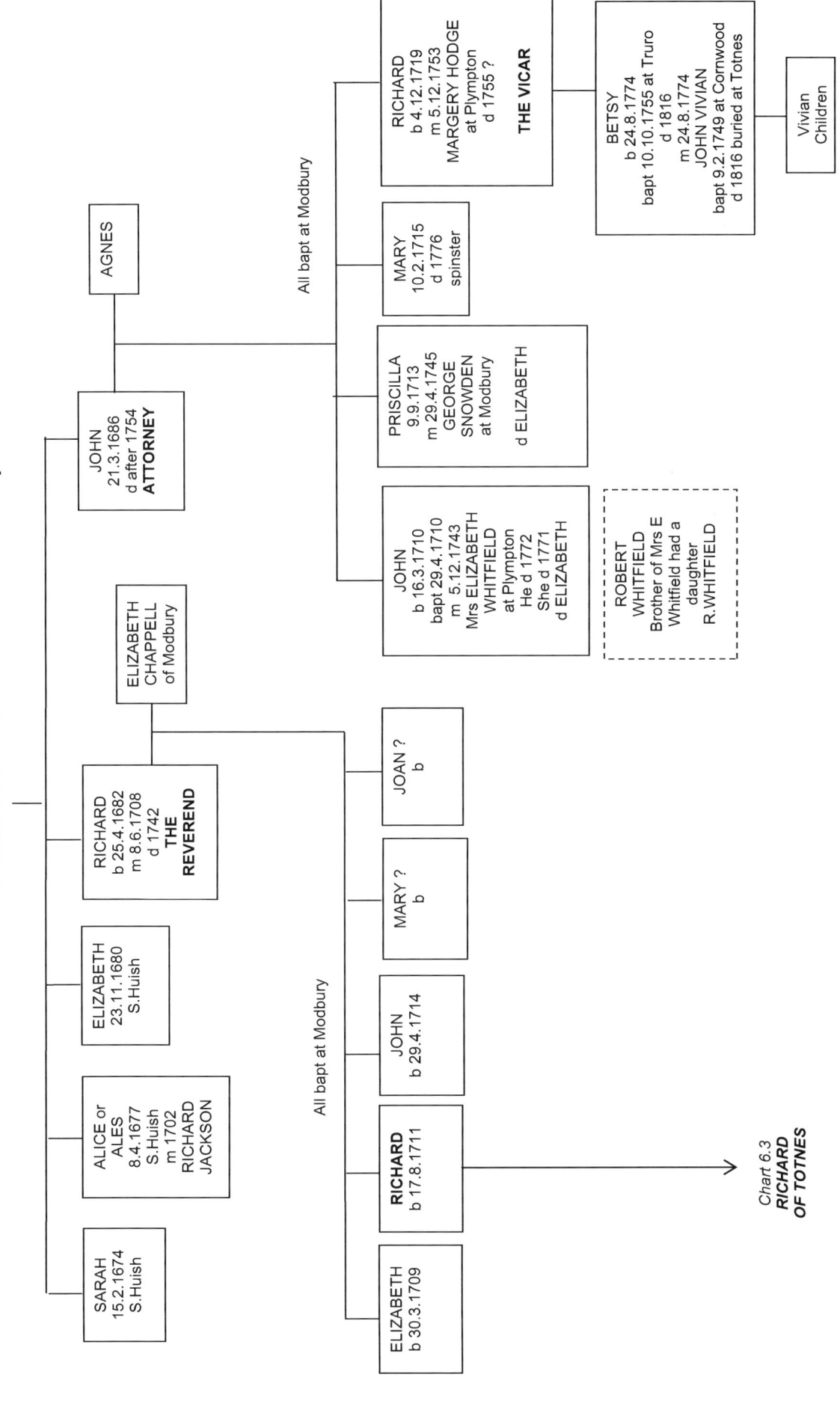

6.2 Chart   RICHARD & JONE

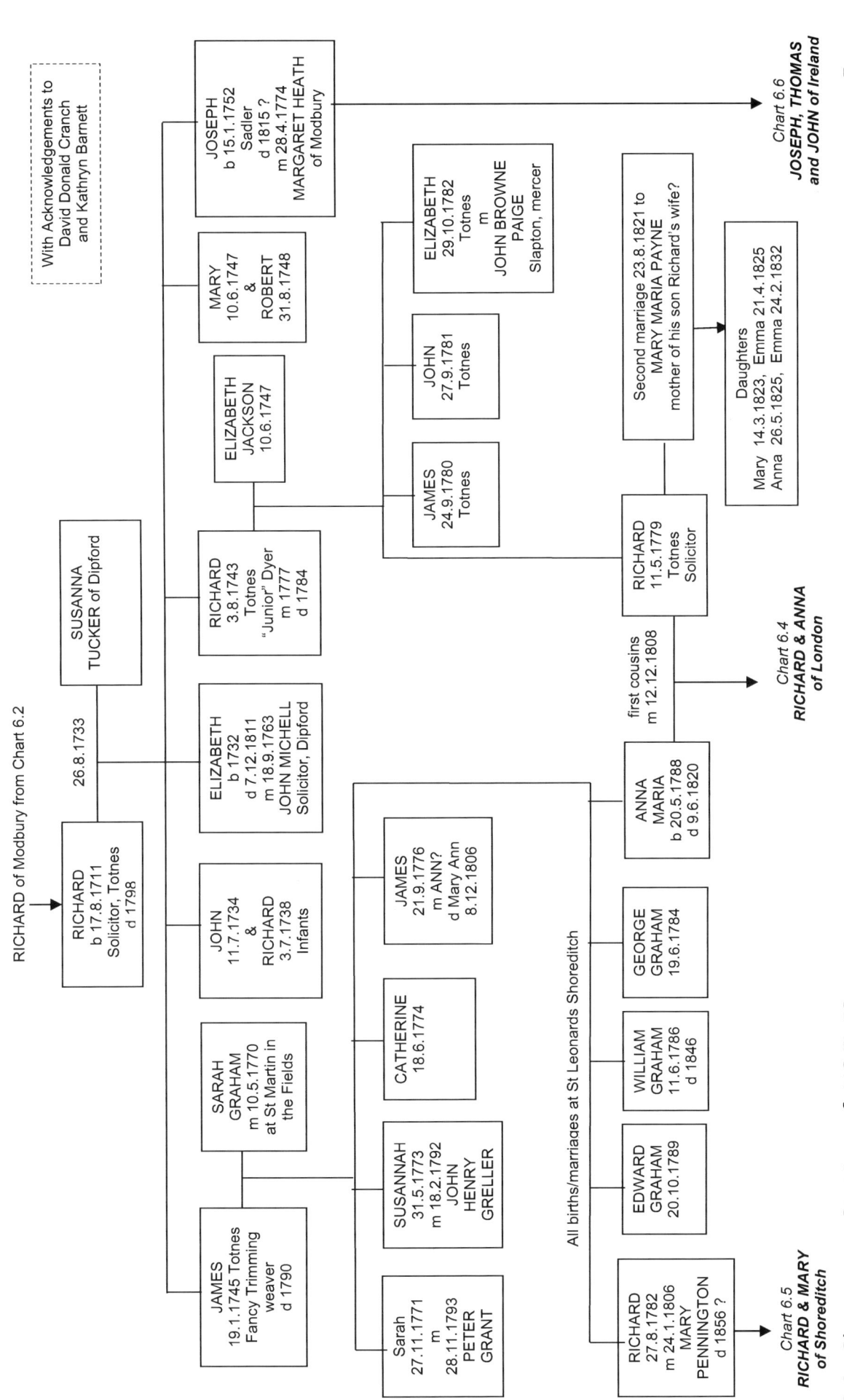

6.3 Chart RICHARD of TOTNES

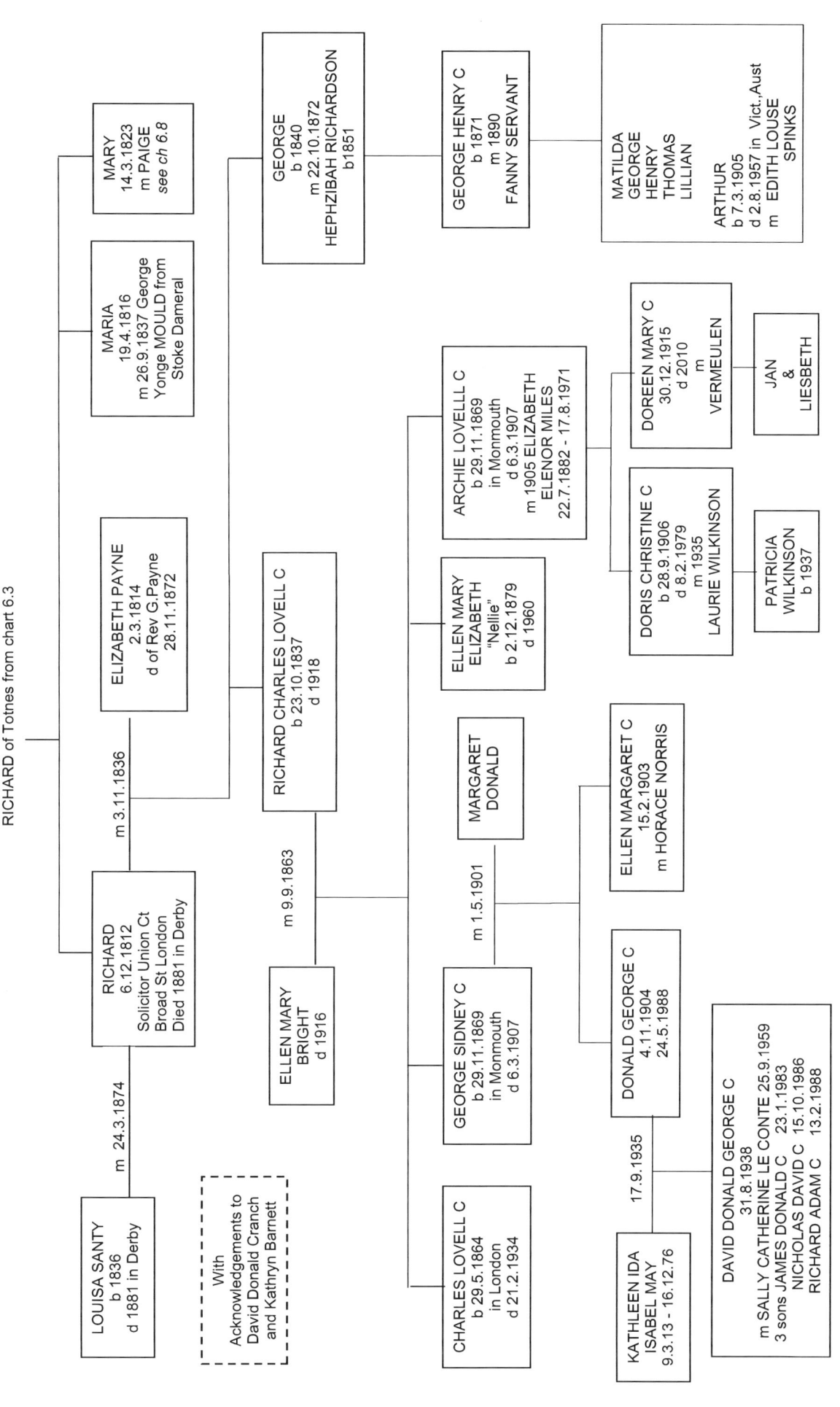

6.4 Chart RICHARD and ANNA of London

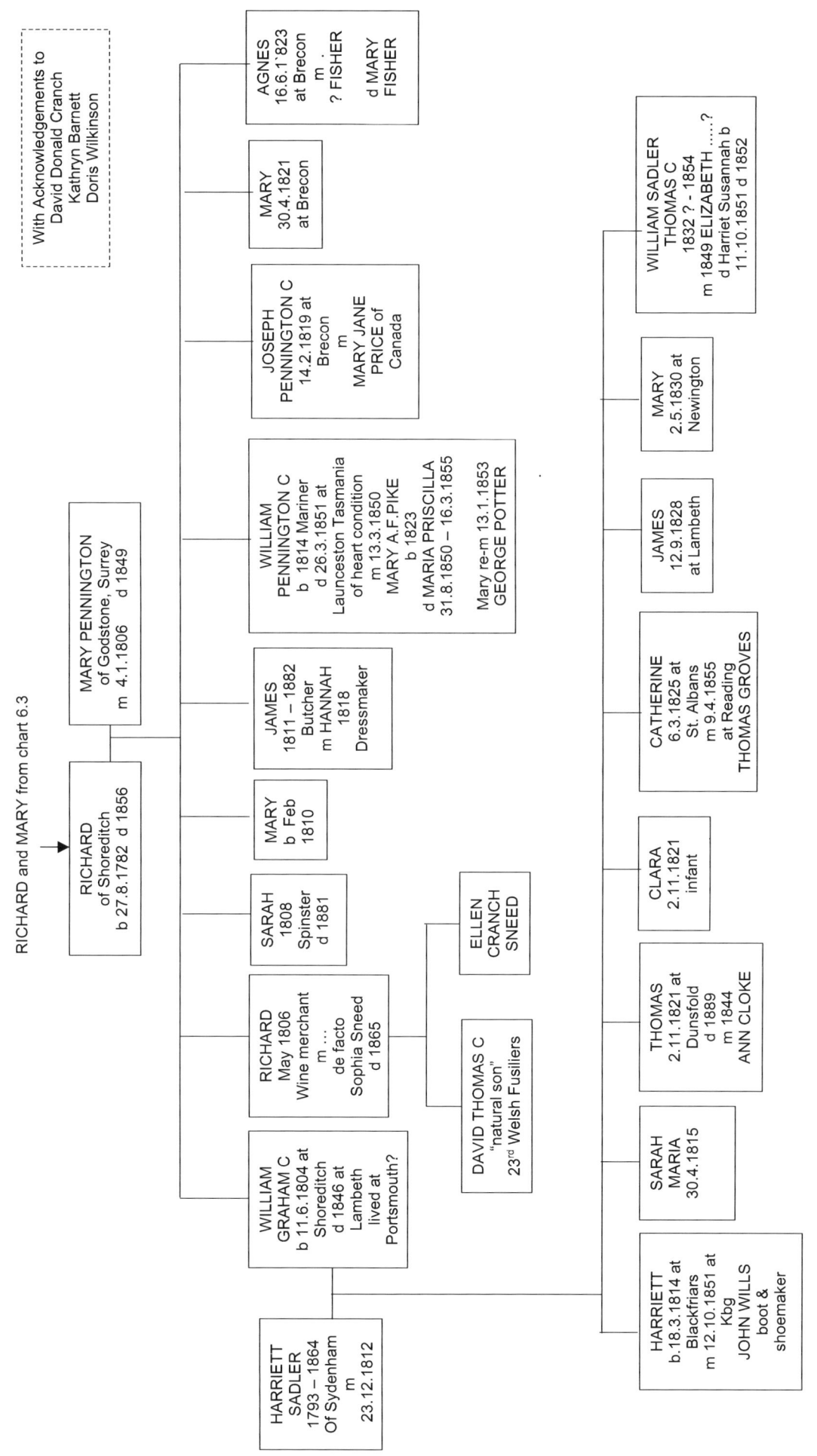

6.5 Chart   RICHARD & MARY of Shoreditch

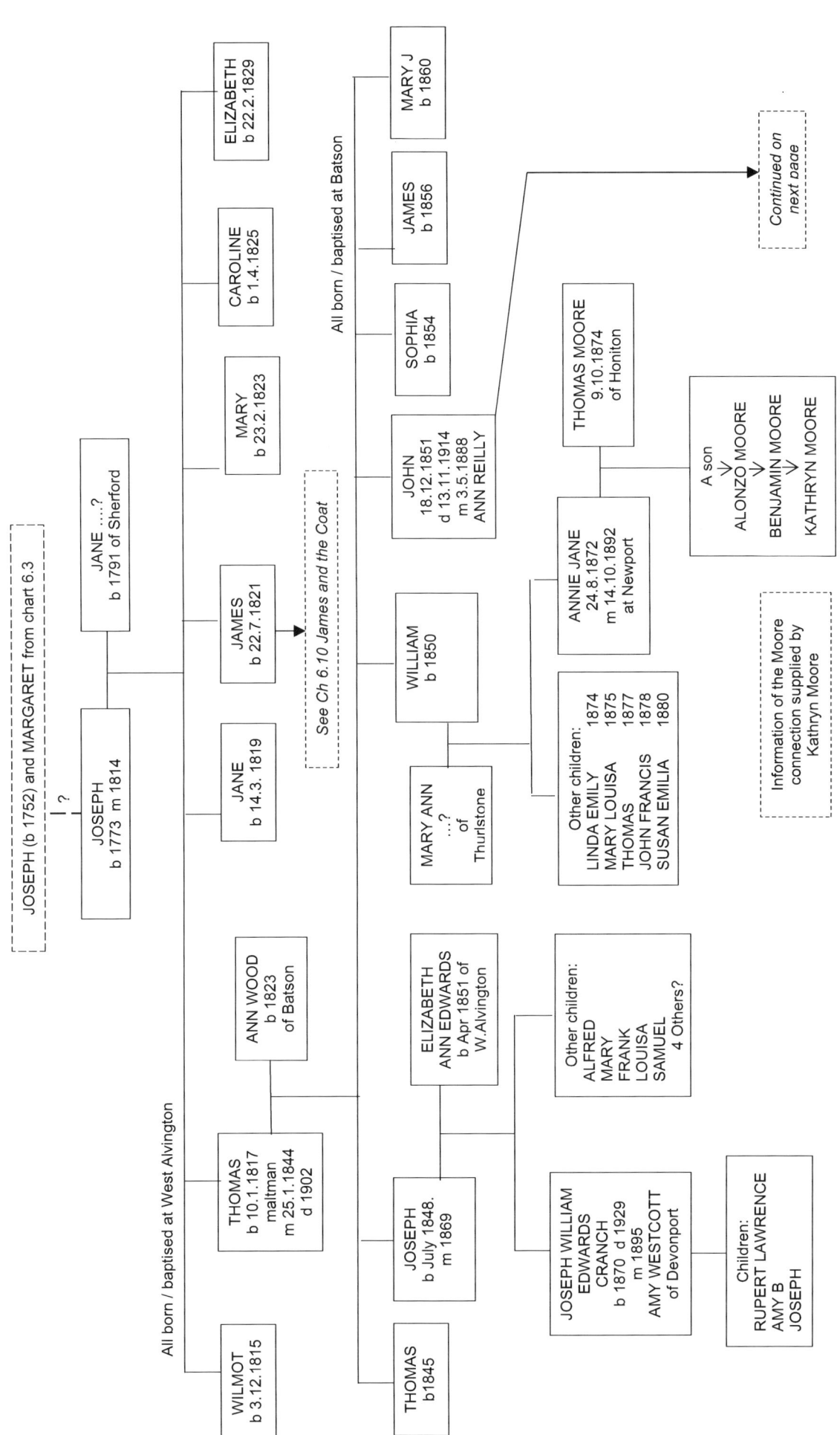

6.6 Chart   Joseph, Thomas and John of Ireland

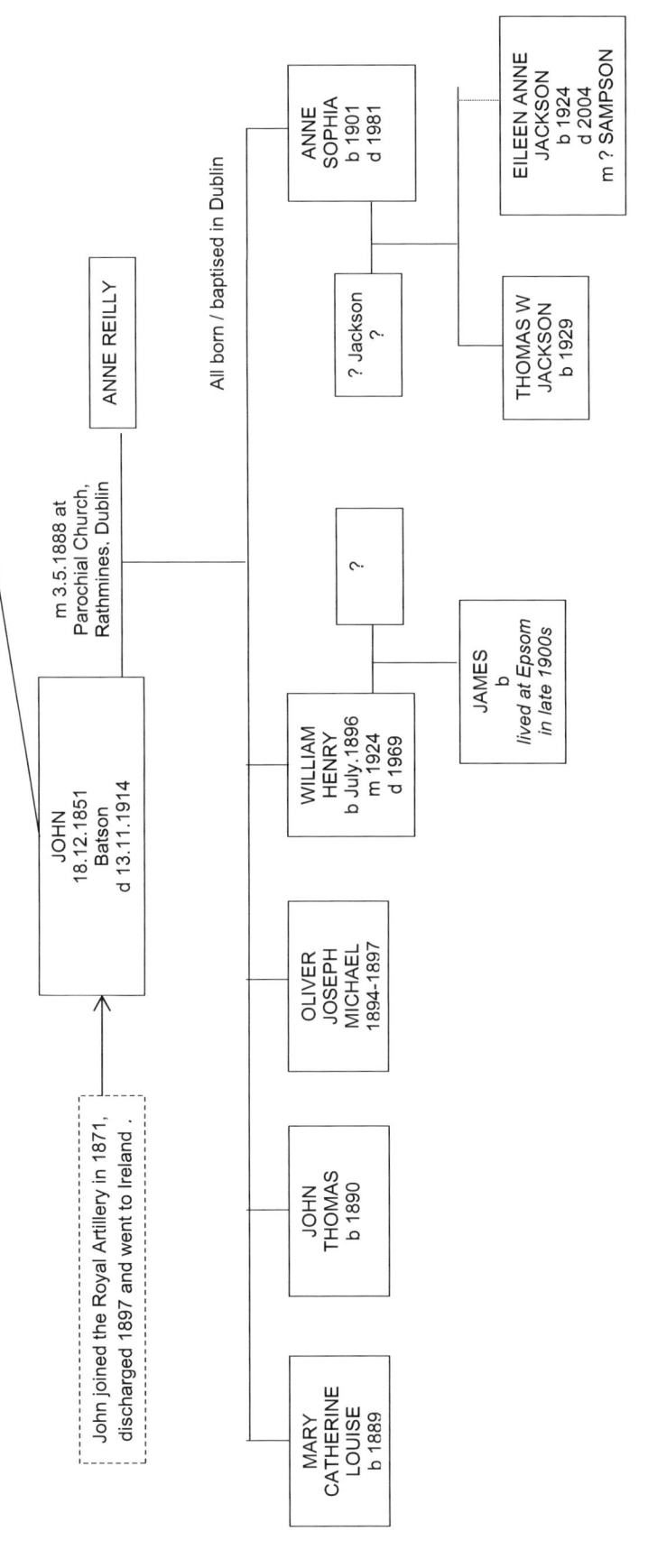

6.6 Chart   Joseph, Thomas and John of Ireland

Ch 6.7 Family of Richard and Jone   *14*

Richard the Elder, The Reverend Richard, Joshua Renolds, Richard's Estate, John the Attorney, Richard the Vicar, Betsey, Mary.

Richard the Elder
Descended from the early Richard Cranches of South Huish (See Chart 4.6)
Born   11.12.1649
Married   Jone Hawkins from Exeter 4.2.1669.
               They had 2 sons (Richard and John) and three daughters
Died 1702
Described as a wool comber and yeoman. He owned considerable property in the region. Some records exist of his legal dealings with his tenants in Bigbury and Kingston (near Plymouth). [a]

His daughter Sarah when she died in 1698 used to live at a cottage at Shabbacombe When his daughter Alice (Ales?) married Richard Jackson, yeoman of Bigbury, she is described as being of Bigbury Her father Richard the Elder made a marriage settlement shortly before he died. In 1707 Alice leased a field at Badstone [b]

(a) National Archives Kew 1686 C series
(b) Calendar of Deeds, Exeter city Library

The Reverend Richard
The Reverend Richard was the older of the two sons of Richard the Elder.
Born 25 April 1682   Died circa 1742, aged about 60

Ch 6.7 Family of Richard and Jone

Education   Went to Exeter College, matriculated 31 march 1701 aged 18
Oxford University BA 1704, MA 1707   *(Alumni Oxonienses 1500-1714)*
From 1721 - 1738 he was the Rector at Dipford (Church of England) of a dissenting congregation.

Married   Elizabeth Chappel of Modbury 8 June 1708. They had three children
She was the daughter of John Chapel the elder. The marriage settlement involved a "moiety of the capital of messuage and lands of Hawelscombe, Bigbury".

Somerset H C ref DD/FS/61/2/16-17

During the period after graduating and before his appointment, he probably assisted incumbent ministers and continued his studies. In 1714 he subscribed to Dr.J.. Walker's "sufferings of the Clergy during the rebellion... at the hands of the protestants". This includes reference to Jellinger (protestant dissenter) evicting Gandy (catholic) from South Brent at the time of the Dissolution.

In 1721 he was ordained at South Huish before becoming Rector at Plympton

References:
1. Certified to be clerk rector of Dipford 31 Dec 1721, ordained in South Huish, DRO ref QS/21/1721/14
2. Rector Dipford (South Huish)   DHC ref QS/21/1721/14
3. Marriage to Elizabeth Chapel : Somerset H C ref DD/FS/61/2/16-17

The Joshua Renolds connection
The Rev Richard is known mostly for his connection with Sir Joshua Renolds. The portrait of him by Sir Joshua Reynolds was sold at auction for £8,400 at Sotherby's in London. He is shown wearing a blue coat and white necktie.

Tony Richardson, Evening Herald, Torquay 24 March 2005

Richard "possessed a small independent fortune, and resided at the town of Plympton" in the 1730's. The families of Rev Richard and the Reverend Renolds lived at Plympton St Maurice and were neighbours and friends. Richard showed interest in young Joshua's abilities and encouraged his development and gave financial support.

Renolds was born in 1723. In 1740 Renold's mother records that she " was last night with Mr Craunch, as he was asking me what I designed to do with Joshua who is now drawing near to seventeen"

Later in 1741 "Mr Cranch advised the father to send his son to London to be placed under the tuition of Mr Hudson a well-known painter of portraits who was also a native of Devonshire". Later Richard paid Joshua to go to Bideford to meet Hudson Joshua was placed with Hudson in Oct 1741. "Mr Cranch when he saw some drawings of Joshua's in his second year he still saw an improvement" and he assisted Joshua with "loans from his old friend Mr Craunch". Richard paid for Renolds to go to study in Italy.

After his return from Italy Renolds, in gratefulness for the Rev Richard's help in getting him the introduction to Hudson, painted Richard's portrait and those of others of his family.

Renolds was "always particularly indebted to Mr Cranch for the good advice by which his father was persuaded to send him to the metropolis . ..and who in grateful remembrance ...many years afterwards had a silver cup made ....for the purpose of presenting it to his judicious friend. However ……Mr Cranch's death prevented this act of gratitude"

References
- *Life and Times of Sir Joshua Renolds by C.R Leslie and T. Taylor 1865*
- *Sir Joshua Renolds by J.Northcote 1819*
- *Sir Joshua Reynolds His Life and Art by Gower 1902*

Richard's Estate

After the Rev Richard died, the Renold's portrait was held by his great niece Betsy who married into the Vivian family and so it became the property of Lord Vivian in Cornwall. The painting passed down through the Vivian family until it was sold to an anonymous bidder at Christie's in 1960, then sold again in 2005 (see above)

Following his death in 1742 County and national newspapers carried sales adverts for Richard's estate. They show he had an estate in Plympton area and property in Church Lane, Chelsea. The solicitor was John Cranch of Modbury, his brother.

DHC ref QS/21/1721/14

John (Attorney) brother of the Rev Richard

Born   21.3.1686
Father   the second son of Richard the Elder
Died   after 1754
Married   Agnes
            They had four children: John, Priscilla, Mary and Richard
Occupation Attorney operating out of Modbury

As a solicitor he was involved in the administration of the estates of the Morley and Bastard families. For example he surveyed the bounds of Lee Moor with Roger Prideaux and Robert Palmer, all three "gentlemen, stewards and tenants" for Morley In 1728 he acted in connection with a fishery and in 1729 he submitted a bill for searches, letters, attending in person, taking minutes etc relating to a "tryall between Barton of Pollexfen and John Pollexfen

1753 Morley estate papers P&WD 69/M/1/79
Pollexfen Bastard P&WD 74/324/12

He is named in several Marriage Allegations in the period 1700 – 1730 as a bondsman, sometimes with his nephew Richard who also followed the profession. After 1730, the references are to his eldest son "John C junior of Modbury" being the solicitor. These examples indicate the type of work involved:

a) 21 April 1721 "Let no licence of matrimony be granted to Robert Watson to intermarry with Elizabeth Cranch of Kingsbridge, spinster, but 15 years of age, before Andrew Cranch her father be first called …."
   This Andrew Cranch is the grandfather of the Seven. His daughter did eventually marry Watson (from the Fursdon Index, DHC):
b) 17 March 1724 "Let no licence be given to J. Ward to intermarry with Nann Jutsham, she being a minor and her father not consenting to the match. Entered by John Cranch, Attorney at Law at Modbury" . A marginal note says ""7 Feb 1726 Revoked by me John C" *(Fursdon Index, DHC)*
c) John 1721 gent An Executor of Will of Francis Furse with Robert Furse got William Mason arrested for non-payments *(DRO 49/9/1/32)*
d) John of Modbury 1739 & 1747 involved with assignment of mortgages with John & Elizabeth Luscombe for messuages at Ford.

Ch 6.7 Family of Richard and Jone

He was a considerable property owner. His will lists him as having property in: Plympton St Mary, Narramore, Barramore, Chappell Wood, Coles meadow, Dodbrooke, Cornwood (Brokers Park, Cora park), Ugborough (Filham, Godwill), Chelsea and another property in Plympton. All his children inherited in varying amounts.

Early in the 18th century an eighth of the manor and lands of Plympton was in his possession, having bought it from Sir Richard Vivian. In 1801 Lord Boringdon, afterwards Earl of Morley acquired all of the various parts of the manor, including the eighth that John's son had inherited. (John's granddaughter Betsy presumed to be the owner then)

Richard the Vicar
The eldest son of John (the attorney) and Agnes was called Richard. Even more confusingly he was also a Reverend though not always called that. He is referred here as "the Vicar" simply to distinguish him from his uncle.

In 1741 he was described as being from Ugborough. He and his father both subscribed towards the establishment of the Devon & Exeter Hospital. Also, in 1741 when taking on an apprentice he was described as "John of Modbury, minister." However when he married in 1753 (aged 34) the Marriage Allegation described him a "clerk".
He was the Reverend at Ugborouigh and "during the 1740s and the incumbency of Richard Cranch, the church was renovated and enlarged."
History of Ugborough Church
He married a widow, Margery Hodge from Truro in December 1753 at Plympton and soon after moved to Truro. The Society for Promoting Christian Knowledge, London 1755 membership lists him as the Rev Mr Cranch the vicar of St Clements in Cornwall.
They had a child Betsey, baptised October 1775 at Truro, but John had already died

Advertisements for the sales of his estate appear in 1756, and refer to him as "very lately died at his living in Cornwall." The administration of his estate was carried out by solicitor Richard of Totnes (his cousin) and his brother "John Cranch junior of Plympton". His will was not very specific, implying that his wife could make whatever arrangements she thought fit. The main beneficiary was his daughter Betsy

Betsy
Betsy was a sweetheart of Wolcot (Peter Pinder) and had her portrait painted by Renolds in October 1762 on one of his return visits to Devon and Cornwall. She married John Vivian who was baptised at Cornwood, son of Rev Thomas Vivian and Mary Hussey of Truro. He became a J.P. & deputy warden of the Stanneries. The Vivian family seems to have inherited most of the Cranch material via Betsey and her mother.

Mary, sister of Richard the vicar, is referred to in connection with a sketch by Renolds in the late 1700's . She with her father arranged for the release of a tenement at Brixton, witness John junior (her brother).

Ch 6.8 The family of Richard of Totnes

Richard of Totnes (solicitor), Richard (dyer), James (weaver), Grandson Richard

Richard of Totnes
Born   17.8.1711
Father   Eldest son of the Rev Richard Cranch of Modbury
Mother   Jone Hawkins
Married   Susanna Tucker of Dipford (where his father was the Minister)
             They had three surviving sons Richard (dyer), James (weaver), Joseph and a daughter Elizabeth
Died   1798

There is a Lease document 1733 in which Richard the son of the Rev Richard Cranch is described as "clothier of Totnes". Evidently later he also practised law, probably aided by his uncle John. (His cousin John was also a solicitor at Modbury). Richard became a town Councillor in 1766 and mayor in 1768 and 1776.
In 1766 the Mayor's allowance was £50 p.a. with Feast days expenses at about £15
By the time Richard became a mayor again, the corporation had decided to curtail the amount it spent on feasts because of the expense and the corporation's debts.
In 1776 he pledged surety for another to be a guild merchant and in 1777 he admitted his son James as a freeman of Totnes.

References: TDA 36 493,495,499 & 705
The Muniments of the Corporation of Totnes by E. Windeatt

Richard (dyer) Eldest son of Richard of Totnes
Born 1743 he became a dyer in the woollen trade, no doubt based down by the river and its mills in Totnes. By 1780-1781 he had men working for him as a tinman and as a peruke maker. He married Elizabeth Jackson in 1777 and they had three sons: Richard (junior), James, and John.

According to the will of Richard (dyer), his wife inherits "property in lower quarter of Totnes, herb garden, orchard" in trust for his eldest son Richard (junior) who also got "the equipment for trade of dyer" and the residue of the estate. Richard (junior) was aged 5 at the time.

Son James got the "estate purchased off Edward Rollwell". It could be that this included the pub referred to in a marriage settlement in 1784 - the Kings Arms. It could also be that James tried his hand at the brewing busines as there is a Journal of Brewings 1799 -1804 kept by a James Cranch   *DHC ref 1659 M/F 11*

North Gate, Totnes
Circa 1900
Cookworthy Museum

JAMES (Weaver)

Born	19.1.1745
Father	Second son of Richard Cranch of Totnes
Mother	Susanna Tucker
Married	Sarah Graham at St Martin in the Fields, London in 1770
	They had nine children, one of whom was Anna Maria
Died	1790

His father had James admitted as freeman to Totnes in 1777, his trade being as a weaver in the woollen trade. It is possible he went to London to learn or improve his craft and there met his future wife

A notice in London Gazette of 28 Dec 1773 announces that the partnership between Robert Hooks & James C of Middle Moorfields, St Leonards, Shoreditch, Gauze and Fancy trimming weavers was dissolved 25 Dec 1773. Any claims of Debts and outstanding payments to be made to R. Hooks by 1 Jan 1774. Mr Cranch to continue on his own at No 10 Middle Moorfields

In the Daily Advertiser 26 Ap 1776 is an advert that James C seeks a shopman to a haberdasher and that enquiries should be made to Mr James Cranch, Trimming Weaver.

He is listed in the Trade directories of 1776 & 1790 and in Kent's directory as living in Middle Moorfields

His will describes him as a Fancy Weaving Trimmer.

RICHARD grandson of Richard of Totnes

Born	11.5.1779 in Totnes
Father	Eldest son of the Richard (dyer)
Mother	Elizabeth Jackson
Married	1) in 1808 Maria a daughter of his uncle James i.e. this Richard and Maria were first cousins. They had seven children
	2) in 1821 Mary Maria Payne, who was probably the widowed mother of his son Richard's wife. They had four daughters
Died	?

He was articled in 1795 in Totnes as solicitor to John Michell, his uncle

He is the solicitor quoted as being involved with mortgages of a South Milton property in 1803 *(DHC ref 1768 M/T/ series)*

He is also involved in cases in 1802 in Kingsbridge with relatives:
- James Roope and John Cranch relating to tenements
- Joseph Cranch as a Feoffee in Kingsbridge
- William Cranch as a Feoffee in Kingsbridge

DHC ref 215M/O/T/ ..

The record of his activities as a solicitor in Totnes ceases shortly after, when he moved to London.

The papers of his practice in which he worked (and his grandfather before that) eventually were held by the solicitors Foster of Wells, now at the Somerset Heritage Centre

His son (another Richard !) was also a solicitor in London.

Ch 6.9 The Family of Richard Charles Lovell Cranch and George

Richard C.L.C., , Ellen Mary Bright, Charles, George, Archie, Doris, Patricia, Doreen, George Cranch (brother of R.C.L. Cranch), Mary (daughter of Richard and Anna)

Richard Charles Lovell Cranch (Richard CLC)
Born   23.10.1837
Father   Richard, grandfather Richard of Totnes, then London
Mother   Elizabeth Payne (died 1916)
Married   Ellen Mary Bright
             They had three sons Charles, George, Archie and daughter Ellen
Died   1918

The following information is based on the memoirs of Doris Christine Wilkinson (nee Cranch) granddaughter of Richard Charles Lovell Cranch latterly of Exeter who wrote The Story of the Cranches 1720- 1978 and gave a copy to RAMM. Undated but probably written in the 1970's She identifies herself :

> My great great grandfather was Richard Cranch who died 1798, manager
> of the solicitor's office connected with the Westminster Bank of London

It is not clear from this where, but assume it to be Totnes. His grandson Richard was also originally of Totnes and also a solicitor but soon moved to London

Ricard Charles Lovell Cranch   Ellen Mary Bright

Richard CLC was a real Londoner, and very proud of being a cockney, as he'd been born within the sound of Bow Bells. On a visit to her husband Richard Cranch in his office at 14 Fenchurch Street , Elizabeth Cranch *(nee Payne,)* fell down some stairs. RCLC was born shortly after.
He went to the Blue Coat School in London and then Ashburton Grammar School probably on the recommendation of the Devon relatives. He had the most beautiful copper plate writing and could draw extremely well.
He returned to London and was apprenticed to the bank. He hated it – top hats, stiff collars and full dress - and the staid and conventional way of living. He rebelled with wild parties. He became friendly with Henry Thomas Bailey, engineer, whose firm

Ch 6.9 The Family of Richard Charles Lovell Cranch and George

made circular iron staircases and eventually the Bailey bridges used in the invasion of France in WW2.

Richard CLC became wealthy, met and after a while married **Ellen Mary Bright**, a daughter of a Director of Railways at Euston Station, London. This pleased everyone as they thought Richard CLC would settle down but he still hated working at the bank. They moved to Monmouth. A little later Henry Thomas Baily married the other daughter Rose Ann Bright.

At Monmouth they bought a large house, had a son Charles. Richard CLC started his wild days again, this time with the officers of the militia stationed there. He was generous with his money and collected cronies around him. On one occasion he hired a train to take them to the races. On another, when he arrested for being drunk and driving a horse and carriage on the footpath, he insisted on being put in the local jail. The police, knowing him, tried to calm him down and wanted him to go home. He treated it all as a joke, but the incident brought an end to his banking career.

His wife, Ellen, was so shocked she would not go out or have friends to the house. They moved house, and Mrs Bright came to live with them. She was wealthy and with her help Richard CLC bought the saw mills in Monmouth which became prosperous and soon employed 15 men. Money was invested in several schemes but also lost on the stock exchange and extravagant living. He managed to keep his exploits discrete from his domestic life but his wife still did not go out and did not wish to receive people to the house. She was an extremely proud but loveable lady.

Charles Lovell Cranch (1864 – 1934)
The eldest son was quiet and conventional. He and his sister Nellie (Ellen Mary Elizabeth Cranch 1879-1960) helped to keep an orderly house. He worked in the bank, but lived at home all his life, mostly to look after his grandmother Elizabeth. His holidays were spent in Torquay and Totnes during which time he escorted two old aunts – the Misses Payne, sisters of his grandmother– to the theatre and concerts. They left him quite a lot of money so that he was able to buy the best equipment for his hobbies (photography, fishing).

George Sidney Cranch (1869-1907)
The second son was born and grew up just like his father. One day he availed himself of the "special services" of a certain fair-haired damsel attached to the militia officer's quarters. Being broke George said "put it on the old man's bill". This caused an unholy row. RCLC horse-whipped George, who pushed his father down the stairs and he broke his leg
George left home, joined the army, went to India and eventually Malta. He married and had two children, Donald and Ellen ("Nellie"). Later the whole family visited Monmouth which delighted his father Richard CLC. In spite of everything George was the favourite son. He was then with the ordinance survey and wrote to the family from Malta with drawings of various places there.
Unfortunately George contracted Maltese fever and died. Richard CLC and Ellen were broken-hearted. Richard CLC gave up drinking and carousing for evermore, which made for a happier household. Ellen died in 1916, Richard CLC in 1918

Archie Lovell Cranch (1885 - 1907)
He was the youngest and last son.

He went to Monmouth Grammar school but spent most of his time on photography. He left home and his uncle Henry Thomas Baily loaned him enough money to set up as a photographer. When he was 20, he married Elizabeth Eleanor Miles, whose garden backed on to the gardens of the Cranch house. She had just started teaching but continued although married women at that time were not allowed to do so. Their daughter Doris born 1906. When the first World War came they were on holiday at Brighton. He wanted to join the war as a balloon observer, but also applied as a radiographer in one of the war hospitals where he was a volunteer. Daughter Doreen was born Dec 30th 1915. The War Office sent them to Neath 3rd Western General Hospital, then Cardiff

Doris Christine Cranch (1906 – 1979)
She had an erratic schooling because of the war. She worked in medical laboratories helping to illustrate books, then enrolled to train as a nurse as way into radiography (being unable to afford to be trained at Guy's in London). She passed her SRN and promptly resigned to take up a position as radiographer at Prince of Wales Hospital, Cardiff. She was there 6 years, travelled a lot in her holidays. Met Laurie Wilkinson a P & O engineering officer. Married 1935. Many WW2 "adventures" in Bristol, London, Cardiff and Exeter. After retirement, resumed her education and took up painting.

Patricia (b. 1937)
Daughter of Doris attended St Margaret's School and wanted to become a radiographer at an early age. She married Derek D Southron who worked at Rolls Royce in Bristol. Two children Ann and Hazel.

Doreen Mary Cranch (1915 – 2010)
Second daughter of Archie went to Cardiff High School, University, Cardiff Medical school to become a Doctor, then University College London to get her D.A. in Anaesthetics. Married Dutch Naval officer George Vermeulen and went to live in Amsterdam. Two children Jan and Liesbeth. She became Professor of Anaesthetics at the University and was given an MBE for her work in anaesthetics. He became a Director of the Haarland Shipping Line.

GEORGE (b 1840)
George, the younger brother of RCL Cranch, was sent to boarding school at Edmonton and then trained to be an accountant.
By 1871 George and his father had moved to Nottingham. His brother Richard remained in London. His mother died in London in 1872.
George married Hephzibah Richardson at Nottingham and had a son George Henry. George Henry married Fanny Servant in 1890 and they lived in London. They had 6 children: Matilda, George, Henry, Thomas, Arthur, Lillian
Arthur married Edith Louise Spinks and died in Victoria Australia 1957

MARY (1823 – 1894)
Daughter of Richard and Anna married ….? Paige (chart 6.4).
Their daughter Elizabeth Cranch Paige died in Kingsbridge 1894. In her will she bequeathed considerable to her Paige relatives and referred to many Cranch relatives including Richard Charles Lovell C, George C and Charles Lovell C

An Amusing story, Binnicknowle

An Amusing Story

David Murch was a local shipping historian and founder of the Salcombe Historical Society. At a meeting with him circa 1993 he passed on the following amusing incident

James Cranch was a farm labourer at Linkum farm. He had a son who was a ships carpenter and died at sea. He had two daughters:
- Polly who went to Australia
- Ellen, born 1862, married Aaron Murch of Kingsbridge on her 18th birthday in 1880. She was a dressmaker and died in 1939. They lived in the West Alvington / Salcombe area and had three sons. Aaron was the grandfather of David Murch

The local families would "inspect" the result any shipwreck. At a local beach on the eve of Ellen's wedding a ship came to grief. James took a fancy to a coat and got it before another could. This person informed the local Protection officials who raided James' home on the wedding day whilst the feast was in progress. They were offered and accepted drinks and invited to search for whatever they were looking for. On returning to Batson, they charged the informant with wasting the equivalent of police time. James was of course wearing the coat throughout the wedding !

Some research indicates that James had a third daughter – "Lizzy"
And his wife was called Jane.

Binnicknowle

There is a property at Avonwick called Binnicknowle, owned until 1890 by William C.S.Cranch, builder of South Brent.

By co-coincidence in the 1920s Binnicknowle was farmed by another Cranch family - John Partridge Cranch, his wife and four of their sons. It is believed this John was born in 1853 at Sherford, son of the James and Jane Cranch referred to above. According to the 1831 census, James then aged about 20 lived with the Partridge family at East Portlemouth.

Confusingly another James Cranch aged about 10 was also listed as living with the Partridges in 1821 and in the 1920s there are two people called John Partridge Cranch with birth dates about 5 years apart.

Other members of the Partridge Cranches lived in Salcombe in the 1920s.

In 1904, in Balkwill's warehouse, at The Quay Salcombe, J.P Cranch and his son Alfred used the first floor for their business. They were carpenters and undertakers.

CHAPTER 7

THE SEVEN CHILDREN OF JOHN [2]

Introducing the Seven

The remaining chapters of the book mostly concern members the Andrew Tree. This chapter follows on from the chart shown on Ch 4.4 Andrew the Elder which ended with showing that a descendent of his, John [2] had seven children.

John[2] was born about 1680 and took over his father's business. He married Elizabeth Pearse of Shaugh (i.e Shaugh Prior) in 1714. Peabody describes him as being "of Shaugh" so he may have worked there initially but by 1717 he was living in Modbury and then probably lived at Norden. He retired to live in Dodbrook. He raised 7 surviving children, their birth records being lost. The dates of birth shown are those given by John the Painter in one of his notebooks.

There is a chart for each child of John [2]. Those for sons John, Andrew and William are simpler and include the relatively little information available about them.

Sons Nathaniel [1], Joseph [2] and Richard [2] have chapters dedicated to them as there is considerable information about them and their descendants. They are notable and important in their own right. Mary is included with the chapter on Richard.

The following table is a summary and guide.

Child	Brief History	Further Information
John [3] 1709 - 1746	became a Dissenting minister. 5 children, 3 went to America	Chart 7.2 John[2] of the Seven Ch. 12.3 Richard and America
Joseph [2] 1710 – 1781	had 9 children, one of whom was John the Painter. Direct ancestor to the Cranches of South Brent, Bond of America	Chart 11.2 Joseph[2] of the Seven and subsequent charts Ch. 13 John the Painter
Andrew [2] 1711(?) - 1787	married into the Bowring family. 4 children Some accounts give Andrew as older than Joseph	Chart 7.3 Andrew [2]
Nathaniel [1] 1715-1764	had 5 children. Grandfather of John the Naturalist, whose daughter was Jane Bowring Cranch	Chart 8.1 Nathaniel [1] of the Seven Ch. 8 The family of Nathaniel [1] Ch. 9 John the Naturalist Ch. 10 Jane Bowring Cranch
Mary 1719 - 1789	married General Joseph Palmer and went to America. 3 children	See Ch. 12 Richard and America
William 1723 (?) - 1788	married, wife died after 6 weeks. No children	Chart 7.4 William of the Seven
Richard [2] 1726- 1811	went to America. Married sister of Abigail Adams. 3 children.	Ch. 12 Richard and America

In general the themes described in previous chapters continue with this generation and their descendants.

JOHN[3] was the first of the seven children of John[2]. He was born about 1709. He was "educated by Messrs H. Grove & Dr. T. Amory at their Academy at Taunton for the education of young gentlemen intended for the ministry among the dissenters. He was ordained a minister over the dissenting congregation at Modbury and afterwards at Ilminster where he was soon taken sick and died in 1746".

(Richard[2] *of America).*

He initially studied under the Rev Flavel (Dartmouth) and attended the Assemblies of Dissenting Ministers, Exeter and was listed as a Protestant Dissenting Minister of Modbury

(James Manning)

The original of his sermon on Day of Judgement at Modbury 1737 is held by Peabody
He married Anna Garland of Totnes on 17 October 1735 (by licence). He was described as then being from Ermington. They had 5 children.
In 1739 when "of Plympton", he subscribed to John Warren's sermons. He moved to Illminster in the early 1740's

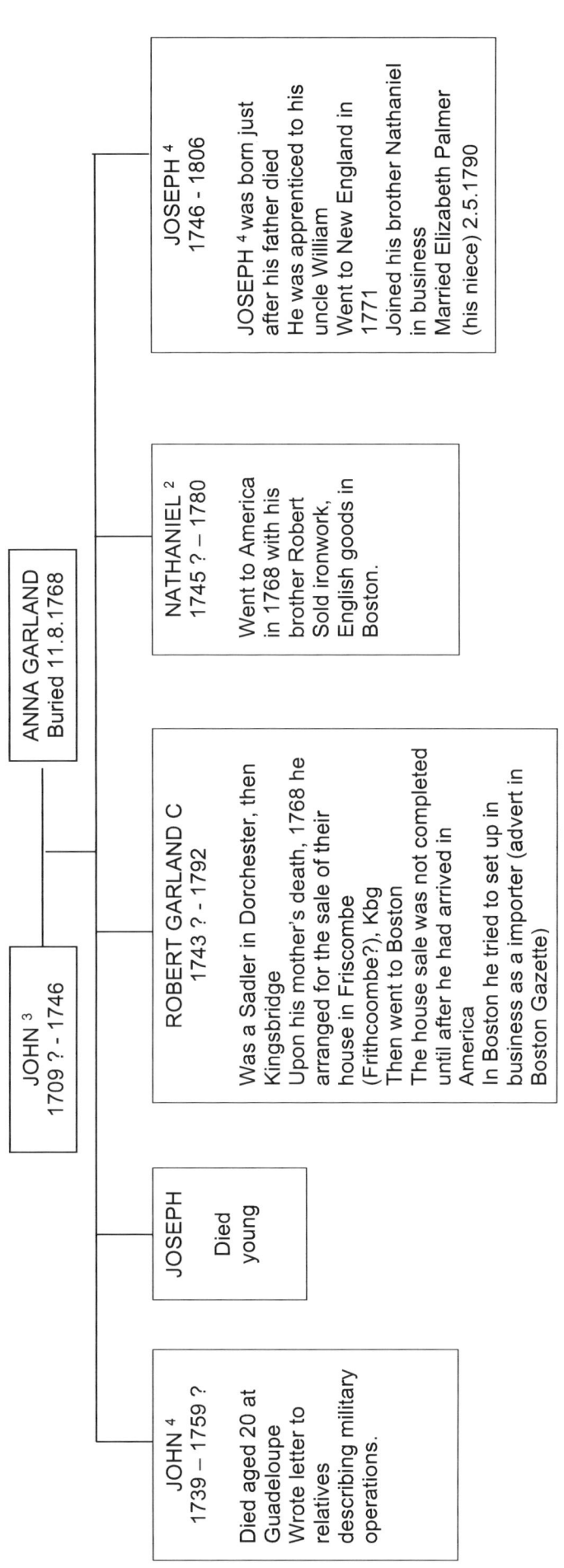

The life of the three sons who went to America is further described in Ch. 12 Richard and America

7.2 Chart   JOHN[3] of The Seven

Andrew [2] is third of the seven children of John [2]
He was apprenticed to a fuller in Exeter in 1731 and became a freeman. He voted for John Baring in the parliamentary election Nov 1776
He (and his daughter) married into the Bowring family and lived in Exeter. They had four children

ANDREW [2] called on John and Abigail Adams who were staying at William Bowring's house in Exeter in the summer of 1787. Abigail describes Andrew [2]: " ...the old Gentleman came, with some difficulty, for he is very lame and infirm... I think he must have had a paralytic stroke as his speech is thick. He has not been able to do any business for a number of years, and I believe he is chiefly supported by his son, who is in the clothier's business with Mr Bowring."

letter by Abigail to her sister dated 15 Sept 1787

```
                    ANDREW [2]─────────SALLY BOWRING
                    of Kingsbridge
                    1711 – 14. 8.1787
                    Buried in Dissenter's graveyard
            │              │                    │
    CHRISTOPHER      JULIA or               SARAH ──── WILLIAM ──── MARY
    1737 – 1787     JUDITH                 m 31 Dec 1769  BOWRING   ANN
    Fuller           ?
    Holy Trinity Parish, Exeter                    │
    m at St.John's Exeter                  SALLY BOWRING &    RICHARD
    Buried in Dissenter's graveyard        THOMAS BOWRING      CRANCH
                                           Infants d 1772     BOWRING
                                                               b 1777
    JANE HUTCHINGS
    1733-1788
    of Mortonhampstead

    JULIET    WILLIAM         GEORGE
    b 1766    b 1768 ?        PALMER C
              d 1770           1770
                              Was at Cambridge
                              univ. in 1784
```

Note: there are various connections between the families of Cranch and Bowring. See Ch 10

7.3 Chart   ANDREW [2] of The Seven

William was the 6th child of John [2], born about 1725

He married   ELIZABETH HORSECOMBE of Marlborough

She died 6 weeks later
He became despondent and finally imbecile
He lost his voice in 1783 and in 1784 his memory failed him
He died 21 Feb 1788
He was an intellectual man, a lover of art and of noble presence

According to John the Painter, he lived at Halwell (near South Pool and Frogmore). John the Painter had a chance meeting with him at Exeter in 1772 when John was a young man on his way to his clerical position at Axminster.

Abigail described William (in a letter 15 Sept 1787) when John and Abigail Adams escorted by John the Painter visited him at Brook (3 miles outside Ivybridge)

"... There is some little property in the hands of the family who take charge of him, sufficient to support a person who has no more wants than he has. He appeared clean and comfortable but took no notice either of the conversation or persons. The only thing which in the least roused him was the mention of his wife. He appeared to be restless when that subject was touched. The character of this man as a given by all his friends and acquaintance leads one to regret, in a particular manner, the loss of his intellect. Possessed of a genius superior to his station; a thirst for knowledge which his circumstances in life permitted him not to peruse; most amiable and engaging in his manners; formed to have adorned a superior rank in life; fondly attached to an amiable wife, who he very soon lost, he fell a sacrifice to a too great sensibility: unable to support the shock, he grew melancholy and was totally lost."

7.5 Chart   WILLIAM of The Seven

CHAPTER 8
THE FAMILY OF NATHANIEL [1]

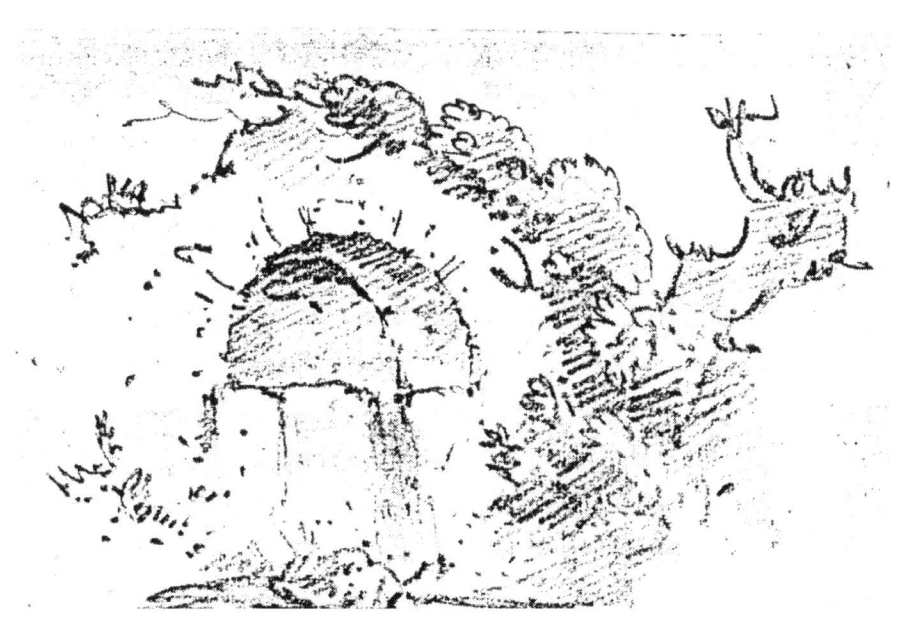

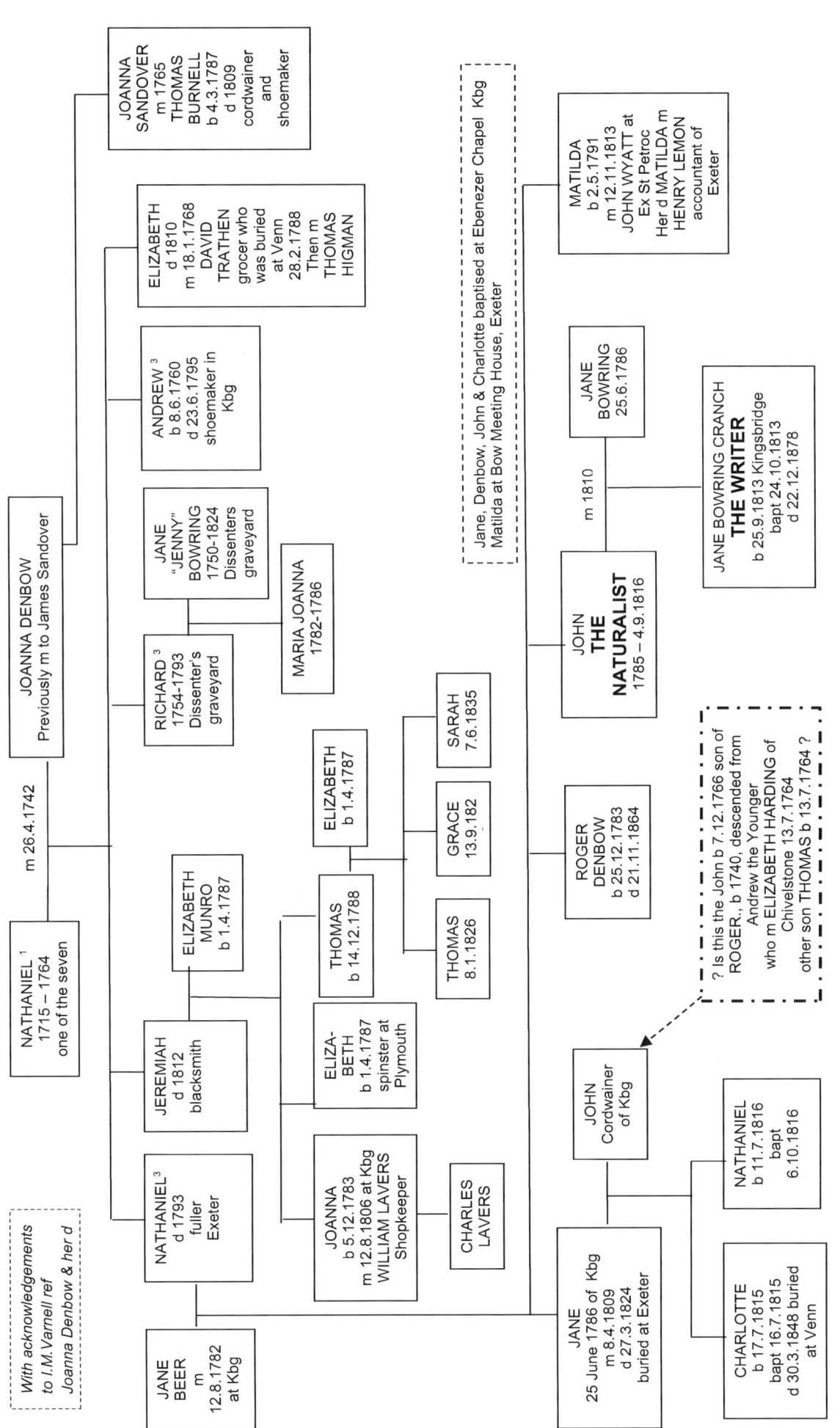

8.1 Chart   NATHANIEL [1] of The Seven

Nathaniel [1] and his Descendants

Nathaniel [1], Salcombe Castle Key, Exeter contingent, His sons, Jackson the Organist, His Daughters, Roger Denbow C, grandchildren, Charlotte, Abigail's visit.

Nathaniel [1] of the Seven
Born   1715
Father   John [2], clothier of Shaugh and Kingsbridge
Mother   Elizabeth Pearse
Married   Joanna Sandover (nee Denbow) of Modbury in 1742 at Kingsbridge
            They had four sons and two daughters.
Died   1764

Based in Kingsbridge, Nathaniel was involved with the clothier business. His ancestors and parents lived (and a brother still did) at Norden. Nathaniel lived in Mill Street, Kingsbridge, a property referred to in Andrew the Elder's will of 1623, and close to Norden. The Town Mills were in Mill St. convenient for Nathaniel who must have been a fuller.

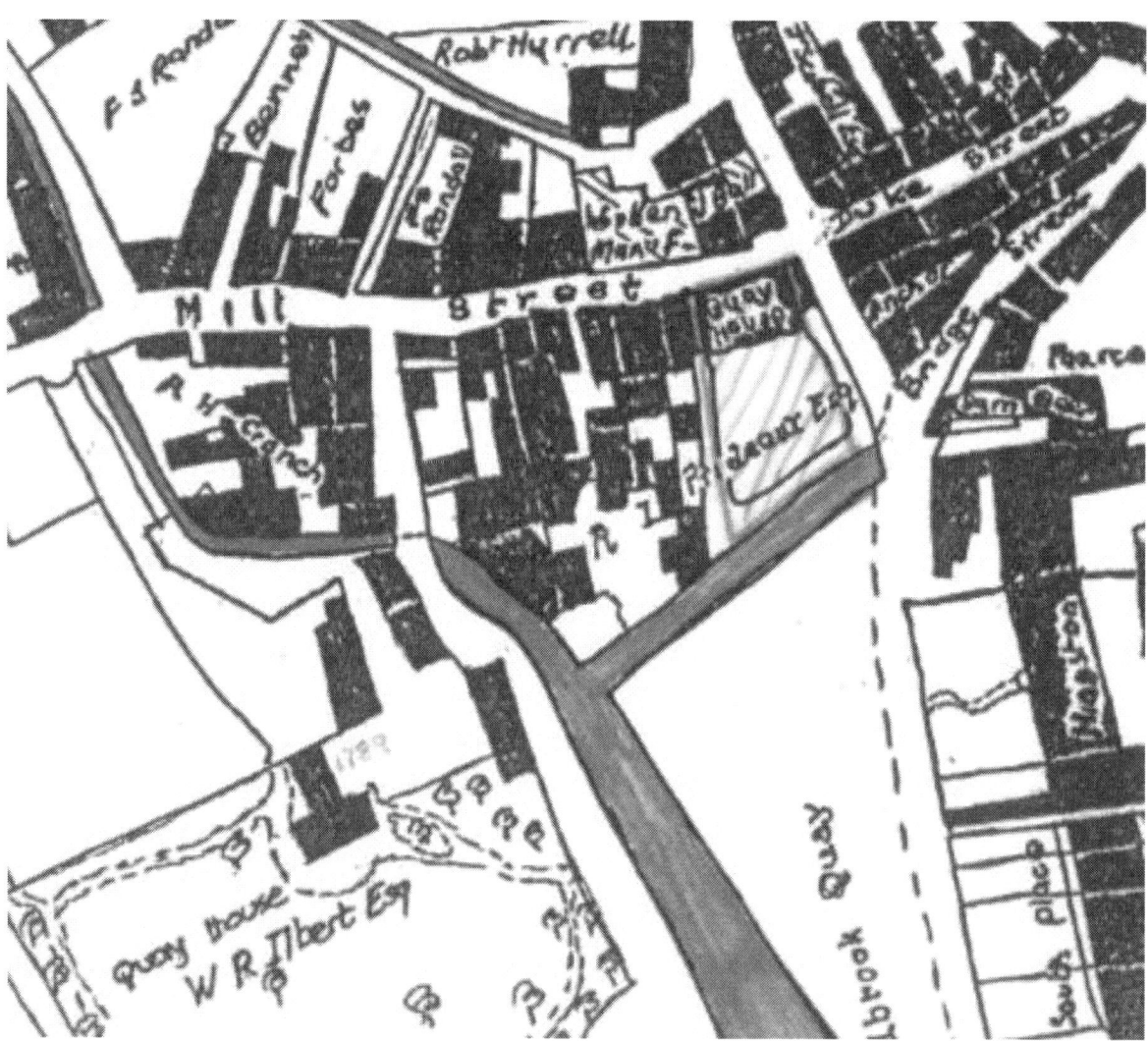

Mill Street was still owned by R.D Cranch in this map of 1841. Nathaniel lived where Quay house was built.
Map and information Courtesy of Kingsbridge Town Council, Cookworthy and A. Lidstone

Ch 8.2   NATHANIEL ¹ and his Descendants

Through his work and that of his father and brothers he would have had contracts with the traders of Exeter which would be one reason for his eldest son taking up business there, along with several other relatives. Another reason would be that Exeter by then had become the centre of the woollen trade.

A feature of the period in which Nathaniel lived was the relationships, connections and associations between the families descended from his brothers and sisters i.e the Seven. Even though two (Mary and Richard) emigrated to America followed shortly by the sons of the eldest (John), there was still contact between them and the other four who were largely still based in Kingsbridge and district.

As time went by, this mostly revolved around the families of Nathaniel and Joseph in Kingsbridge and that of Andrew in Exeter. Indeed Exeter became quite a focus.

The Key of Salcombe Castle
As already described the Cranch family witnessed the events relating to the Civil War and Dissent. This association continued years after as the following account shows. It features Nathaniel [1] and a grandson of Joseph [2]
Some doubt has been cast over a drawing made by John the Painter of the large key attributed to be that of Salcombe castle, the subject of much interest during the Civil War and since. The following letter written by "J. Cranch, London" is important and confirms the accuracy of the claim:
> "Being myself a native of Kingsbridge, I remember William Cranch my father say frequently that this key at one time, when the "old mansion" (long since taken down) had been left in care for a short period (about 1760). They made a collection of old things lying about as their perquites. "The snappers up of inconsiderable trifles". The key included in the batch of things brought to Kingsbridge for disposal. Mr Nathaniel Cranch, the ancestor of Miss J.B. Cranch, now residing at South Place recognised the key and took measure to having it restored to its former position in the old hall.
> This Nathaniel Cranch was the one who lent his oak table for George Whitfield to stand upon. He was related to John Cranch the first scholar at Duncombe's school and was witness to codicil of his master's will."
> *Kingsbridge Gazette 12 December 1868*

Notes:
1. The drawing of the key is in a Notebook of John the Painter, and reproduced in chapter 13. It is described there as follows:
    > "Drawing by Joseph Cranch, dated May 27 1818 of "the Key of Fort Charles the ruins of which are now commonly called Salcombe Castle". Taken from a drawing made from the original subject at Fallapit by John Cranch 25 Sept 1799"
2. The J. Cranch who wrote the above letter is the Joseph Cranch who married Margaret Lakeman, and grandson of Joseph [2], one of the Seven
3. The Nathaniel referred to is Nathaniel [1] of the seven
4. John the Painter was a nephew of Nathaniel [1] and at that time (1760) was a young boy living in Kingsbridge probably still at Norden.
5. The story of the table is related in the chapter on Jane Bowring Cranch (a descendant of Nathaniel)
6. The authenticity of the drawing is now surely beyond doubt.

The Exeter Contingent

In Exeter there developed a sizable contingent of Cranches and their relatives (mostly from the Andrew tree. See Chart 10.2)
From the Seven (see Chart 4.4) there were:
- Andrew[2], bother of Nathaniel [1,] was a prominent fuller and freeman there, marrying a Bowring. He was probably the first "arrival" but being in the clothier business where Exeter had become a significant trading centre by that time, it would be fairly certain that the Cranch family knew many of the people of Exeter quite well through their business contacts.
- Nathaniel's son Nathaniel [3]
- Richard the third son of Nathaniel also married a Bowring

Not only was there this common bond of family and being in the same trade but also the bond of being Dissenters. They retained close ties with the family left in Kingsbridge, as evidenced by John the Painter's letter home in 1742

The Sons of Nataniel

Nathaniel [3]

Born about 1750, the eldest son Nathaniel [3] "was fond of music, and benefitted by the instruction of **Jackson, organist of Exeter Cathedral** whose influence created a musical taste among Exonians. "The Exeter organ was as famous as that of Haarlen, Holland". *Ancient Exeter and its trade TDA vol5 (1872)*
Jackson excelled in painting as well as music and was a prominent Exeter figure known by the Cranch family generally

A Mr Cranch (Nathaniel?) is in a list of supporters of the 1788 Exeter Committee of the Society for the Abolition of the Slave trade. Supporters came from a wide area of E & N Devon. Many were dissenters. Plymouth also had a committee
Devon and the Slave trade by Todd Gray

Nathaniel had married John Beer's daughter Jane and had six children. All were baptised in Exeter where Nathaniel worked as a fuller but he seems to have kept in close touch with Kingsbridge where his mother still lived.

In his mother's will (she died 1784) Joanna describes a property in Kingsbridge referred to in Andrew's will of 1723. After his mother's death, Nathaniel (then described as blacksmith) agrees to sell the lease to John Beer, ironmonger, Kingsbridge of
> "mansion or dwelling house, little garden, stable, backside herb garden and parcel of land in Dodbrooke" *DRO 52/12/9*

The date was 20 Jan 1790 and probably refers to the property his father retired to. Nathaniel presumably used the money to acquire his own premises in Exeter. John Bowring of St Leonard, Parish of Trinity, Exeter insured the property occupied by Nathaniel [3] in 1790.

Nathaniel[3] died in 1793. In 1796 in the publication Exeter Pocket Book Journal there is reference to his widow Mrs Cranch being a cheesemonger, of Broadgate.

Jeremiah
Born about 1755 and the second son
Jeremiah started as the journeyman to first son Nathaniel. It was his mother's wish that he remains there "until he found betterment". Sometime after this, probably when his elder brother sold up the Dodbrooke house, he became an ironmonger and blacksmith. In 1791 he took out a bond of indemnity to use 92 Fore Street "for peaceful use of site". He took the bond out with his cousin Thomas Burnell "cordwainer". Jeremiah is listed as "Blacksmith". For a while he was also at Plymouth.

Andrew
The fourth son Andrew was a shoemaker in Kingsbridge and a bachelor. He was the "miser" who brought up his nephew John the Naturalist after Nathaniel died. (see Chapter 9)

Daughters
Nathaniel's daughter Elizabeth married David Trathen.

His other daughter married Thomas Burnell. The Burnells were prominent dissenters.

The Presbyterians in 1790 erected on the East side of Fore Street near by subscription a new meeting-house of the Independent persuasion. It was subsequently endowed in the beginning of the 1800's by Thomas Burnell, cordwainer who also appointed the trustees to hold this legacy. The first Register from 1774 has been lost. The present one starts from 1792.
Hawkins

Roger Denbow C (1783 – 1864)
Grandson of Nathaniel [1], he lived in Mill St, Kingsbridge which he inherited from his father. He was a member of the Ebenezer church where he was a trustee.
He with John Cranch (his brother-in-law?) in March 1837 signed the Kingsbridge Independent Register (copy at DRO) :
> "We the undersigned have examined the above entrants and compared them with the original register, this day sent off, to be deposited in the office of the Secretary of state and find it correct"
> H. Watts, J. Cranch, R.D. Cranch

On some land belonging to Mr R Denbow Cranch of Dodbrooke Hills ....
> "Many years ago, a young farmer labourer on the Gerston estate turned up with the plough a large gold coin of the reign of Edward III. He immediately exclaimed "this shall be a wedding ring for my wife". Unfortunately, he died unmarried. The person who inherited it also never married. It has been bequeathed in succession to others and always has been followed with the same result – they never married! It is now in the possession of Mr R Denbow Cranch – a bachelor!
Fox book

In 1814 Denbow, described as yeoman, with a dozen others was involved in acquiring land for Loddiswell Congregational Church. Some familiar names: Willing brothers, the Lavers, plus some Reverends, a woolcomber, a blacksmith, a mason, and labourers.
Congregational Federation, Nottingham

It was to this church that the table and chair was sent after the meeting house in Fore St was bombed in WW2 (see chapter on his niece Jane Bowring Cranch)

In the Robson Commercial Directory 1840 and the White Commercial Directory 1850 Roger D. Cranch is listed as a coal merchant living in Mill St, Kbg

Other grandchildren of Nathaniel [1]:
- Jane who married a John Cranch who was 40 years old at the time. They had two children : Charlotte and Nathaniel. Their father John died when they were young and Charlotte probably then lived with aunt Elizabeth Trathen
- John the Naturalist who had a daughter Jane Bowring C
- Matilda

Charlotte 1815 - 1848
She became the postmistress of Kingsbridge. In a letter in 1845 (to John Roope C) Charlotte refers to postal delays, blaming weather conditions. From 1810 for over 30 years the mail between Kingsbridge and Salcombe was carried at first on foot and then up and down the estuary by boat (except in 1837 the mail bags were conveyed by a donkey).
Charlotte was buried in the (Baptist) Venn cemetery as was David Trathen.
At her funeral in 1848 were "uncle Trathen, uncle and aunt Higman, Philip Burnell, Denbow and John Cranch and son: (i.e John Roope C. and his son William)

The Visit of Abigail
Abigail Adams (and entourage) visited the Trathens when she came to Kingsbridge in 1787. She wrote:
> " Mr & Mrs Burnell & Mr & Mrs Trathen both offered us beds but we were too numerous to accept…though we engaged ourselves to dine with Mr Burnell and drink tea with Mr Trathen the next day".

She noted that Mr Trathen was a grocer on good circumstances; and that Mr Burnell was a shoemaker worth £5,000.
Philip Burnell was a descendant of the Thomas Burnell who married Charlotte's great aunt.

Note:
Abigail Adams was the wife of John Adams and they toured the West Country. At the time he was first U.S. Ambassador to England, later to become the second President.

CHAPTER 9
JOHN THE NATURALIST

Ch 9 John the Naturalist 1

Family Connections, Barrow's Account, Visit by British Museum, Appointment as Collector, Appointment to the Congo Expedition, The Congo Expedition, John's letter, Recognition, Newspaper report, Notes and References, Monod's Account, a Recent Booklet

Family Connections
John C   Born 1785   Exeter
              Died 4 Sept 1816 Boma, Congo
Father   Nathaniel [3], who was a "journeyman fuller" of Exeter
Married   Jane Bowring.
Daughter   Jane Bowring Cranch, writer.

He is referred to as John Cranch the Naturalist to distinguish him from the many other Cranches named John.

John Cranch the Naturalist
John is known for his contribution towards the natural history collections of his day and for his participation in the ill-fated Congo Expedition of 1816
This account of him is by Sir John Barrow[1] :

"John C was self- taught. He was born in Exeter in 1785 of humble but respectable parents. At aged eight he lost his father, leaving his mother in circumstances which did not enable her to provide for all her children. He was taken charge of by an uncle in Kingsbridge whose main object in life was the accumulation of wealth and he almost denied his nephew the benefit of a common education. The miserable guinea which procured him a year's instruction in reading, writing and arithmetic was wrenched from him with so much grudging and in a manner so unkind as to be severely felt and never afterwards forgotten.

At 14 John C was apprenticed as a shoemaker. The strength of mind which he showed from his early childhood was now constantly and obviously struggling with the adverse circumstances of his situation. Every moment which could be stolen from his daily labour was devoted to the few books which he had found the means to collect. He delighted in the study of natural history and even at this early period of his life he was able to draw up correct and classical descriptions of all the types of insects he could find around Kingsbridge

Without assistance other than from books he acquired a sufficient knowledge of Latin and French to enable him to use them in describing objects of natural history. He also acquired a general knowledge of astronomy. But while eagerly endeavouring to grasp at science everything tended to depress him and did nothing to encourage him. However, he persevered to nourish his passion, the love of knowledge, silently and sedulously, unnoticed and unknown, in spite of every obstacle,

When his apprenticeship ended, he went to London with the professed view of improving his shoemaking skills; but in reality with higher aspirations; though he hardly ventured to own them himself. The manners and morals of his fellow workmen were ill suited to his feelings and pursuits and served only to increase his dislike of his profession. It was some consolation to him to reflect that he was in the great mart of human knowledge and though unfriended and a stranger he found information flowed to him on every side. His mind was filled but unsatisfied. Every museum, auction room, and bookstall, every object which attracted his attention he visited with a rapid and insatiable curiosity, gleaning information wherever it was to be had and treasuring it up with systematic care.

His account of what he observed in the capital is said to exhibit an obvious and striking proof of an inquisitive, diligent and discerning mind. A kindred spirit he met said

> "our conversations and philosophical rambles …. marked a vast comprehension …. in an intellect which seemed …. to grasp magnitude and minutiae with equal address and which could at once surprise, delight and instruct"

After some time he returned to Devon but discovered how little chance the "bootmaker from London" had in eclipsing even his humble rivals. …… His labours produced little more than a bare subsistence and every spare moment was dedicated to his favourite pursuit. However, his circumstances were improved by marriage. He consigned his workshop to his journeyman while he sedulously and successfully collected objects of natural history

In his researches he climbed rugged precipices, was lowered down from the summits of the tallest cliffs, waded through rapid streams, explored the beds of the muddiest rivers and sought the deepest recesses. He frequently wandered for whole weeks from home and often ventured out to sea for several days entirely alone in the smallest fisherman's skiff. In all weathers, no vicissitudes of "storms and sunshine" prevented his fatiguing pursuits: the discovery of a new insect amply repaid the most painful exertions"

Visit by the British Museum
John the Naturalist wrote several papers in the "Kingsbridge Weekly Entertainer" on natural history subjects. This and his natural history collection gradually made him better known and his talents were duly noted by the most able naturalists.
Dr. Leach, British Museum, wrote:

"In 1814, Mr Montague[4], Mr C. Prideaux and I visited John C to see his museum. We were astonished at the magnitude of his collection of shells, crustacea, insects, birds etc collected entirely by him and still more so with the accuracy of their classification and with the remarks and conversation on all subjects of natural history by this self-educated and zealous individual. Quite delighted with having made his acquaintance, I left him with a resolution to cultivate a correspondence with him on the subject of a our favourite pursuits. The following morning I received a note from him offering me specimens that he could supply.
Soon after I was appointed to the British Museum and John C applied for a position but there was no vacancy. However, his pay requirements were within my own ability so I proposed he should undertake to find marine specimens from the coasts of D & C and then later make a tour of G.B. At the same time I promised to recommend him for the first available situation."

Appointment as Collector (Leach continues):
"On receiving my letter he immediately discharged his journeyman and converted his premises to receive and preserve the items he collected. He kept up a continual communication with Plymouth fishermen and constantly received from them baskets filled with the rubbish they dredged from the bottom of the sea. He examined,

Ch 9 John the Naturalist

preserved and described all the new objects so discovered. He visited the Brixham, Plymouth and Falmouth fishermen and made excursions with them.
He very often left Kingsbridge in an open boat for long periods during which he dredged when the tide was full and examined the shore when it was out. At night he drew up onto shore and slept in his boat. When the weather was too stormy he would leave his boat and examine the countryside for insects, birds etc. The remarks about the infinity of new objects which he discovered are invaluable."

Appointment to the Congo Expedition (Leach continues)
"In this way was John C employed by the B M. to collect natural history specimens at the time when the expedition to the Congo was planned. Dr. Leach recommended him to Sir J Banks as a person suited in every way for the undertaking. For his part the position was the height of his ambition and he at once accepted it, though not without some foreboding. His conduct during the voyage out does not appear to have been influenced by this foreboding, nor was his exertions diminished by occasional lowness of spirits, owing partly to the gloomy view of Christianity taken by his church. His friends declare him to be a sincere Christian, an affectionate parent and a kind friend.

The Congo Expedition
John C received "instructions for the Collector of Objects of Natural History" but he used his own numbering procedures which "remain singularly incomprehensible"
He was based in the transport ship Dorothy that went with the sloop "Congo". John C seemed not be an easy character as "his absurd conduct will diminish the liberty of the Captain towards us and was too much the object of jest "

John C's "small net" which was always suspended over the side of the vessel would have been the modest origin of a whole line of devices increasingly perfected. Monod claims that Darwin aboard the Beagle did the same as John C 15 years later and may have benefited from any lessons from the expedition

Going up the Congo the transport ship had to stay in the estuary and a flotilla of landing boats went up stream as far as the rapids of Yellak. During this river period John C was disappointed by the "extremely scanty and not easily obtained animals, fish and reptiles". But he did shoot many birds.
After about 3 weeks the difficulties of land travel were so great that they decided to turn back, getting back to the Dorothy 18th Sept by which time many had died.
Bowring's account continued:
> "John C was taken ill on 23 August 1816 on the march between the towns of Cooloo and Inga and was carried back on the shoulders of the natives to Cooloo and from thence in a hammock to the place of embarkation below the rapids, but it was the tenth day before he reached the ship in a canoe.
> His symptoms are generally now regarded as being those of Yellow Fever. His condition worsened and he died three days later after uttering "a devout prayer for the welfare of his family and wife" aged 31. He was buried at Embomma in his own burial ground with full military honours alongside other victims."

All the expedition died except Leach. 56 people travelled, 21 did not return.

Letter written by John C

In his diary during the expedition John wrote (presumably to the British Museum) from the transport ship Dorothy 29 June 1816.

Sir:

The duties of the situation I have the honour to hold in this expedition demand I should embrace any opportunity that presents itself to communicate such observations as have occurred and at the same time to transmit a specimen of each object of Natural History I have preserved during the voyage.

I have therefore accordant to those parts of my Instructions selected such as are needful and transmit with them a copy of my Journal to this day. I have endeavoured as far as circumstances would permit to keep an individual or more of every specimen taken and I trust it will appear by the condition of the specimens sent that nothing has been omitted on my part to endeavour to preserve them as far as possible. Many of the mollusca tho' extremely interesting when alive could not be preserved but my friend and companion Dr Smith has very kindly taken some correct drawings of the most remarkable and which will hereafter answer every purpose to identify those species in future.

I have endeavoured as far as my abilities will permit to retain in description some of those characters which are perishable in spirit etc. The dates also and peculiar circumstances under which some of these animals were taken are noticed. This may hereafter tend to assist in ascertaining the Geography of a few but in my opinion it would require many voyages to ascertain with a degree of certainty the places and under what circumstances in general many species of animal appear

The slight knowledge I have of General Zoology will I hope plead sufficient excuse for my not entering minutely into description as I should otherwise do if I were well acquainted with the subject itself. I flatter myself however that the species now sent will hereafter meet the attention which perhaps their peculiarities may deserve.

I remain your obedient servant John Cranch

Apparently the specimens he sent back were received in poor state – many birds for instance totally destroyed by insects and most of the insects "were entirely destroyed by insects and damp"

Recognition

Dr Leach reported on the results of the expedition and gave due recognition and credit to John Cranch's work. As in for example:

> Observations on the Genus Ocythoe of Rafinesque, read by Dr Leach before the Royal Society

Also a species of mollusc Cranch found in South Devon's waters was named after him by Leach.

Newspaper Report

In one of John the Painter's notebooks is a reproduction of what is apparently a newspaper report (origin unknown, but presumably a Kingsbridge paper). The extract is undated but Joseph [6] on 7 Feb 1817 writes in the notebook "From this statement as well as others of this a sad affair we find that cousin John Cranch is "numbered among the dead". (John the Naturalist and Joseph [6] were second cousins) :

> "The detailed accounts of the expedition to explore the river Congo or Zaire have reached the admiralty. Melancholy as the result has been..... the journals ..... are ...highly interesting and satisfactory ... It would seem ......that the mortality was entirely owing to the land journey beyond the

rapids and that Capt Tuckey died of complete exhaustion, after leaving the river and not from fever. .... The total number of deaths amount to 18 of which 14 were in the land expedition. ...... The Dorothy lost but one man and he fell overboard and was drowned.... (the Surgeon of the Congo claims) .....the causes of death were due to ..." mental anxiety and disturbed rest as the sole causes ..."brought about by an anxious zeal and over eagerness to accomplish the objects of the expedition ....which led them to attempt more than the human constitution was able to bear......"

Notes and References:
1. *The account of John Cranch's Life written by* **Sir John Barrow**, *Secretary to the Admiralty, narrator of the Congo Expedition of 1816, was published March 1818: and based on material furnished by Sir John Bowring contained in the introduction to Hawkins: History of Kingsbridge 1819*
2. *Bowring said the fostering uncle was called John. There was not an uncle John. It was Andrew [3] who was the uncle, shoemaker and bachelor.*
3. *John was evidently influenced by and worked with Col. George Montague (of Montague's Harrier fame) who was an eminent naturalist and author and lived at Knowle House, Kingsbridge. After he died the British Museum purchased his large and valuable natural history collection.*
4. *The curios that were brought back were held by his daughter Jane Bowring Cranch. When she died, her great friend Miss S.P. Fox purchased most of them.*
5. *John belonged to the Independent Chapel in Kingsbridge. Jane installed a tablet there to him. The chapel was destroyed by WW2 Bomb*

John Cranch, Zoologist on the Expedition to the Congo 1816 by Theodore Monod.

Professor Monod discovered that Dossier MS 681 in the Natural History Museum in Paris contained a whole series of papers by John C, a journal, with a list of publications and water colours relating to the expedition. It is thought that Dr. Leach took the material with him when he went from the British Museum to Paris in 1817 to study the zoological results of the expedition.

Monod considered John C had such a standing in Natural History circles as to justify his publication :

"in memory of a zoologist who would have been the first to make what today would be called a biological oceanographic expedition".

Bulletin of the British Museum (Natural History) Historical Series
Vol 4 No1 London 1970, in French.

Afterwards the British Museum were interested to find out more about John and wrote to the family with a copy of the booklet

"as the man I am interested in was so remarkable ...."

Unfortunately the family were unable to provide any further information.

John and Jane Cranch of Kingsbridge: The role of natural history in a Georgian domestic crisis"

This booklet again credits John for his endeavours and throws light on the domestic consequences of John's obsessions with natural history. The part describing John's family relationships are not quite accurate in my view: see Chart 8.1

Ian M. Varndell PhD CBiol FRSB.
Rep. Trans. Devon. Ass. Advmt Sci., 151, 219–244

CHAPTER 10
JANE BOWRING CRANCH

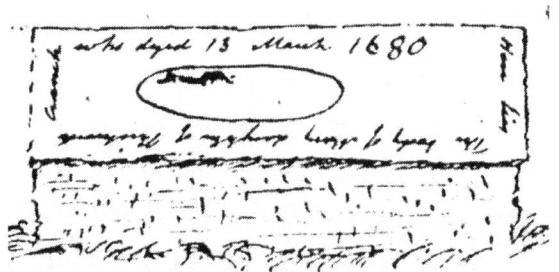

Ch 10.1 Jane Bowring Cranch

Family Connections, Property, Her Will, Bowring-Cranch Connections, Sir John Bowring, Collected and Other Poems, Saltstone, Bolt Head, Poems in Newspapers

Family Connections
Born   25.9.1813 in Kingsbridge and lived there all her life
Died   22.12.1878, age 66
Father: John the Naturalist, who died when she was only three years old.
Mother   Jane Bowring
Occupation Writer and Poet, Family Historian, Spinster.

Jane was part of the network of Cranch family relations based in Kingsbridge and Exeter, mostly those of the Andrew tree. She became a family historian and kept in touch with her various co-families and continued the puritan tradition. She had a great knowledge of the areas around Kingsbridge and its people particularly the period of the civil strife and religious turmoil which engulfed Kingsbridge. Her writings and poems greatly reflect their and her views, her knowledge of the family and its location, although the Cranch name is hardly ever mentioned

The book for which she is particularly noted is "Troublous' Times" which records the exploits of the Rev. Hicks and was based on his diary. It is clear that she used both intimate family and local knowledge when writing it and so it contributes greatly to our knowledge of Cranch family history.

Her literary efforts were undoubtedly encouraged and promoted by her cousin and godfather Sir John Bowring. In a paper on "Ancient Exeter & its Trade" read at Exeter July 1872 shortly before he died, Sir John said:
> "The daughter of John Cranch (Naturalist) has also taken her place in the literary world and has written some observant descriptions of the persecuted Puritans with whom her ancestors were associated"

She was elected member of The Devonshire Association in 1877 which met that year in Kingsbridge. She contributed a biography of John Cranch the Painter (Notes and Queries Vol 1). This biography is almost word for word the same as that written (but unpublished) by James Davidson in 1832.

Two poems of particular local interest are the ones about the Saltstone and Bolt Head. The latter was the subject of one of John the Painter's "expeditions", but as far as we know she took no great interest in him otherwise.

An example of how Jane was steeped in local history relates to a shipwreck. In 1772 the *Chantiloupe* floundered in Bigbury Bay. Only one man survived. A lady dressed in all her finery did make it ashore, only to be stripped of her clothes and jewels and left to die by the looters. "There is in the possession of Miss J.B.Cranch, a corner of the ill-fated lady's apron which was ..... given on the evening following the wreck to her grandfather who preserved it ....The fragment is a beautiful specimen of fine embroidered muslin."   *Kingsbridge Estuary etc S.B Fox 1864*

Property
She was a lady of independent means, inheriting the property in Mill St. which originally belonged to her great-grand father Nathaniel [1]

She bequeathed some land in her property to the adjoining Independent Church, Fore St, Kingsbridge. She was responsible for the plaque to her father which was in the church. Unfortunately, the church and its records were destroyed by one of the few bombs that hit Kingsbridge in WW2

Nos 3 & 4 South Place today

Mill Street today

She lived at No 3 South Place Dodbrooke. The property was put up for auction in 1870 and was described a comprising front and back parlours, drawing room and 4 bedrooms, kitchen and curtilage. She was a yearly tenant.
She then lived at 59 Fore Street which she owned.
Following her death, there was a public auction of her household furniture, books etc at 59 Fore Street.   *Notices in Kingsbridge Gazette 11 June 1870and 4 Jan 1879*

Jane's will
In her will she named Henry Lemon of Exeter, husband of her cousin Matilda, as her executor. It names at least 16 beneficiaries (nearly all relations) and illustrates how her life revolved around the Cranch family. As far as can be ascertained, all items that might have been of family interest were either sold at the auction or inherited by Miss S.P. Fox. who was a great friend.

She seemed to regard the tree of Andrew the Elder as the only true Cranches as she wrote to Peabody saying she was "the only one left – no-more Cranches in Kingsbridge !" What she probably meant was that there were no other direct descendants of Andrew the Elder left in Kingsbridge, which was probably true. She certainly was not the last Cranch !

Cranch – Bowring relationships
There was considerable connections between the Cranch family and the Bowrings over the years:
- Three generations back on her father's side, a Kingsbridge Cranch (Andrew) married a Kingsbridge Bowring (Sally) in about 1730
- Two generations back another Kingsbridge Cranch (Sarah) married an Exeter Bowring (William) in 1769
- Jane's mother was a Jane Bowring from Exeter, her father John the Naturalist Cranch from Kingsbridge, married about 1810
- In her lifetime an Exeter Cranch (Richard) married an Exeter Bowring (Jenny) in about 1780

The chart that follows attempts to show these various (complicated) linkages.

In John the Painter's letter of 1772 he refers to meeting many relations at Exeter: he met Bill Bowring and cousin Dick on their way to a meeting; stayed at Bowring's house where he spent time with "uncle Andrew" and "Bill and his wife"; went to see Mr Bowring; went to St Peter's Church where he saw "Mr William of Halwell" and met several other family friends. (Andrew and William were Cranch uncles, Bill was a Bowring.)

The Cranch and Bowring families were not only inter-related, but also were in the cloth trade and shared common beliefs – Protestantism in its various guises. Many of the Cranch and Bowring members belonged to meeting houses such as
- Exeter, Bow Meeting (orthodox Presbyterian):
- Exeter, James (later Georges) Meeting (Unitarian)
- Moretonhampstead, Cross Meeting (Presbyterian)
- United Brethren (orthodox Presbyterian)

Some are buried in the Dissenters Graveyard 1824 – 1837 for the Georges meeting. Jane herself was a staunch member of the Kingsbridge Congregational church.

Sir John Bowring
The influence of the Bowrings on Jane and other Exeter Cranches in late 1700 - 1800's was considerable. Prominent was her cousin and godfather Sir John Bowring.

Sir John Bowring 1792 – 1872 was a descendant of an old puritan family and an ardent disciple in the school of Unitarian and political radicalism. He was an eminent linguist, political economist, writer and student of literature. He was an M.P., British Consul to Hong Kong and superintendent of trade in China. He was knighted in 1854 and sent to Hong Kong as Governor where his high handedness led to war with China. He was elected FRS, FRGS and received several foreign degrees and decorations. He retired to Exeter and was prominent in various societies. There is no doubt his views coincided with Jane's and that he encouraged her to publish.

The Bowring business in the late 1700's included insurance (used by the Cranch fullers in Exeter). It eventually became an international business. The family historian Miss Michell received a reply to an enquiry which confirmed that the Cranch and Bowrings were related and " our forebears certainly come from Devonshire and were particularly associated with Exeter, Mortonhampstead and Kingsbridge"
Letter written by Edgar Bowring, The Bowring Building, London 6 July 1978

Collected and Other Poems
A booklet of a collection of 15 poems composed over many years was produced a year before she died. Her interest in the "Troublous Times" period and social causes is evident. *Poems published by Provost & Co.1877*

The Saltstone is a rock frequently referred to in her book "Troublous Times"

She explains line 5 : *"Gaze reverently upon yon islet the ebbing waves leave bare"*
"There is a rock near the middle of the Kingsbridge estuary, called Saltstone, on which the persecuted Non-conformists, in the reigns of Charles II and his brother James, used, when Tide and weather permitted, to meet for worship; and this rock being claimed by no particular parish, here they could assemble unmolested."

The sun is in the west, and beneath his radiance bright
The headland's soft brow seems a "hill of light"
Calm at its feet primeval the slumbering waters lie,
A sea of glass reflecting the glory of the sky

Gaze reverently upon yon islet the ebbing waves leave bare
For godly men of old were wont to gather there
Proscribed, despoiled, and harassed, to worship god they met
By eager foes surrounded and cruel spies beset

The waves around its sedgy sides, the greenwood on shore
The beach o'erhung with trees, are now as when of yore
The voice of winds and waters joined to swell their solemn hymn
Till the moon beyond the hill disclosed her golden rim

In suffering knit together, on this sequestered rock
Some hunted pastor oft rejoiced to meet his scattered flock
O hallowed spot ! to such thou wert an island of the blest
A moment's breathing space to them, of peace, and joy, of rest

The grace of God, it is a panoply to shield from earthly fear
These Christians bravely proved whilst steeped in sorrow here
They held the truth as those had done who death himself withstood
And joined the martyr army that sealed it with their blood

In suffering meek, in faith triumphant, let no scoffing tongue deride
These pastors of the olden time; for men so true, so tried
Might well be called *successors* of their prototypes
In bonds and cruel mockings, imprisonment, and stripes

Of their grave visages, and sober doublets, and solemn speech we read,
Yet in those dauntless souls, the steadfast will begot the glorious deed
They smote the pride of princes, and left to kings a legacy
Of the "rights divine of men" till Time himself shall die

In many a grand church, I've scanned with curious eyes
The gorgeous tombs where pomp in dust by worms forgotten lies
Despite the painter's blazonries, the herald's quaint design
The sculptors' rarest art, the scholar's choicest line.

But here's a monument which shall not perish whilst pious hearts revere
And scared hold the rights of conscience to peasant as to peer
Firm as this rock on which they knelt, the memory shall endure
of them who fought the good fight valiantly, and kept the faith so pure.

Fishermen having picnic on Saltstone before it became a reserve.   Cookworthy P0505

The Bolt Head, Salcombe.
Another area of Kingsbridge area featured in a poem is this tribute, produced in recognition of John the Painter's trip to this area "in search of antiquities".

> O *thou* majestic relic of a world where Adam wept,
> The flood has swelled against thy front, the deluge o'er thee swept;
> O everlasting hill, in calm and silent progress fast
> Were thy foundations laid, ay, perhaps a million ages past!
>
> When "without form and void" this ancient earth was looming dim
> In darkness, shrouded through time measureless to all save. Him
> Whose "Spirit moved upon the waters," swift unveiled then-face,
> And the great shoreless, soundless deep then knew its destined place.
>
> Our monuments of eld, the pyramids or columns still
> Erect of Thebes, piled up at some Osiris despot will,
> Works of a race of yesterday they seem compared with thee,
> The stony secret of whose age is kept by earth and sea;
>
> For thou might'st, when thy stately head was kissed by heaven-sent light,
> Which dawned on Eden's morning, melted into Eden's night,
> And the morning stars first shone, and the tender moon was told
> With her fair face to guide the ocean, then be grey and old.

Poems in Newspapers
Many of her poems first appeared in newspapers and other publications:

True Greatness is a poem concerning **John Pounds and his Scholars**. She explains:
> "John Pounds, who has been called the true founder of the Ragged Schools, died several years since at Bristol…… His attention being drawn to the miserable condition of the young neglected children around him, he …established a school for their instruction on his own premises. …… The instructions he gave were, of course, wholly gratuitous – the poor little creatures he taught to read and write …….had no HONEST weekly pence to pay……….."
> *W. & F. G. Cash, [1855],*

The Young Working Man's Address To His Books probably reflects her own views. This is from *British Workman Vol. 1, No. 20 (1856), a C19th Business, Temperance & Trade Periodical.* The opening verse and last verse:

My Books! there's magic in these words!
My books have been to me
As sunshine to the grateful earth,
Or flowers to the bee.

For what the sun is to the earth
Or rain to plant and tree
Or fair winds to the prosp'rous bark
My books have been to me

True Greatness (this time about Whitfield) is an ode to the Rev Whitfield. A sample is verse 6 :
> Let him preach, as Paul of old did
> Shelter'd by the heavens alone
> With no earthly limit round him
> Save the blue horizon's zone
> And his kindl'ng glance to meet
> Breathless thousands at his feet
> *Whitfield Preaching, a Tract* Published by: W. & F. G. Cash, [1856], London

Burns. She produced a poem to celebrate the birth of Robert Burns in *The Western TImes 29.1.1859*. There was a competition held at Chrystal Place (not without controversy) to celebrate his birth, but this was not an entry.

The Riches Of Poverty was another poem dedicated to John Pounds, published in the *Western Times 25 July 1857*. This one much shorter:

A poor lame man, and a toil-worn man,
Wrought from break of day till the sun
went down
Where he saw young children
Cast vagrant wise on the swarming town,

And it moved him so, their infant woe,
He began what a nation now joys to see,
I'll do my best: leave with God the rest
But the poor can help the poor," quoth he.

A lonely an aged woman,
Watch'd patient, where sickness and
death were rife,
The groan of the soul, in its parting dole,
The wail of the babe new born to life

O, who for the poor can feel like the poor
And though mine the widow's mite must be,
Yet there's One will bless, even to littleness,
And the poor can help the poor," quoth she.

A hard-work'd man, and weary man,
with his wife, and children seven
When a weak voice cried, their door outside,
"A morsel for the love of Heaven."

From the little store, too scant before,
They gave, and the beggar did say,
"now God be thank'd." "Ah God be thank'd,
that the poor can help the poor," quoth they

Other References and sources
Devonshire Association, Wikipedia
Western Morning News
Western Times
The Exeter Dissenters Graveyard Trust.

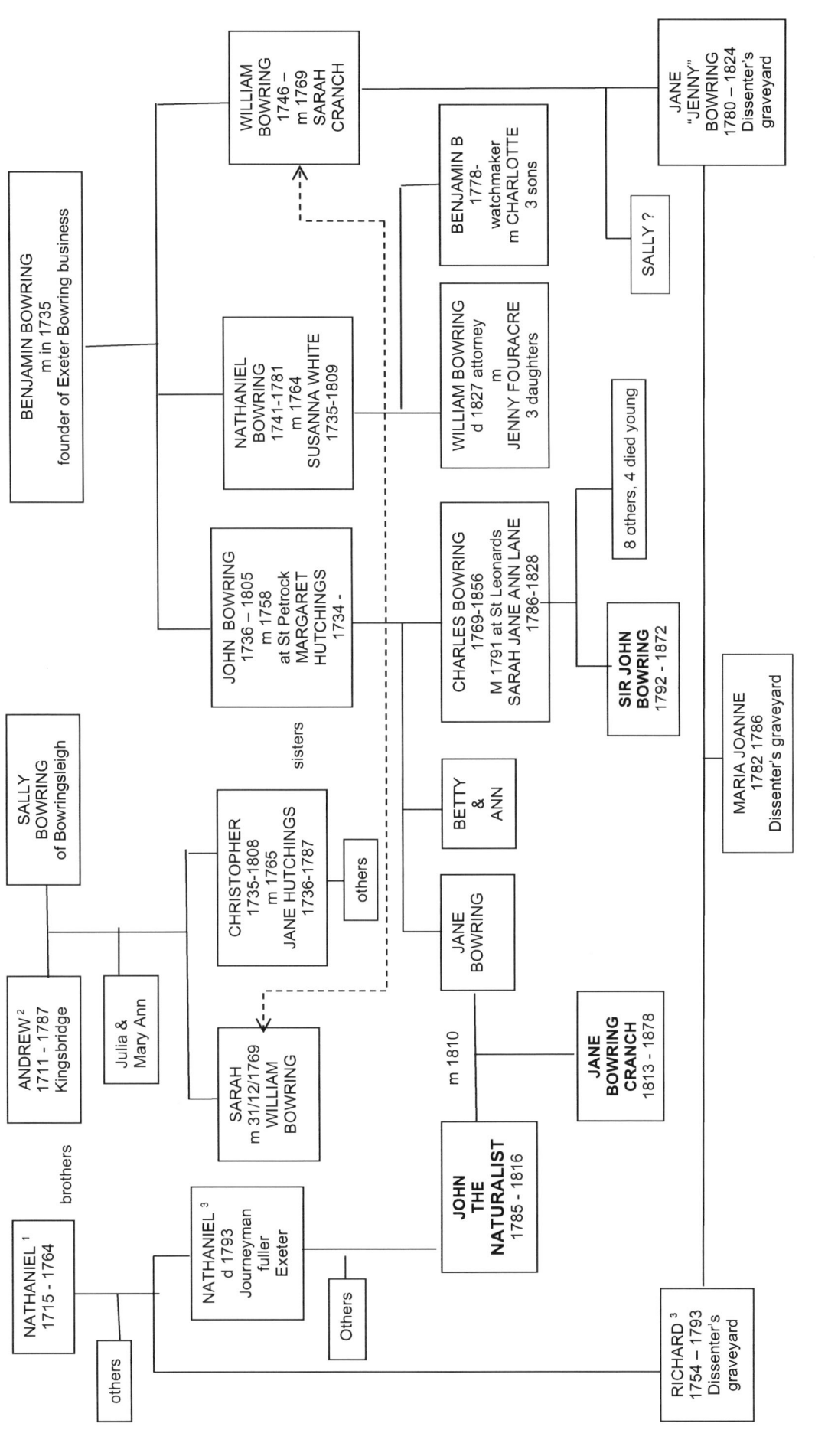

10.2 Chart   BOWRING and CRANCH Connections   7

CHAPTER 11
THE FAMILY OF JOSEPH 2

Ch 11.1 Family if Joseph [2]

Introduction

This chapter is one continuation of Chapter 7 where the Seven children of John [2] of the Andrew Tree were introduced.

This chapter discusses the second son Joseph [2]. He married Elizabeth Lidstone and they had eight surviving children as shown in the following chart 11.2 and they created quite a network of relatives. This is summarised:

Child	Brief History	Further Information
Mary[2]	married James Wilcocks	chart 11.3 see also Ch 14.1
Elizabeth	married James Elworthy	Chart 11.2
Hannah	married William Bond (senior), went to America	Ch. 12 Richard and America
Joseph [5]	married Rebecca Elworthy	Ch.17 Joseph [5] and his Families
John	the Painter	Ch.13 John the Painter
Ebbet	went to America with her sister Hannah	Ch 12 Richard and America
William N.	married Mary Roope	Ch. 14 William N and family
Francis	Spinster lived with brother William N.	Ch 11.2

Information about the two daughters Elizabeth and Francis is limited and contained within the main chart 11.2

Mary's family and descendants is shown next in chart 11.3

Subsequent chapters cover the considerable information concerning the others. The first stop is America!

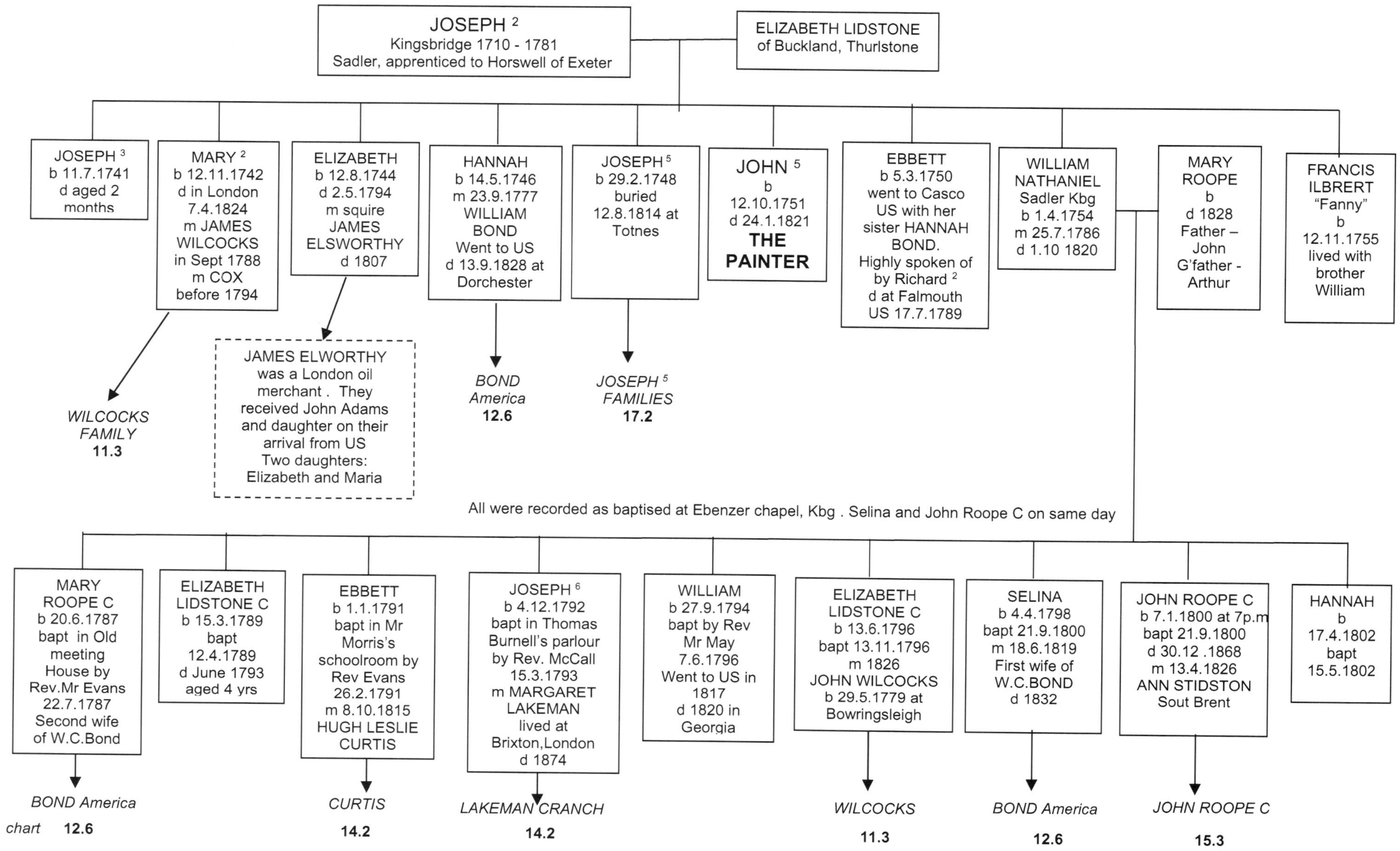

JOSEPH² of The Seven

JOSEPH² Kingsbridge 1710 - 1781, Sadler, apprenticed to Horswell of Exeter — m **ELIZABETH LIDSTONE** of Buckland, Thurlstone

Children:

- **JOSEPH³** b 11.7.1741 d aged 2 months

- **MARY²** b 12.11.1742 d in London 7.4.1824 m JAMES WILCOCKS in Sept 1788 m COX before 1794 → *WILCOCKS FAMILY* **11.3**

- **ELIZABETH** b 12.8.1744 d 2.5.1794 m squire JAMES ELSWORTHY d 1807
  - *JAMES ELWORTHY was a London oil merchant. They received John Adams and daughter on their arrival from US. Two daughters: Elizabeth and Maria*

- **HANNAH** b 14.5.1746 m 23.9.1777 WILLIAM BOND Went to US d 13.9.1828 at Dorchester → *BOND America* **12.6**

- **JOSEPH⁵** b 29.2.1748 buried 12.8.1814 at Totnes → *JOSEPH⁵ FAMILIES* **17.2**

- **JOHN⁵** b 12.10.1751 d 24.1.1821 **THE PAINTER**

- **EBBETT** b 5.3.1750 went to Casco US with her sister HANNAH BOND. Highly spoken of by Richard² d at Falmouth US 17.7.1789

- **WILLIAM NATHANIEL** Sadler Kbg b 1.4.1754 m 25.7.1786 d 1.10 1820 — m **MARY ROOPE** b d 1828 Father – John G'father - Arthur

- **FRANCIS ILBRERT** "Fanny" b 12.11.1755 lived with brother William

Children of WILLIAM NATHANIEL & MARY ROOPE:

- **MARY ROOPE C** b 20.6.1787 bapt in Old meeting House by Rev.Mr Evans 22.7.1787 Second wife of W.C.Bond → *BOND America chart* **12.6**

- **ELIZABETH LIDSTONE C** b 15.3.1789 bapt 12.4.1789 d June 1793 aged 4 yrs

- **EBBETT** b 1.1.1791 bapt in Mr Morris's schoolroom by Rev Evans 26.2.1791 m 8.10.1815 HUGH LESLIE CURTIS → *CURTIS* **14.2**

- **JOSEPH⁶** b 4.12.1792 bapt in Thomas Burnell's parlour by Rev. McCall 15.3.1793 m MARGARET LAKEMAN lived at Brixton,London d 1874 → *LAKEMAN CRANCH* **14.2**

- **WILLIAM** b 27.9.1794 bapt by Rev Mr May 7.6.1796 Went to US in 1817 d 1820 in Georgia

- **ELIZABETH LIDSTONE C** b 13.6.1796 bapt 13.11.1796 m 1826 JOHN WILCOCKS b 29.5.1779 at Bowringsleigh → *WILCOCKS* **11.3**

- **SELINA** b 4.4.1798 bapt 21.9.1800 m 18.6.1819 First wife of W.C.BOND d 1832 → *BOND America* **12.6**

- **JOHN ROOPE C** b 7.1.1800 at 7p.m bapt 21.9.1800 d 30.12 .1868 m 13.4.1826 ANN STIDSTON Sout Brent → *JOHN ROOPE C* **15.3**

- **HANNAH** b 17.4.1802 bapt 15.5.1802

All were recorded as baptised at Ebenezer chapel, Kbg . Selina and John Roope C on same day

11.2 Chart   JOSEPH² of The Seven

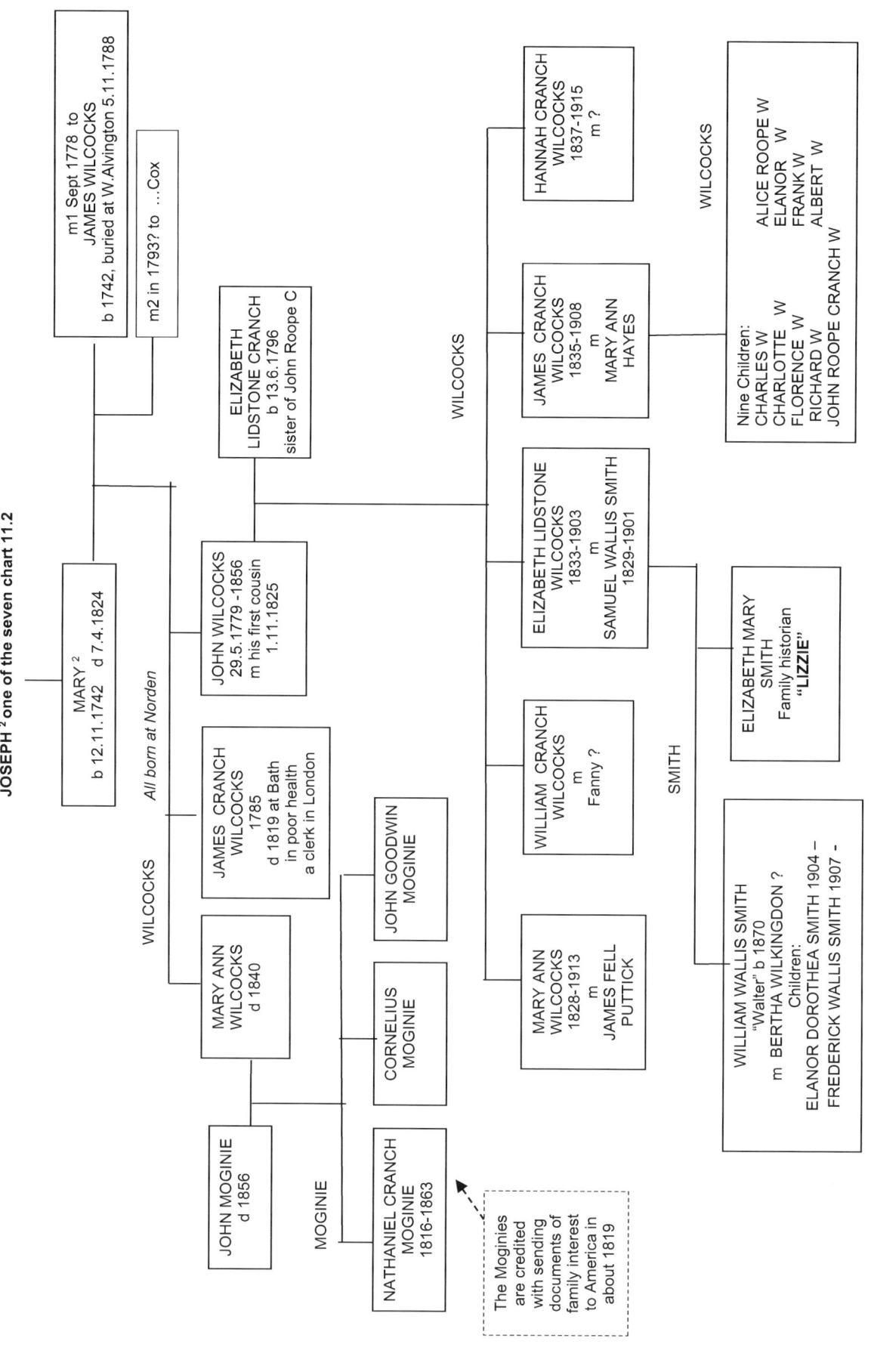

11.3 Chart   MARY and the WILCOCKS, SMITH, MOGINIE families

CHAPTER 12
RICHARD AND AMERICA

12.1 The First Cranches in America

Richard's Claim, Migrants after 1640, the Cranch Exodus in the 1700's, Mary, Joseph Palmer, Robert Garland C, Nathaniel [2], Joseph [4], Migrants after 1800, T.S. Eliot.

Hereafter in this chapter Richard's superscript is not used.

Richard's Claim
Richard was the youngest of the eight children of Joseph [2] He claimed he was
> "..as I suppose the first person of the name of Cranch who has a family of children in America.."

Note the wording. He may well be correct but he certainly was not the first Cranch to go to America when he went in 1746; in fact several Cranches went to America) before him (mostly to the Boston area).

The coming of the puritans began in 1620's . However according to the governor at the time English people
> "began to navigate and plant in these lands well-nigh 40 years ago
>
> *Bolton: The Real Founders of New England*

According to Brown
> "Devon was third amongst the counties of England to send emigrants to the New World, most came from coastal communities especially in South Devon where the tradition of the sea was very strong. .... There was no severe oppression forcing several thousand Devonians to leave in the 1620's and 1630's but personal factors promoted the desire for advancement.......Members of the yeoman class provided the backbone of this emigration ...."
>
> *Brown: Devonians and New England Settlement before 1650 (RTDA 95 ; 1963)*

The Topographical Dictionary of English Emigrants 1620 – 1650 gives the figure as 175 emigrants from 73 Devon parishes
An Encyclopaedia of World History, W Langer, Ed., Harrap 1987 claims that between 1630 – 1642 there were over 16,000 migrants to the Massachusetts Bay Colony.
Hotten: Original Lists of Emigrants 1600-1700 gives the muster of Capt. W. Pierce's servants attending Mulbury Island on 24 Jan 1624 to include:
> "John Cranich came in the Marygold"

The Marygold in 1619 sailed from Plymouth, 30 tons, no ordinance. In 1627 the Marygold sailed 90 tons, no ordinance, 2 decks. She was one of the ships used for carrying the thousand men under the Earl of Holland.
> *The Early Stuart Mariners and Shipping 1619 – 1635 (D & C R Soc. vol 33; 1990)*

Migrants after 1640
The religious situation in Devon after about 1640 radically changed. The "no severe oppression" in Brown's article above no longer applied. The desire to escape was a seriously consideration as the following quotations dating from about the mid 1600's from the diaries of the Rev Hicks show (*from "Troublous Times"*):.
> "…to join the little company of godly folk who have made arrangements to sail next month from the port of Plymouth to New England"
>
> "…and though that to which we think of going may seem little better than a wilderness by comparison with this we are driven out from, yet shall we and our children find there the ….freedom to worship God"

12.1 The First Cranches in America

"...in New England, the brave and godly sons and daughters of the Old (... whom tyrants banish ...) can dwell in safety and have laid the foundation of a free and gracious polity"

According to the Rev Burdwood:
" My sons ...desire to build homes ...in that New World. I was once along with several other brethren in misfortune upon the point of embarking for. Yet ... Providence ....constrained me to stay behind"

Peabody asserts:
"There were Cranches in New England nearly a hundred years before Richard, who esteemed himself the first one who had a family here, came over. Andrew Cranch's name is found among those of the early settlers of N. Hampshire, previously to 1690".

There is some evidence for this:

J. Farmer, Genealogical Register of 1st Settlers of New England gives
Andrew Cranch, born about 1646, arrived in New Hampshire in 1687. Subsequently this Andrew features as a witness to some wills in 1688 & 1690 *(American Ancestors: Maine: Early Wills etc)*. He may well be the Andrew Cranch quoted by Peabody

The Boston Globe 21 Apr. 1769 reports that a Mary Cranch, a widow from Salem "being intoxicated fell backwards downstairs and broke her neck". The previous year she was reported as being in court because of debt.

Records of Falmouth (now Portland) N.E. Hist & Gen Reg vol XVI gives a Samuel Jordan as marrying Francis Cranch 2 Mar 1734

The Complete Book of Emigrants by P.W.Coldham reports that on 12 Oct 1685 the rebels convicted after Monmouth's rebellion and designed to be shipped by John Rose, merchant to Barbados or Jamaica, included "John Crance"

The Cranch Exodus in the 1700's

The main source of information about later settlers comes from Peabody.
There were probably three main motives for the emigration. Almost certainly one would have been to escape the on-going dissent and its consequences.
Secondly the desire to create a "better World". The colony of Massachusetts had fashioned in the 1600's a civil commonwealth along congregational church lines. Not without problems but the Puritan principles would have attracted those members of the Cranch family with similar views.
Thirdly, since the children of John[2] were "all brought up to trade" we can assume that the dissipation of the family and a gloomy outlook for those who did not inherit contributed to the desire to "try for another life elsewhere"

Richard went to America in 1746 on the ship Wilmington with:
- Mary his sister who had married General Joseph Palmer and their two children. The General had chartered the ship so he could also take cargo.
- William Pearse Mead who went as a young boy with Gen Palmer (Richard's cousin once removed by John)
- Edward Pearse (cousin of William Mead)

Later the sons of John [2] the Minister went (nephews of Richard [2]):
- In 1768 Nathaniel and Robert Garland C.
- in 1771 their brother Joseph[4] and Hannah (Richard's niece by Joseph) who had married William Bond) and her sister Ebbett.

The details that follow, in the charts or text, are based mainly on Peabody's record.
Life does not seem to have been easy for any of them.

12.1 The First Cranches in America

Mary (1719-1789)
Mary was born at (Dod)Brooke, one of the seven and only daughter of John [2] She married Joseph Palmer in 1745 (?) and went with him to Boston in 1746 and lived at Germantown, Quincy
She is described as a "lovely and accomplished" woman. The General, her husband, himself accords to her high qualities as a woman and wife. In her later years she lost the sight of one eye and did not see well with the other (1784)
Her temperament was nervous. (Abigail says she was prone to angry outbursts). A few days before her death in 1790 she was struck speechless.
She was residing at the time in Quincy near her brother Richard. Richard in his letter giving an account of the deaths of her and her husband speaks of them as persons of "exquisite feelings".

Mary wrote a letter to her brother Joseph [2] on 29 Aug 1746 whilst on board the ship Wilmington, anchored in Cawsand Bay, Plymouth that she "expects signal to sail every moment". This indicates that the Wilmington sailed at the end of August. Since she arrived in Boston on the 2nd November the voyage took a full two months.
Another letter from Germanton to a relative named Tozer in Ashburton dated May 1765 "mentioning many interesting things and among them a high tide which had risen over the wharf at Germanton doing much damage".
Mary received a letter from her nephew John Cranch the Painter 19 June 1788 with money. She was then in straightened circumstances; he had recently inherited.

Joseph Palmer (1716–1788) *(information from Wikipedia)*
He was born at Shaugh Prior, a son of John and Joan Palmer, née Pearse. He married Mary Cranch in 1746, at Ermington and emigrated to Massachusetts later that year with his brother-in-law Richard Cranch.
In 1752 they built a glassworks and founded a colony of German workmen, which became known as Germantown, now part of Quincy, Massachusetts. Later they built a chocolate mill and spermaceti and salt factories. Their ventures failed. By the 1770s Palmer had become a supporter of American independence. He fought in the Battle of Lexington and served in the Massachusetts Provincial Congress and on the Cambridge Committee of Safety. He sent Israel Bissell on his ride to warn that the war with Britain had begun. He received a commission as a colonel in the Massachusetts militia and as brigadier for Suffolk County, Massachusetts, in 1776. He went on intelligence-gathering missions in Vermont and Rhode Island and, as brigadier-general, led a failed attack on Newport, Rhode Island. After the war, he returned to his businesses. Heavy debt forced him to leave Germantown and he started a salt factory on the Boston Neck in 1784. He died four years later at his home in Dorchester, Massachusetts on Christmas day

Robert Garland C (1743-1792)
Robert was a sadler and one of the sons of John the Dissenting Minister who died early. The family would have witnessed a difficult life, so it is not surprising that they followed the example of their uncle Richard in going to America
Robert went to Boston in 1768 almost immediately after his mother died, and probably in same ship as his brother Nathaniel. The sale of their home in Kingsbridge UK continued after he arrived in America. He advertised his wares the Boston Gazette. After his wife died in 1779 he became melancholy and intemperate. He was temporarily taken in by Gen Palmer in 1789, then moved to live with his brother Joseph at West Point 1791. He died in the winter of 1792

12.1 The First Cranches in America

Nathaniel [2] (1745-1780)
Nataniel was also a son of John The Minister and probably worked with his brother before they went to America in 1768.
He sold ironwork, English goods imported into Boston. An advert placed in The Massachusetts Spy - June 11 1772 with Joseph[4] said that they
> "lately from England, Ironmongers and Gunsmiths ….. hereby inform the Public, that they have taken a shop near the Lamb, in where they now have for sale, a variety of Articles……"

He took the Oath of Allegiance to State of Pennsylvania and was in service of the Quartermaster General Miffin, Philadelphia during the revolution
> *A Linn & Egle, Names of persons who took Oath of Alegiance to State of Pennsyvania, Westminster, M.D , Willow Bend Books 2000*

He was betrothed to Elizabeth Palmer (first cousin) but died in 1780. According to the *Boston Globe 19 Apr. 1780*:
> Nathaniel Cranch lately returned from public employment at Philadelphia and while passing over the parapet (?) ….leading to Roxbury fell from the battlement and was instantly killed.

Joseph [4] (1746-1806)
Born 1726 just after his father's death. He went to New England in 1771 and joined his brother Nathaniel [2] in business
In 1781 he was Commissary General of Military Stores Department (armourer) a position obtained with help from his uncle Richard. This was a prominent position as shown by the following: a letter from Henry Knox to Joseph Cranch at West Point on 20 July 1791 for 2000 gun stocks etc
> *(Henry Knox papers, New York Public Library)*

He married Elizabeth Palmer (daughter of Mary & Gen Joseph Palmer, his niece) in 1790 and lived in West Point with her sister Mary Palmer.
In 1800 they returned to Milton, N. England. Then in 1805 to Jamaica Plain.
Joseph was described then as a small feeble-looking man. He died in 1806 after at least 16 years as an invalid.
> *Jamaica Plain near Boston was founded by Boston Puritans seeking farm land.*

Migrants in the 1800's
Two notable later family migrants ones are Selina and Mary Roope Cranch. *(see chapter on The Bonds)*
Other Passenger & Immigration lists show:
- Another Nathaniel landed Pennsylvania 1779
- Thomas age 25 and William age 23 landed at New York 1821 & 1822
- Joseph age 38 and Mary age 43 landed N.Y 1832 with son Charles and family

The Eliot connection:
From *First families of America*, there is an entry for C.R Eliot born 20 Jan 1856 that gives him as descended from the Andrew tree. T.S Eliot is a descendant of C.R.Eliot and therefore was related to the Cranches (remotely!).
T.S. Eliot lived in England. His ashes, by his request, are in St Michels's Church, East Coker, Somerset which he claimed to be the home of Andrew Eliot who emigrated from there in 1667.
> *Wikipedia*

Ch 12.2 Richard ²

Portrait, Family Connections, America at that time, Outline of his Life, Family Life of Richard and Mary, Eulogy

Thomas Crane Public Library, Mass

Richard C 1726 – 1811 from Kingsbridge in 1746.
Settled in Braintree (later part of Quincy) watchmaker, republican & senator
Member Massachusetts General Court. Judge in Court of Common Pleas

From First Families

Ch 12.2 Richard [2]

Family Connections

Born   1726 in Kingsbridge, the last of the "Seven" of the Andrew Tree
Died   16 Oct 1811 in America
Father: John[2], clothier, died in 1746
Mother   Elizabeth Pearse
Married   Mary Smith (1741 – 1811) in 1762. He was 36, she 21.

Mary had two sisters:
- Abigail who married John Adams, second President of the United States
- Elizabeth who married Rev John Shaw and after his death Rev Stephen Peabody (also his second marriage). A descendant Peabody recorded valuable information about the Cranch family

The Smith sisters were well connected as their mother was a Quincy, wealthy farmers who it is said virtually ran Braintree at that time.

Richard became an influential participant in the development of America through his marriage, living in Massachusetts, his intellect and his beliefs.
The following is designed to give an outline of his achievements, his family life and the circumstances in which he lived.

America at that Time

Richard arrived in 1746. Public opinion in Boston began to go against Britain in the early 1760's over taxation. Thereafter Boston featured frequently in the conflict with Britain e.g. in 1770 the Boston Massacre in which John Adams defended the soldiers involved and in 1773 the Boston Tea Party. The American War of Independence was 1775 – 1783. These events, the disputes surrounding them and the political atmosphere were witnessed by anyone living in the Boston area at that time. Add to that the constant threat of disease, the problems caused by severe weather, unreliable servants, poor transport and roads – it soon becomes apparent that life was not easy.

An outline of his Life

Richard was one of six sons. He was bound as an apprentice to a maker of wool cards. At age 19 when his father died he bought himself out and went to America in 1746 with Gen. Joseph Palmer who had married his sister Mary. Initially he and the Gen. had joint ventures which failed and deterred him from any future partnerships

He opened a card manufacturing shop. In an advert in a Boston newspaper 1748 he described himself a "card maker from London", Then he went into the watch trade. He left Boston in 1750 and lived thenceforward in Braintree.

He was a great student and a man of much mental force. He became a learned man, received an honorary degree from Harvard University, was elected a member of the American Academy of Arts & Sciences, sustained several important public offices, was a Representative Senator and was for many years a member of the legislature and a Judge of the Court of Common Pleas

He supported independence and practiced a rationalist monotheism denying the divinity of Christ. Today he would be Unitarian.

His wife Mary was a lady of most benevolent character and was described as the "mother of orphans" by one of her nieces. She died the day after Richard.

They had four children. All married into notable American families. The son William Cranch followed his father into the legal profession and became a significant person in his own right. He in turn had 13 children.

Richard himself wrote "A Short Memorandum about Richard Cranch and his family written in 1805 ....at the request of his daughter". The memorandum is invaluable as it specifies a number of Cranch family relationships, shown in the charts that follow. They for the most part are excluded from the following extracts:

"I Richard Cranch of Quincy in the County of Norfolk and State of Massachusetts, Esquire, being, as I suppose, the first person of the name of Cranch who has had a family of children in America would for the information of posterity give the following short account of myself and family.
I was born at Kingsbridge .... My ancestors were born in the same town or its neighbourhood and were chiefly if not wholly concerned in the woollen manufacture. My grandfather Andrew Cranch carried on the business of serge-making largely in Kingsbridge. My father John Cranch was his only son by his first wife Ebutt and was born in Kingsbridge. His grandfather Richard Cranch after whom I was named.... was a rigid puritan and belonged to the church of the Rev John Flavell of Dartmouth. My mother ...was Elizabeth Pearse. .... The late general Joseph Palmer had married my only sister Mary Cranch and came from England in 1746 with me ...in a large ship called the Wilmington .... I was then just 21 .... (having spent his 21st on board ship)
As to my life both public and private, ... I have lived for nearly 60 years ....in or near Boston. I was formally honoured with a seat in the General Court for a number of years as a representative for the old town of Braintree which then contained what is now divided into the three towns of Braintree, Quincy and Randolph. I was afterwards chosen and served as a Senator of the Commonwealth of Massachusetts and also for a number of years one of the judges of the court of Common Pleas. I am now in the 79th year .... what the future is known only to god to whom I commend myself. ....
New England Genealogy and History Register vol 27 (1873)

Sources and other references:
- *American Archives 1847 Sketches of Alumini (by his son William)*
- *Peabody*
- *His son William also wrote the Introduction containing a longer biography of his father in ... Laws of U.S. Relating to Patents and Patent Office .... Opinions of Hon. William Cranch, Chief Justice of Circuit Court of U.S. for D.C..........*
- *Dictionary of American Biography*
- *William Pattee's "History of Old Braintree & Quincy" has entry for Richard as an immigrant.*
- *The first Census of America – Mass – gave for Richard Cranch's residence Men 2, boys 1, females 4, other 1, slaves 0*
- *Index of Court of Common Pleas, Suffolk County, Mass, 1756 – 1776 and the Boston Globe give various accounts of cases where Richard was the Judge.*
- *American Academy of Arts and Science 1794: president John Adams, a councillor was Richard C*
- *Ratification of the Federal Constitution by Massachusetts 1788 : yeas recorded by Richard C of Braintree and Capt Joseph Palmer of Falmouth. (N.E.Hist Gen Reg 1.)*
- *Massachusetts Historical Society : Adams papers*

The Family Life of Richard and Mary

Abigail Adams wrote numerous letters to her sister Mary. They show how deeply inter-twined the Adams and Cranch families were and provide much of the information which follows.

Dear Abigail, D Jacobs, Ballentine Books, New York 2014.
New Letters of Abigail Adams 1888-1801 S Mitchell 1947

Richard spent his early years in Boston in various ventures which mostly failed. He seemed to have no flair for business matters. He moved to Braintree (to live with his sister Mary and the Palmers?).

There he met the Smith family and evidently made such an impression on them that he became the tutor to the three girls, even though he was of no social standing, poor and unqualified. Abigail later wrote

> "to our own and inestimable brother Cranch do I owe my taste for letters and refinement……. the books he pulled from father's shelf".

At the time others said of Richard: "He was tall and lean with a high forehead, delicate features and a long open face .... he attracted men of rank and learning, a quiet ardour, "loving and compassionate" and "acutely sensitive"

Whilst trying to earn a living selling cards for wool-combing and repairing watches, he taught himself Greek, Latin, ancient Hebrew, and developed ingenious theories about the prophesies in the bible. He had enormous intellectual powers and acquired great knowledge, both scientific and classical. His frail health prevented him from manual work. His intellectual pursuits detracted from his business interests.

Richard and Mary Smith married in 1762. They complimented each other. He was a dreamer, she the pragmatist. Her sister Abigail (later to become a Federalist) then began to be courted by John Adams (also a Puritan recently graduated from Harvard), who had also by this time heard of Richard. Adams married Mary's sister Abigail.

In 1764 Mary's first child was born. In those days, one out of five New England women died from complications. Infant mortality was one in ten. Men were banished until the outcome was known. The agony of childbirth was often attended by a mid-wife with her own methods, many ladies and much wine!

By 1766 they had moved to Salem (partly it was said to escape his sister Mary Palmer). In the autumn Richard was very ill and then snow trapped them in.

By 1774 they were back in Boston. Tory hostility had chased them out of Salem, but life in Boston at the time of the disputes with Britain was hardly secure, nor peaceful. Mary wanted to leave Boston. Richard's sales of watches and clocks had been poor due to the import boycott of British goods, but demand for locally made wool-combing cards boomed. Mary wrote "Mr Cranch is so hurried with work that he does not know how to spare time to see after anything …. "

There was a smallpox outbreak in early spring 1775 and fearing an epidemic the Cranches moved their 3 children back to Braintree while they carried on in Boston. Then they were trapped when Boston was garrisoned by the British. Richard had to get a visa to get out. Small pox raged in Boston in 1776. The advocated diets to counter it and the recently introduced inoculation procedures against it were controversial.

Richard's upturn in business meant he could buy a 32-acre farm with a "commodious farmhouse" in Braintree in 1777. Abigail wrote to her husband John: "You would smile to see what a farmer our brother Cranch makes. His whole attention is as much engaged in it as it ever was with watch work or prophesies."   He made several tons of hay with his own hands and built a new barn practically by himself.
The farmhouse was so near the Adams' house that the Cranch and Adam's girls "were in and out of each other's houses". This close association between the two families continued for the rest of their lives.
Richard did not make a success of his farm any more than of fixing watches or selling cards. He was repeatedly and unanimously elected to the county court and the Massachusetts's House of Representatives. The long commutes to court and congress in Boston left Richard with little energy for farming.
Abigail wrote: "I know very well that a small farm must afford you a scanty support …. but I know your prudence & economy has carried you along tho' not in affluence, yet with decency & comfort"

To make ends meet, Mary took in boarders (uncommon practice for a married woman). She did this as well as coping with three children, her household and a husband prone to ill-health, absent-mindedness and whose priority was to serve his country at the expense of all else.
When he lived in Boston for his work he longed to be in Mary's company at Braintree. As his children grew up he would counsel them to endeavour. To Billy his eldest: "you may in future …have many opportunities for prestigious jobs" (because of John Adam's contacts for instance)

Throughout Richard's life he suffered ill-health. 1782 spring he became mortally sick, several colds, serious lung infection, then pneumonia then edema nursed by Mary. Amazingly he recovered in late summer and went back to court early October. Abigail wrote ; "the doctors say he owes his life to the incessant, unwearied, indefatigable watchful care of his wife, who almost sacrificed her own to save his"
However Mary too had health problems over the years. For instance she fell seriously ill in the summer of 1800 and was helped in her long recovery by Richard. Richard showed the Cranch family trait – a regard for family.

Contact between the Cranches (Richard's as well as the later Cranch arrivals), the Adams, the Bonds and the Palmers was continuous within America then and for generations afterwards. Richard also maintained contact with the Cranch family he left behind. This is an example – a letter written by Richard from Boston 1773 to his nephew John the Painter, then at Axminster:
> ……(please) enquire …into the origin of the name and family of Cranch…….who our ancestors were before my grandfather Andrew Cranch of Kingsbridge ….(I am unable to find) the name on any (reference) books or public lists …(or anywhere) except in Devon ….As I am the first of the name that ever had a family in America I have a great curiosity to know where from we sprung….
> I often hear from your brother-in-law Elsworthy and have lately received a letter from cousin Richard at Exeter acknowledging receipt of a watch I gave him ….
> From your sincere friend and affectionate uncle Richard Cranch.

In 1787 the Adams arrived back in America and stayed with the Cranches for a week. Whilst in England they had toured Devon to see Cranch relatives, so no doubt had

Ch 12.2 Richard 2

much to relate. Whilst away, Abigail had written to Mary that John Adams says that to Richard " any of his books are at his service"

In 1789 Abigail requested "Richard to make out his account which he has against Mr Adams". Abigail "had lent Mary some money (in advance on account) ... and will re-reimburse Richard in full as "it was my own money". In the same letter she wishes "…it was in John Adam's power to help Mr Cranch to some office ….Mr Adams expressed the same …" but John Adams was against patronage.

In 1790 Mary's own financial circumstances were as pressed as ever, due to Richard's poorly paid public service but the happiness and wellbeing of her family was paramount and what she strived for. In April of that year there was a virulent strain of influenza and hardly anyone escaped. Abigail writes about general illness in all families at that time, moans about the state of roads, and "wishing perfect restoration to health of Richard".

The church ministers held great sway over their communities, so the appointment of the successor to an incumbent was a key decision. In 1797 Quincy (by then incorporating Braintree) asked Richard to lead the search for a new minister. In spite of his ill health and business failures, he was the most revered man in town. However his wife Mary was a master expediter. Eventually after 23 months of dispute between various factions and personalities, in January 1800 the Rev. Peter Whitney accepted the post of minister at the First Church of Quincy, Massachusetts. This was as much a reflection of Richard's views as the Rev. Whitney's abilities to win the votes. It led to Whitney getting to know Richard well which in turn gave Whitney the inside knowledge for the eulogy he later delivered.

Ironically a report (on the death of Hannah Cranch Bond in 1870) states that
> " Richard acquired considerable property, part of his estate is still known as Cranch's Farm"

In all probability he would take some personal satisfaction with that, in spite of living most of his life poor. He had established a Cranches Farm in America.

Eulogy
The Discourse Delivered at Quincy October 19, 1811 at the Internment of the Hon Richard Cranch who died October 16, 1811 and of Mrs Mary Cranch, his wife, who died October 17, 1811 by Peter Whitney.

Whitney begins by exploring the theme of "the righteous shall be in everlasting remembrance" *(American King James Version psalm 112 line 6,)* which Peter Whitney considered did Richard and Mary justice. The following is an extract of the eulogy.

Richard Cranch was descended from reputable parents who were Puritans. He was early instructed in the great principles of religion, and had continually before him an example of strict adherence to the practice of the gospel. Their piety and sincere attachment to what they conceived to be the truth were always the subject of his admiration.

He was deeply impressed by the advantages of his religious upbringing. He said in my last conversation with him, "for more than 60 years I have felt the value of early religion, and of an early profession of Christianity. At a period when no worldly considerations could be supposed to influence my conduct, I made a public profession of religion. I have never found any reason to lament this part of my conduct. It has always given me pleasure on reflection, and brightens my prospects into futurity.

On arrival he resided for several years in Boston, and soon became acquainted with some of the most distinguished clergy and laity. His mind was naturally vigorous and comprehensive, thoughtful and inquisitive. His friendship was sought by the wise and virtuous and in their society he laid the foundation for an honourable and useful career. He continually improved himself by reading and conversing with the intelligent His taste led him principally to the knowledge of God, of his works, dispensations and particularly to Christian theology and the Bible. The prophesies of scripture forcibly impressed him which led him read more on the subject. From the prophesies which describe the antichrist he designed an ingenious theory. Unfortunately he could not be prevailed to publicise it.

In 1750 the prevalence of small pox meant he moved to Braintree, then he moved to Weymouth and he belonged to its church for the rest of his life. In Weymouth also he met his wife which led to a very happy marriage.

His talents and his virtues soon recommended him to the confidence of the people. In public office, the fidelity and intelligence he displayed are universally known.

Among all his excellences his piety perhaps was the most prominent. He felt in every action that he was in the presence of God and accountable at his tribunal. In his family devotions he was uncommonly fervent; and in his life there were as few aberrations from the strictest integrity as have ever marked a man. He was a constant and serious church attendant and professor of Christianity. With him vice could find no shelter. It was frowned upon with indignation. Though pleasant and cheerful as a companion his cheerfulness never degenerated into levity; nor in the moments of greatest relaxation did he forget his character as a Christian. His conversation was replete with apposite and entertaining anecdotes and with the richest fund of intelligence. The wise delighted to mingle in his society and always benefited from the full stores of his mind.

With the clergy he was in the highest estimation and few have ever surpassed him in their knowledge of Christian theology. He was regarded as a sound divine.

Though not attached to the sentiments of the Catholics, he viewed them with an eye of candour, and beheld them to be men of sincerity and virtue. He never erected himself into a standard for others; but was willing to believe that, however widely Christians might differ, they might have the honesty and fidelity to recommend them to God and hoped that eventually every country and every religion would meet together in heaven. He abhorred bigotry.

In the domestic relations of life, he displayed every virtue that could be desired. Let us imitate his piety, his meekness and humility and live as he did.

All his faculties except that of hearing he retained until shortly before his death. His wife died shortly after and the passage of scripture which is placed at the head of this discourse, was I believe equally appropriate to her character.

The scene is rarely found. Having lived together for almost half a century this happy pair are scarcely divided by death. It was his earnest desire that he might not survive the death of his wife; and hers that she might live to behold her dearest friend "gathered in peace to the dust of his fathers". When she was informed of the dangerous condition of her husband she observed that all her desires of living were on his account and that she was now ready to die with him. Within a few hours of his death, she died. As their tastes, their habits, their virtues and their prospects bore so near a resemblance we trust they are both now joined together again in heaven.

Mrs Cranch was born in Weymouth [America] in September 1741. She was the daughter of the Rev. William Smith, pastor of its first church and had a pious education. Her mind was above the ordinary level which she improved by reading and the society of the wise. Few of her sex have surpassed her in useful qualifications and none perhaps in the virtues which she will be in "everlasting remembrance". As a companion she was cheerful and entertaining; as a friend she was affectionate and faithful. As a wife she was everything that could be desired. "She looked well to her household and her children have reason to call her blessed". The sick found in her a ready and consoling visitor and the poor were made partakers of her bounty.

As she had early made a public profession of religion, so she endeavoured uniformly to live as the "gospel teacheth". Habitually serious and devout, death and eternity were no strangers to her thoughts and she met it without terror. Never have I witnessed more perfect resignation, more triumphant hopes, more settled composure of mind than she displayed in her last sickness. Sensible of her imperfections she depended for salvation on the mercy of God through the Redeemer. Every step to the grave seemed to give additional firmness to her faith and fresh vigour to her hopes. I doubt not she "shine as the brightness of the firmament and as a star forever and ever".

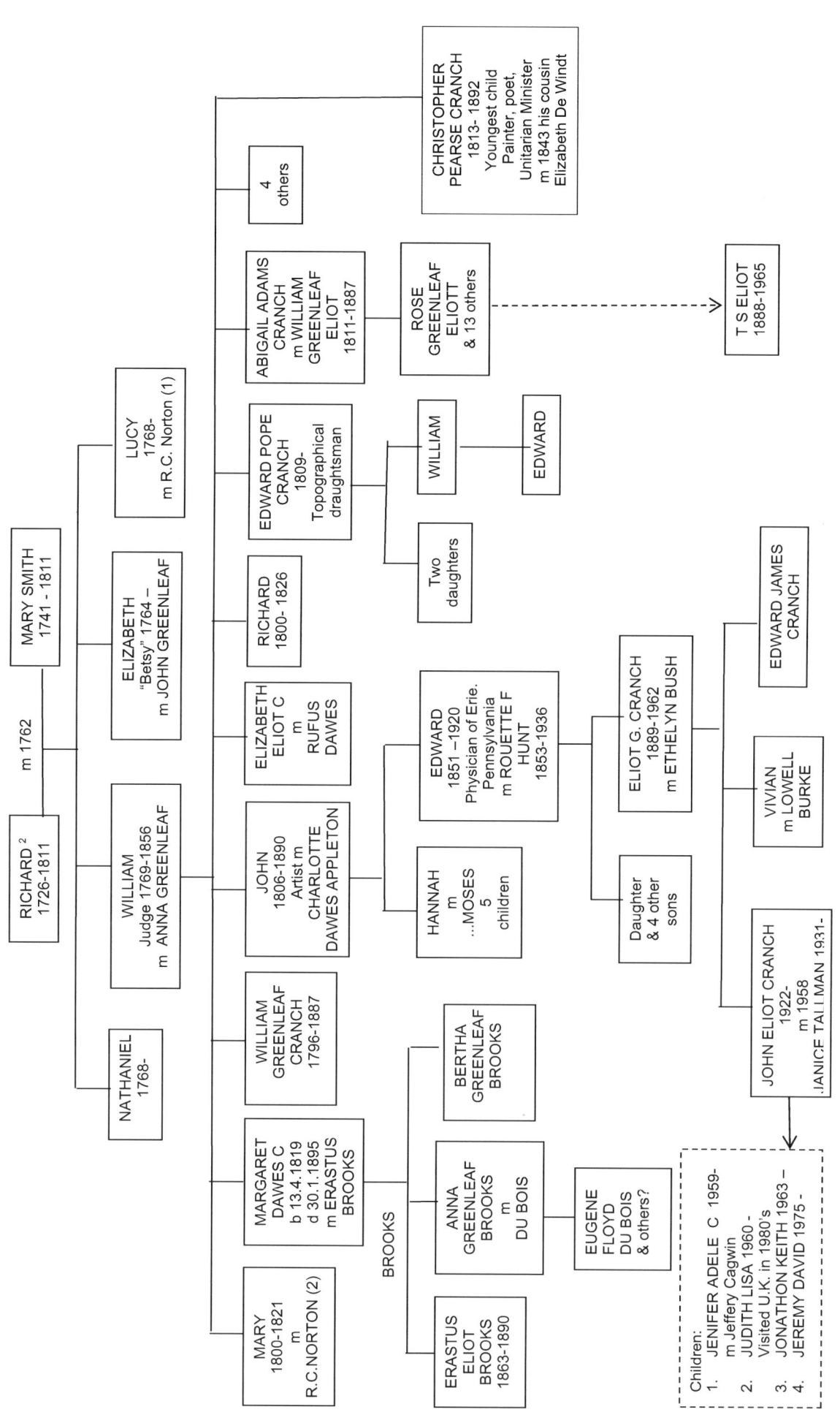

12.3 Chart   American Family of RICHARD [2]   13

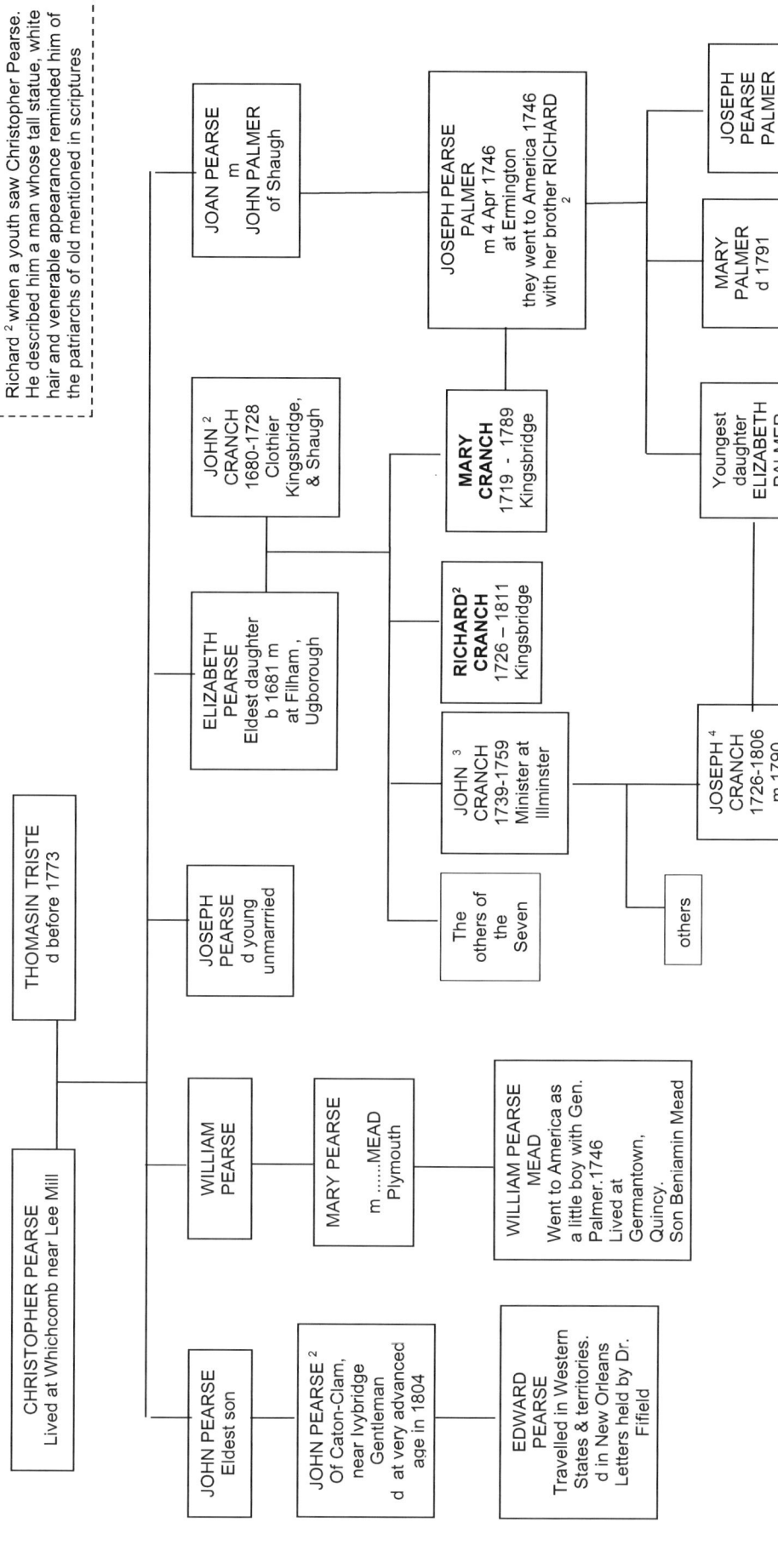

12.4 Chart MARY CRANCH, PEARSE, MEAD & PALMER FAMILIES

Ch 12.5 The Bonds

William Bond, W.C Bond, Selina Cranch, Mary Roope Cranch, Cranch - Bond Connections, Mrs Brooks' Letter, Memorials

The initial Bond family in America were part of the Richard "migration" and were related. They were pioneers in their own right. Their descendants have visited Devon at various times

William Bond (1754 – 1848)
Born in Plymouth (England), his father was an eminent chemist and surgeon and related to t
he Brendon family who could trace possession of their estate back to the time of William the Conqueror.

"The family of Brendon and their descendants of Brendon and Westcott In St. Dominick, Cornwall" by J. Brendon Curgenven, 1903:

William Bond was a true Cornishman – fiery, impulsive, generous, affectionate and indulgent to his children, but subject to violent outbursts of passion. His true Cornishman's taste for mining led him to lose money in American mining ventures.

He married **Hannah Cranch** (niece of Richard [2]) in 1777. He had visited America in 1784 and was urged by the Cranches there to emigrate. He went in 1784 and in 1786 charted the brig *John* to bring his family over – Hannah, their two children and Hannah's sister **Ebbet.** Richard, uncle of Hannah and Ebbet, spoke highly of Ebbet.

After unsuccessful ventures, he and family were back in Boston in 1790 where he began business as a silversmith and watch and clockmaker, trades he had learned in London in his youth. It took time to build up the business and his family had a long hard struggle with poverty.

His wife Hannah was a woman of great force of will, a stern sense of justice and integrity and a marked vigour of intellect; an uncompromising Puritan housewife, strict on the performance of every duty, and equally strict in exacting of others their dues. In her presence the children of the family never spoke except in subdued whispers; and when she entered a room all rose and remained standing until she was seated. These were the manners of the age, but she is said to have been peculiarly strict in enforcing them and even her grown children stood in awe of her.

He and his wife never ceased to regret their emigration to America. A loyal, love of England was characteristic of the family for many years. On household customs, manners and traditions, they were thoroughly English. In his latter years he was regarded as a quaint figure, with rosy cheeks, bright sharp eyes, brisk and vehement.

W.C.Bond i.e. William Cranch Bond, (1789 – 1859)
Son of William, born in Portland, Maine. He was a mild mannered boy, good tempered with remarkable mechanical ability, At the age of 10 he made a wooden clock. He was not strong physically but constant exercise established his health.

He left school at an early age to work in his father's shop. By 1812 most of the chronometers used in Boston trade were derived from his instruments, requiring a high degree of skill. He also became an avid astronomer.

The hardships of his circumstances gave him despair at times but his mother sympathised with his aspirations even though she could not relieve the adversity. He discovered and observed the great comet of 1811 for months before it came to the knowledge of universities. In 1815 (aged 26) he was commissioned by Harvard College to make "examinations of the building and instruments at Greenwich and to consult instrument makers". Since he was paid, it meant he was not pennyless, so was able to see England.

During another visit to England in 1819 he married his cousin Selina Cranch in Kingsbridge. They had six children. She died in 1831. Afterwards he married her elder sister Mary Roope Cranch.

The parlour of his house was converted into an observatory. He worked by day in his business and in the evening at his workbench as a watchmaker to earn enough to meet the current household expenses. Apparently he had no financial acumen.

His "business" (largely unpaid) was in undertaking assignments connected with astronomy, meteorology, magnetism and chronometers. His fame spread. He was made Astronomical Observer by the government in 1838. By 1839 he was "well established in a profitable manufacturing business" when approached to join the American Academy at Cambridge by "his constant friend the Hon. J. Quincy". There was constant entertainment of scientific colleagues and friends in an "open house", including the descendants of Richard [2] and other relatives. Being a close friend of the Quincy family was not insignificant. His whole family were bound up in his interests. Later one of his son's George Phillips Bond carried on these interests.

In due course of time he received an Honary degree of M.A. from Harvard College, was the first Director of the Observatory of Harvard College, Professor of Practical Astronomy, was a member of the American Academy of Arts and sciences, of the American Philosophical Society, member of Royal Astronomical Society of London and of other such institutes. He was awarded a Council Medal at the Great Exhibition 1851 (Crystal Palace) for apparatus to record observation of Mars electrically and was the first to photograph the moon's disc.

In old age he was a gentle, kindly old man and deeply religious. He died aged 95. The American Academy of Arts and Sciences resolved that:
> "... the simplicity and sincerity of his Christian life, ...imparted that serenity and tranquillity which charmed his friends and was manifest in the modesty , neatness and integrity of his various communications to the public... which we have lost"

Selina Cranch was a beautiful woman with a soft and gentle voice and manners. Her father William Cranch 1754 – 1820 refers to her in his home-made diary for 1819:
- 14 May Wm Bond & Selina came home (*maybe from visit to Bonds at Plymouth?*)
- 12 June *(wrote and posted letter directly)* to Selina at No 7 St James's St., Clerkenwell (home of the Elworthys)
- 18 June Selina married W.C.Bond, (then *they*) went to London on 21 June

Other entries relate to letters sent to and received from Wm Bond
The registration of her marriage was sworn on 12.7.1819 and gives Selina as spinster of Kingsbridge, W.C Bond of Boston a batchelor, both over 21 years of age,

witnessed by her father. The actual marriage was on 18 June 1819 at Dodbrook church.

Mary Roope Cranch was Mary's eldest sister and W.C. Bond's second wife. She was a woman of strong determined character, capable, and very ambitious. The household expenses were willingly cut down to save the money needed for the purchase of costly books and instruments. She was ready to make any personal sacrifices for the science to which her husband was devoted.

She was the eldest of the siblings and would be expected when growing up in Kingsbridge to look after "the young ones" for her mother and generally help run the large household. She appears to be a very capable lady and it would seem natural for her to look after her youngest sister's children all under the age of 10 when their mother Selina died.

Her youngest brother John Roope C evidently revered her as he wished she were with him in his hour of need following the death of his own daughter Hannah aged age18.

The Cranch – Bond Connections

The following charts show the relationships between the Cranches and the Bonds, the beginnings of the American Cranches (i.e Ricard's family) and how Mary Cranch (of the seven and sister of Richard) was related to the Pearse, Mead and Palmer families. The following letter gives much information about the various connections and members of these families

Mrs Brook's Letter

In July 1892, Mrs Margaret Dawes Brooks was in Plymouth, Devon on a UK visit. She had evidently contacted her South Brent relatives on arrival and received a letter from Richard Stidson Cranch. There is no indication that she or any of her party ever met up with the relatives in South Brent during her visit. The letter was started just after she arrived in Devon and completed just before she left Southampton to continue her "search for health" on the continent.

Mr Dear Sir

I received your kind letter this morning & hasten to answer & thank you for it & for the beautiful memorial card in memory of your respectful father.

I begin by telling you that I am 73 years old & afflicted with muscular rheumatism & can only by help of my stick & the arm of my faithful maid travel about. I came from New York by the German Lloyd steamer accompanied by my two daughters Anna Greenway du Bois and Bertha Greenway Brooks & my niece Rose Greenway Eliot & a friend Miss Disowery & my grandson Eugenie Floyd Du Bois. We were in search of health as the physician said a sea voyage was needed by both my daughters.

I lost my husband Erastus Brooks 5 years ago & my only son two years since at the age of 27. My good son-in-law also was taken from us a year ago. Their characters were spotless and they are both honoured by the community in which they lived. A beautiful Rectory is now being suited with money bequeathed by my son Erastus Eliot Brooks at West New Brighton Staten Island. Surely as Wordsworth says:
   "the good go first" . And those whose lives are dry as summer dust
   Burns to the socket"
I am left!
I said that I had an old letter but it was not from John Cranch but from our relative Mrs Fifield who was born Bond & sister of our very scientific relative Wm Cranch

Bond, astronomer at Cambridge, Mass. Their ancestors were Cranches from Devon. No doubt are quite as familiar with that Cranch of your family as I am.

My father was Wm Cranch son of Richard who sailed from Plymouth 1746 with his only sister Mary & her husband and cousin whom she had married. He was titled "General" Palmer, what that title implied & how or why applied I have never known. Some descendants are in America, namely Peabody and Putnam.

As to our name few remain as my father was an only son. His two sisters took the names by marriage of Greenway & Norton. My mother's name was Anna Greenway. She had 13 children of whom I was the 13th born 1819.

My eldest brother Wm Greenway died a bachelor, a man of spotless character and called Brother Wm by the whole community of Washington City where he was born 1796. He was a janitor burger and so was my brother John artist with his cousin James and my sister Elizabeth Eliot who married her cousin Rufus Dawes. He had no children.

My brother Richard Cranch was drowned in Lake Erie while surveying that lake preparatory to the opening of the Grand Canal connecting the great lake and New York City in 1826. He was a fine man & loved by all, his age was 26. I was only five years old at the time but remember him.

My brother John was a portrait painter and a student in Italy. He died two years ago aged 84; he left two children a daughter who married & has five children & a son Edward Cranch who lives at Erie Penn is a physician in good practice. He has five fine boys all young and a daughter born a few months ago. We hope these boys will stay the name Cranch for many years in America!

My only surviving brother Edward Pope Cranch is a lawyer by education but an artist by choice. His talent for characters is great & he writes the best letters even now at 83. He is loved and respected by all; he lives near Cincinnati Ohio; he has one son Wm Cranch & a grandson Edward. I regret to say their father married with a R. Catholic mother, went over to that religion. Their uncle became Archbishop Wood of Philadelphia, my brother however & his wife & two daughters remain staunch Protestants. (I fear I do not make this clear, but it not important)

If any of your family should ever visit New York we should be glad to welcome them at our home (for we honour the name of Cranch)

My grandfather married Mary Smith whose father was the Rev Wm Smith of Mass. Her sister Abigail married John Adams our second President & at the close of our year of Independence was sent as Ambassador to Great Britain in 1784. His wife accompanied him & his son John Quincy Adams afterwards elected President in 1796.

I think my father had taken up his home as a lawyer in Washington City. He married in Boston and soon after lived in Washington City. His uncle John Adams having appointed him Judge at the early age of 36 as his office continued until his death in 1856. He held office longer than any other person - 56 years ! He was and his memory is honoured and beloved by all who knew him and by family and friends. He wrote the reports of the Supreme Court & his name is familiar to all legal men through "Cranch's Reports" throughout America. Having only his salary he left no property, giving his sons a college education and his daughter a good education. His grandchildren had to make their own way in life. My sister who is named Abby Adams married his cousin Wm G. Eliot a descendant of the distinguished Eliot who died in the tower imprisoned for conscience sake.

Wm Greenway Eliot was a man of great energy & did more than any other man who lived in St Louis & founded the Washington University in St Louis Mo. He had 14 children one of whom is with our party Rose Greenway Eliot.

I am confined pretty much to my rooms in this hotel which is very comfortable but my daughters are exploring the neighbourhood seeing much that is lovely in Devonshire. I have visited Salisbury with its grand Cathedral and Wells and Exeter and now tomorrow go to Bristol and on to Oxford and then on to London to remain a week at the Montague Mansion in Great S Russel St. Are there any Cranches in London? We are sorry our stay is not longer and my health better so we could have seen your mother and self. Our children may in the future. We shall be or I with my maid hope to pass the month of August in the Isle of Wight while some of us go to the continent. I am not sure just where we shall stay while there. (This poor writing will I am afraid try your patience and eyesight)
With great respect for the family name and thanks for your letter
I remain yours very truly

Margaret Dawes Brooks Aug 30 1892
She gave her address as: Mrs Brooks, West New Brighton, Staten Island, New York

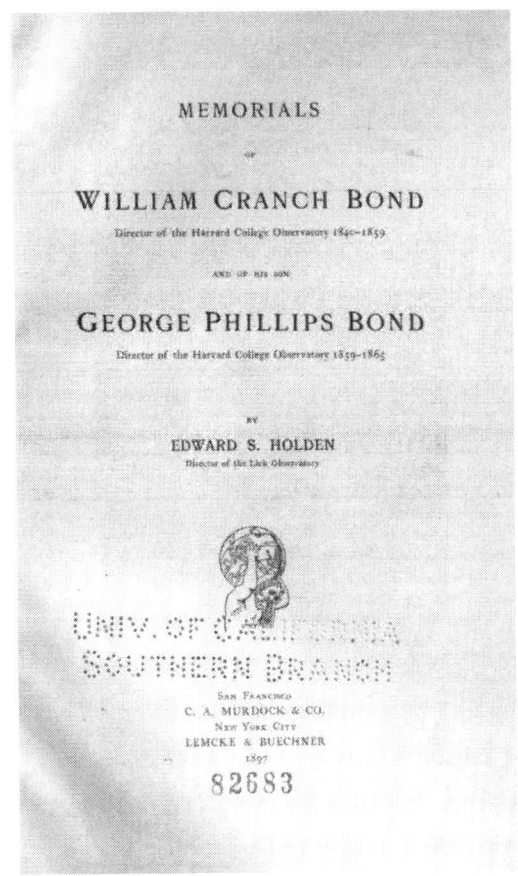

"Memorials of William Cranch Bond
Director of the Harvard College Observatory and of his son"
by E.S. Holden 1897

Richard [2] Cranch had brothers Joseph [2] and William. Joseph [2] had 9 children. Two of them were Hannah and Ebbet. (see Chart 11.2)

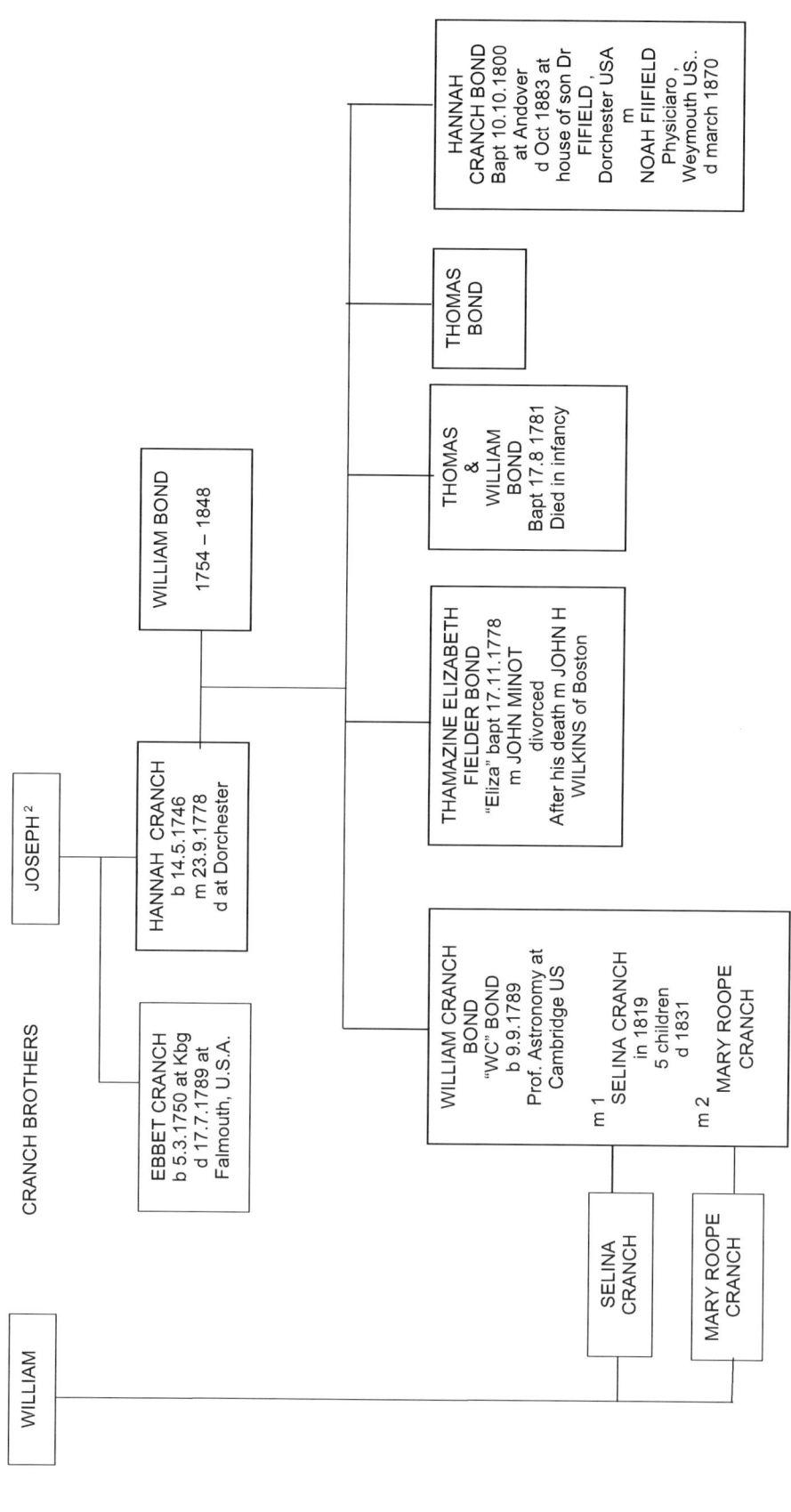

12.6 Chart   The BONDS of America

CHAPTER 13
JOHN THE PAINTER

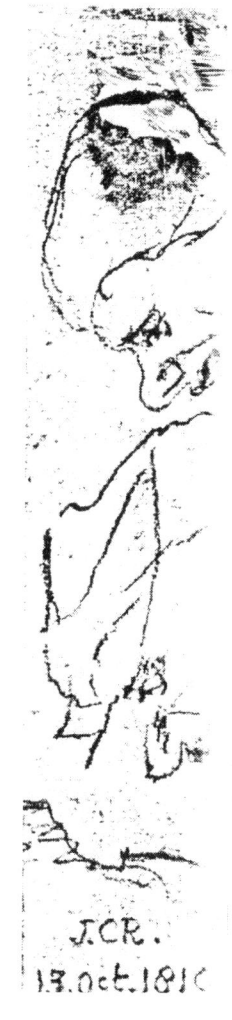

Ch 13.1 A Summary of the life of John Cranch

Portrait, Outline Of His Life, Self-Portrait, Character, Wit, Views, Travel and Friends, Later Years

Portrait and engraving by J. T. Smith published 10 Oct 1785, as described by him:
JOHN CRANCH
Born at Kingsbridge in Devonshire 12th Oct 1753 Aged 44
Fellow of the American Society of Arts & Sciences, Painter of an unique Picture of
The Death of Chatterton & author of the Economy of Testaments etc
Engraved from a Picture, which with the Death of Chatterton, is in the possession of
Sir James Winter Lake, Bart., F.S.A.

(note his date of birth was not as stated by J T Smith)

Ch 13.1 A Summary of the life of John Cranch

John Cranch (the "Painter")
Born   12 Oct 1751 in Kingsbridge
Father   Joseph, Sadler of Kingsbridge
Mother   Elizabeth Lidstone of Buckland, Thurlestone
Died   24 Jan 1821

John Cranch "excelled as a boy in writing, music and drawing" and probably attended Kingsbridge Grammar school.

From the family he would have known that his relative, the Rev. Richard Cranch of Ivybridge, had sponsored the aspiring painter Reynolds but the Rev died (in 1756) before John could expect any similar support.

His early employment after leaving school is not known, but it is possible he was engaged in some capacity by Lord Petre, owner of Norden which is where his family lived until about 1770 . At 21 (1772) he was engaged as a clerk in Axminster to an estate steward (Mr Knight). Here he learnt Latin and developed his artistic skills under the guidance of a Roman Catholic priest.

After three years (1775) he became the clerk to an attorney (Simon Bunter) and gained his accreditation as a Solicitor. Bunter came to regard him so much that he made him a co-executor in his will and left him an inheritance.

John took the opportunity to realise his ambition to be a painter. He went to live in London. He continued his legal work for a while, took up painting, enjoyed his inheritance and indulged his varied interests. This could be said on the one hand, to be to the detriment of taking a disciplined approach to his lifetime's ambition and, on the other, to enable him to display his talents and versatility

He became part of the London scene of artists, satirists and antiquarians. He was called Jack by his friends and was known as a man of much wit and humour and was generous.

He was befriended by Sir Joshua Reynolds who aided him and by Constable who he helped. He painted portraits and historical pictures and was known for his "poker-pictures" (using a red-hot poker on wood). Most of his paintings date from 1791 to 1810, eight of them were exhibited at the British Institution. His best-known work was "Death of Chatterton". The total known paintings of his are about 30

He was elected a Foreign Honorary Member of the American Academy of Arts and Sciences in 1797 and a member of the American Antiquarian Society in 1818, appointments influenced no doubt by his uncle Richard Cranch of America.

His standing as an artist was summed up by a critic as thus:
> " ....Cranch was an enthusiastic amateur ......an artist on a small scale and of small stature, but the savour of originality endows his painting with a sparkle to which the spectator can readily respond. "

He had great interest in "antiquities", inflamed by his friendship with John T Smith who engraved his portrait. He was distracted by the episode of Cromwell's head.

He published several articles, wrote for newspapers, was an editor of a London paper and left notebooks. These show his interest in "antiquities", the civil war and poetry. His letters also show family interest. One of these notebooks indicates he spent some time in his home town in 1799 to view "antiquities" and copy documents relating to the Grammar school and the civil war.

He kept in touch with his family both in this country and America and probably often returned to Devon. He also must have travelled as evidenced by some of his paintings and writings.

There are several indications that he was familiar with the attractions of Bath, and frequently stayed there. He moved there permanently in 1810. He spent a considerable amount of his time there researching Bath's rich history and its antiquities. By this time he had ceased all legal work but his training and learning stood him in good stead as a researcher of Bath's history. He ceased painting for a time, but continued sketches as part of his interest in antiquities.

By his death he was no longer financially independent. He died in Bath 24 January 1821 aged 70 and was buried at Walcot churchyard. He was unmarried, although he apparently wished to do so. He did not go to America, but expressed favourable sentiments of their struggles at the time.

Local obituaries commented very favourably on his personal qualities of integrity, moral rectitude and friendship, whereas an early biography highlighted his alleged failings in later life.

Self portrait
The J.T.Smith engraving seems to be the only known picture of John. Copies are to be found in museums e.g. the V & A, RAMM, in his biography by James Davidson in 'History of the Town and Parish of Axminster' (Exeter City Library) and in America. It was widely distributed among the family. In the Family Archive papers is this self-portrait sketch (undated):

His character

From his letters and the information arising from his activities we can piece together an understanding of his character. The most illuminating description of him comes from Abigail during the Adams' visit to the West Country in 1787 when John was 36:

> This is a curious genius. He is a middle-sized man, of delicate countenance, but quite awkward in his manners. He seldom looks one in the face, and seems as if he had been cramped and cowed in his youth. In company, one so pained for him, yet he is a man of reading and an accurate taste in the fine arts. Poetry, painting, music sculpture, architecture, all of them have engaged his attention. His profession does not seem to be the object of his affections, and he has given up the practice, with the intention of pursuing some other employment. He appears to be a man whose soul wants a wider expansion than his situation and circumstances allow. Dejected spirits he is very liable to. I do not think he is a happy man. His sentiments are by no means narrow or contracted; yet he is one by himself.

Wit

A theme detected throughout his life is one of a person with a lively mind with a sense of humour, which tempered his inherited family background and led to him engaging his attention widely.

There are numerous references to his wit and humour. When in London, he knew or knew of fellow artists and satirists such as Acherman, (he had one of his prints which is now in FA), Cruikshank, Woodward and Wolcott (who wrote under the name of Peter Pindar). Wolcot was also born in Kingsbridge and went to London about ten years before John. Rolandson an artist, caricaturist and satirist was also in London at that time.

Their humour was satirical wit along the lines of Alexander Pope. His notebooks contain many examples, such as this one concerned a landlady in Kingsbridge "whose chief fame lay in drinking, swearing, whoring, bull baiting etc":

> Beneath this small hillock lies the famous Moll Palmer
> Who has changed this cold climate (perhaps) for a warmer
> Speak no ill of the dead says the Rev.d St Paul
> As little as I can Sir: two lines shall hold all
> Her life was a scene of noise clamour and riot
> And never till now could be said to be quiet

Several other poems appear in his Notebook circa 1810 such as "to my old friend N.D.Bishop for his present of a fowl":

> Thy pullet, friend – thy pullet
> Fit for a royal gullet
> We've pick'd the bones of and hereby protest
> The chickabiddy had so fine a beast
> That while we carved and cramm'd, one hinted t'other
> That (God willing) could have pick'd another   etc

His letters are full of wit and asides, but he tends to "waffle" (to use a modern expression). They contain many references to smoking a pipe and having "ale".

Views

His family background was one of religious dissent, puritan beliefs and with strong connections with those who sought a new life in America and American independence. He gave the following pamphlet to John Adams, reflecting the family's views of the time and maybe its Flemish origins .

> *The true interest and Political maxims of the Republick of Holland and West Friesland by John De Witt 1702*

John wrote on it:

> *To his Excellency John Adams Esq ambassador from the United States of America , to the court of Great Britain 1787 J.Cr.*

Travel and Friends

It is evident that John travelled. He knew the West Country well; his account of his travel to Spa in 1785 showed he already knew about Bath; he painted the river Shannon in Ireland, Ely church, a house in Cornwall; visited and stayed at Frome and London (before moving there). He had a passport which described him as "gent" *(according to Graeme Cranch)*. He did not go to America though was interested in it. He evidently enjoyed living in London (several addresses) for about 20 years and the company of some fellow spirits.

Through his travels, work and background he came to know a wide variety of people who became friends and who he stayed with and / or corresponded. This was in addition to his numerous relatives both here and in America

He did not marry. He did express his love to Mrs Fielding a widow in a letter but was unsuccessful it seems.

His later Years

In a letter to his brother Bill in 1816 (John was 65) he reflects on his old age and his present state of affairs:

> "It is no small consolation to me …. a poor isolated unlucky fellow that has been so long suffered "from post to pillar" in this strange and ill governed world [that I am] still capable of sympathizing …….[with the] ..pleasant prospects …[and dreams of others]…. I can almost venture to say I rejoice in them, though Jury and I have so long ago "shook hands and parted".

He then admits to no longer being flush with money by saying that he will pay his own postage but not that of others (this was before the 1d stamp):

> "it is heart rending to me …….. It is an infallible sign that I am <u>not in quid</u>"

He needed to raise funds and so:

> "I am painting away at such a rate as [I] …. never wanted ….I have at length took heart and with introductory assistance from friends, …., have obtained some channels for sale. An acquaintance has lately sold a pair for me at Bristol and encouraged me to send more. [He regards this as] … more infatuation to entertain than hope. But ….both by necessity and inclination …[rather than write articles]…. what can I do else?

DHC ref: 51/7/8/9

Ch 13.2 Clerical Work 6

John Knight, Simon Bunter and his Will, Travel to Spa, Letters, Adams' visit to West Country, Publications, Lectures, Cromwell's Head.

John Knight (1734-1801)
John's first employment in Axminster was with John Knight who was the Estate Steward for Lord Petre, the then Lord of the Manor of Axminster. Lord Petre and the Knight family were strongly Catholic.
He was engaged in 1772 at a salary of £15 per year as a writer.
The resident priest aided John in his studies (teaching him Latin for example) and developing his artistic skills.
Evidence of John's work is contained in documents such as the Manor of Cossington Counterpart lease: 1773 witnessed by John Knight and John Cranch:

Simon Bunter (1725-1784) and his Will
John Cranch joined Bunter in 1775 and was there for about 10 years. He gained his accreditation as a solicitor's clerk from Bunter. Towards the end of Bunter's life, John probably in effect ran the office.
Simon Bunter was a wealthy man, a church warden and the leading lawyer in Axminster. He had built Oak House in Chard Street Axminster which was later described by Pevsner as the best house in Axminster
His wife was Meliora, considerably older than him. She was sister to the Judge Gundry who died of jail fever 1754. Bunter left Axminster for Lymne Regis in 1774 after his wife died

In his will Bunter named his executors to be: John Cranch and his nephews John & William Clapcott. He left legacies totalling about £3,350. (One was to his niece Mary who had married a Mr.Tucker)
To John Cranch, "formerly my clerk", he gave books and artifacts and the reminder of his estate. This had considerable land and property. It would seem as if John and his co-executors took nearly five years to wind up the estate.
It was claimed (by Davidson and subsequently by others) that John eventually benefited by over £2,000 from this inheritance, but proof seems to be lacking.
In a letter to America John says that "a property of 12 or 15 thousand pounds value had devolved on ..... (the Clapcotts)"
Evidently the various legacies and benefits acquired through his administering of this estate and that of others meant John could decamp tor London.
CC/PREB/49/1-22 is dated 26 Jan 1783, proved 12 April 1785.

Travel to Spa, Germany
John recorded in a notebook a trip he made to Spa, Germany in Aug 1785, no doubt in connection with being an executor. He was accompanied by Mr Tucker and Mr Clapcot.
There they met and brought back George who had been "pent up" in the English School at Liege for 3 years. It is not clear who George was. It's likely it was George Tucker, a nephew of Bunter.
John was pre-occupied during the trip as he "must indispensably return to Axminster by the 18 Aug" for an appointment, presumably connected to the will and / or other pressing legal work. But they were able to do some touring, indicating John was already familiar with Bath:
"…. the waters of La Chaude Fontaine are nothing as hot as those at Bath"

Ch 13.2 Clerical Work

Letters

He wrote numerous letters, particularly in the period he was at Axminster. Some are to Philip Crocker (friend and publisher, Frome) and John Andrews (friend and Attorney at Law, Plympton) concerning his own publications or comments on those of others such as Polwhele's History of Devonshire. In one he says he was the "editor of a weekly miscellany" called "The Guide". Many letters were written to his brother William.

He also established correspondence with his uncle Richard in America after the War of Independence and wrote letters of introduction to him inter alia regarding the efforts of English tradesmen to develop trade with America e.g. Clapcott hoped to sell Dorset beer.

When John had just turned 21 he journeyed to Axminster to take up his position as clerk to Mr Knight. This is an abridged account of the journey.

Dear Father
Having just supped & smoked my first pipe of the excellent half pound of tobacco you gave me I find myself in no bad cue for setting down the journal I promised you & here follows the brief thereof.
I suppose Brockedon has before this informed you of my disappointment with regard to the stage coach: of my stay at Newton on Saturday night & setting out for Exon from thence on Sunday morning at 8 o'clock. I had a very pleasant walk & met nothing worth mentioning besides a sporting of good water in going up Haldon & Dr.Adam's two sons in going down. I walked very leisurely & before 12 got to the 7 Stars where I dined & having viewed the New Bridge works changed my stockings & got my shoes polished etc.
I rebetook myself to my staff & bundle & I found myself before one at the Bear in Southgate Street inquiring after my box & the master of the wagon to whose own proper person I resolved to apply on account of the preceding days' mishap, the consequence of which now aked my leg bones,.
This *Monarch* of the highway being deeply encased on business (that is to say) with a rump of beef & fowls in the parlour I waited half an hour before I could get an Audience & as we had settled the necessary preliminaries I sat down by the fire & called for some beer in company with the Waggoner & a drowsy council of Hackney Coachmen & deputy bootcatchers who overheard the treaty & from whom I learnt (soon after the master turned his back) that I had taken a very impolite measure making my agreement with him instead of his prime minister.
However (thought I) the dearer I pay for discretion the longer & better it shall wear. So having drunk I sallied into the Street & met Bill Bowring & cousin Dick under Southgate. They were going to the meeting but accompanied me back to Bowring's house & then left me. I went from thence to Mr. Bowden's to whom I paid a sum of money & took a receipt & afterwards went several times to counsellor Heath's and at last P. him of these two matters & also of the delivery of a letter to Mr knight you'll please to inform Mr Hawkins as they were his commands
I then went to St. Peter's church (where I saw Mr William of Halwell) & afterwards back to cousin Bowring's where I spent the time till 6 o 'clock with Uncle Bill and his wife Dick & Jack Burnell
At 6 o'clock Bowring, Dick & Jack Burnell went with me to the wagon warehouse & with some difficulty got my box, admitted to be fixed outside the wagon, for there was

Ch 13.2 Clerical Work

but tolerable room left for the persons of myself & the other two passengers: a woman & a boy both blacks & natives of Jamaica going to London.

A description of his fellow passengers follows then:

Nearly 13 hours was dragged along without having the least glimpse of house, hedge or sky & under the most melancholy waking apprehensions in regard for my box which all the while hung tottering like a precipice over the front of the wagon the motion of which with the sounds of 6 and 30 bells of different sizes were tied about the horses necks made such dismal & disconcerted noise as served only to increase my vexation

…….Axminster at which latter place to my great satisfaction I got safe with my luggage at half past 8. Having took a final leave of wagons and bid adieu to the poor souls who were going forwards

Met with middling reception at Mr. Knight's who brought me into his clerk's office & with great dexterity counted about 50 skins of parchment of which together with a room a fire place in it & half a set of tools he made me a handsel by way of introduction. I got some breakfast & about noon went to bed where I lay till 9 o'clock this morning.

I have but just seen my Mrs. She is more than 6 foot high & looks pleasant. They have a son 2 years old, a daughter of 6 & another of 4 at home who are all become my playfellows. The eldest son of 11 years is at a boarding school in France. Axminster is a miserable looking place in itself. It lies on the side of a hill & consists of near 20 little dirty lanes which they call streets with here and there a pretty house; a very pleasant country lies around it and upon several small elevations you can see 40 villages at one.

Mr. Knight's is a fine spacious house out of town in the middle of as large square. Champayne of 4 or 5 acres. We are 4 miles from Lyme which is our nearest sea.

  Hark! "The bell strikes one 1
  We take no note of time but from its loss"

Good night & a merry Christmas t'ye   John Cranch

Notes
1. John calls this copy No.1 . It is in his Notebook 3
2. unknown – Brockedon, Mr Bowden, Dr. Adams, Counsellor Heath.
3. The Burnells of Kingsbridge were related. Thomas Burnell married a daughter of John's uncle Nathaniel (Chap 7)
4. Bill Bowring and cousin Dick – see Chart of Bowring and Cranch Connections
5. Mr William of Halwell is William of the Seven, an uncle
6. Hawkins was Abraham Hawkins , author of a book about Kingsbridge

Did he enjoy his clerical duties?
It appears not because in Dec 1773 he wrote of his desire to leave his employers and explore his talents, a sentiment which would surely not endear him to his father.

In Dec 1779 he writes he is homesick and reports he visited London.
When Abigail visited him in 1787 she reported that "his profession does not seem to be the object of his affections" and that he "has given up the practice". This was not quite correct as there are referrals to him carrying out solicitor work when in London, albeit not as diligently as before.

The Visit of the Adams to the West Country 1787

The Adams arrived in England in July 1784 to stay with the Elworthys in London, but John wrote to his sister Elizabeth to say he was unable to get there to meet them. However he did do so briefly in Aug 1784 and then was with them for most of their tour of "Cranch homelands"

In August 1787 Abigail with John Adams, their daughter and entourage went on a tour of the West Country. Later Abigail wrote to her sister:

> "When I wrote you last, I was just going to set out on a journey to the West of England. I promised you to visit Mr Cranch's friends and relatives. This we did ... We were absent a month and made a tour of about six hundred miles."

She describes visiting Winchester (and the family tree of Quincy), Southampton (and her first experience of bathing) and Weymouth. This gave her the opportunity to observe rural life:

> "This whole town is the property of a widow lady. Houses are built by the tenants and taken at life rents, which upon the decease of the lessees, revert back again to the owner of the soil. Thus, is the landed property of this country vested in lordships and in the hands of the rich altogether. The peasantry are but slaves to the lord, notwithstanding the mighty boasts they make of liberty

She goes on to reflect that in a fertile area one could assume all was well and *"the voice of Poverty was rarely heard".* Far from it. She alleges:

> "the money earned by sweat of brow must go to feed the pampered lord and fatten the greedy bishop whist the miserable, shattered, thatched -roof cottage crumbles to the dust for want of repair"

She continues to describe the peasant life, the inequity of land ownership, poverty and comparisons with America. Then onto Axminster.

> "...Here we found Mr J Cranch. He dined with us, and we drank tea with him. ... He accompanied us to Exeter, Plymouth and Kingsbridge. At Exeter ...Mr Bowring came to visit us……. He requested that we would drink tea with him after the meeting; and as our intention was to see Mr Cranch's brother Andrew, he engaged him to get him to his house. The old gentleman came with some difficulty for he is very lame and infirm. He seemed very glad to see us and asked many questions respecting his brother and sister in America. He has not been able to do any business for a number of years and I believe he is supported by his son who is in the clothier's business with Mr Bowring. Mrs Cranch, though is nearly as old as her husband, is a smart, sprightly, active woman and is wilted just enough to last to perpetuity She told me that her husband took it very hard that his brother had not written to him for a long time……Mr Cranch 's daughter married Mr Bowring's brother, they have three sons. She is a sprightly woman like her mother. Mr Bowring's daughter married a son of Mr Nathaniel Cranch so the family is doubly linked together and what is more they all seem united by the strongest ties of family harmony and love.
>
> From Exeter we went to Plymouth…………. Made a stop at Ivybridge. Mr Adams accompanied by Mr Cranch went to Brook about 3 miles distant, to visit his uncle Mr William Cranch.
>
> ...Kingsbridge, the chief resort of the Cranch family. We arrived at the inn about six o'clock ...about eight with a ringing of bells... we were visited by the various branches of the Cranch family ...amounting to 15 persons. ...

Ch 13.2 Clerical Work

> *Mr and Mrs Burnell and Mr and Mrs Trathen both offered us beds and accommodations at their houses, but we were too numerous to accept their kind invitations......we engaged ourselves to dine with Mr Burnell and to drink tea with Mr Trathen the next day. ... Mrs Burnell has a strong resemblance to Mrs Palmer. She is a genteel woman and easy and polite. We dined at a very pretty dinner and after meeting drank tea at the other house, Mr Trathen's. Their houses are very small but everything neat and comfortable. Mr Burnell is as shoemaker worth £5,000; Mr Trathen a grocer in good circumstance. The rest of the family joined us at the two houses.*
>
> *They are all serious industrious good people amongst whom the greatest family harmony appears to subsist. The people of this county appear more like our New England people than any I have met within this country before, but the distinction between tradesmen and gentry as they are termed is widely different from that distinction in our country.*

She continues this analysis, and castigates the ladies of middle rank for lack of morality, and for frequenting the "watering-places" which proliferated.

Persons mentioned:
- Richard of America's brothers Andrew and William; his other brothers John, Joseph and Nathaniel had already died
- Bowrings: see chart 10.2 for Bowring – Cranch connections
- Mrs Burnell (nee Joanna Cranch daughter of Nathaniel[1]) was niece of Mrs Palmer (nee Mary Cranch).

Other relatives at Kingsbridge at that time would probably be John the painter's brother William, possibly brother Joseph, cousins Robert Garland, Nathaniel and Joseph, Mary and James Wilcocks.

John presented John Adams with a pamphlet "The True Interest and Political maxims of the Republic of Holland and West Friesland " written by John de Witt, London 1720 which he inscribed on the front cover:

> "To his Excellency John Adams esq. Ambassador from the United states
> of America to the court of Great Britain 1787   J.Cr."

Since the Adams visit was not long after American Independence, the subject of the pamphlet was a hot topic on both sides of the Atlantic.

Publications

There is not a complete listing of his writings. For example, he edited or wrote for more than one London publication, which do not seem to have survived. Some exist:

A brief Inquiry concerning Pen Pits, in which the origin and purposes of those extraordinary excavations are attempted to be explained and accounted for.
Printed by Crockers, Frome 1820 John calls himself "Archaeologist "

The œconomy of Testaments; Or, Reflections on the Mischievous Consequences Generally Arising From the Usual Dispositions of Property by Will. With A Preface, by William Langworthy, of the Honourable Society of the Inner Temple. The article was originally a letter written 5 Dec 1791. Its sentiments would be based on John's own experiences as a solicitor and maybe in particular as being an executor of Bunter's will
W. Meyler, J. Barratt, and Bull and Hensley, Bath, 1794.
Given to Boston Public Library 15/6/1882 (by Joseph?)

The Gentleman's Magazine Sept 1795 reviewed it thus:
> "The author, a disappointed professor of painting which science he took up at a late period of life, endeavours here to dissuade men from giving in a will any limited or contingent interest to a legatee or devisee and from bequeathing any property in trust to the use of another.
> Whether he had met with a disappointment in this way also we know not, but his editor supports his objections with arguments not always fairly put and with injudicious ridicule of trustees and professional men"

A major article was his "Inducements to promote the Fine Arts of Great Britain by exciting Native Genius to independent Effort and Original Intentions (1811).
Crockers of Frome and another item on antiquities in Dorset in 1820.
In the copy in Bath's Reference Library is a poem entitled "Wrote at Sydney garden *(Bath)* on reading notice against defacing the trees etc". The poem is also reproduced in Notebook 3
Another article: Attempt to Promote the Commercial Interests of Great Britain, and of A Plan for Increasing the Revenue of His Royal Highness the Prince of Wales

Lectures
> "Mr Cranch favoured the Society with the substance of some papers transmitted to him from Dorchester, near Boston in New England, relatively to the account of a MUMMY .... discovered in a cavern in Warren County, Kentucky ."

The bulk of the article is given to describing the mummy and its location
Report by the Bath Literary & Philosophical Society meeting Monday Feb 17 in The Bath And Cheltenham Gazette Wednesday February 26 1817

Cromwell's' Head

A CROWN OR A HALTER?

NARRATIVE

RELATING TO

THE REAL EMBALMED HEAD

OF

OLIVER CROMWELL,

NOW EXHIBITING

IN MEAD-COURT, IN OLD BOND-STREET.

1799.

Ch 13.2 Clerical Work

The following is an abridged version of this article by John Cranch:

Oliver Cromwell was born in Huntingdon 25 April 1599, inaugurated Protector 12 Dec 1653, died at Whitehall Palace aged 62 3 Sept 1658 . He was buried with "more than regal" honours in Henry the Seventh chapel in Westminster abbey.

After the Restoration, Jan 1661, the bodies of Oliver Cromwell, his son-in-law Henry Ireton (Lord Deputy of Ireland) and John Bradshaw, (who as president of the high court of Justice had pronounced sentence of death on King Charles the First) were by vote of the House of Commons to be removed.

The coffins were taken up on at the end of January 1661 from Westminster abbey to the Red Lion Inn in Holborn. They were conveyed upon sledges to Tyburn; the bodies taken out and hanged at the three several angles of the gallows until sunset. They were then beheaded, the trunks thrown into a deep pit under the gallows and the heads set upon poles on the top of Westminster Hall.

It is likely enough that the decapitation was performed in haste amid much tumult and confusion as the nose was broken and the head showing signs of being separated from the body by two distinct, irregular blows.

The tradition respecting the head of Oliver Cromwell is that on a stormy night in the latter end of the reign of Charles, or James the Second, blown off from the top of Westminster Hall, it was taken up by one of those many persons whom the flagitiious conduct of these monarchs, had by that time converted to a less favourable opinion of Cromwell. Soon after it was presented to the Russell family of Cambridgeshire where it remained for many years until, being sold by Samuel Russell to James Cox (proprietor of a private museum)

The head was first seen by Mr Cox about 1780 when exhibited near Claremarket. On that occasion Mr Cox first became acquainted with Samuel Russell (to whom he was related). Russell needed money for his support, which Cox advanced until eventually Russell transferred the head over to Cox by a legal dead in 1787. Cox "lately sold it to its present proprietors", having had to wait 7 years to acquire it and at considerable expense.

Cox purposely concealed it even from his own family in order to prevent the trouble of those incessant applications which he conceived would be made for a sight of it, in case it should be publicly known that he possessed so extraordinary and interesting a curiosity.

It may be noticed that one of its ears is wanting; and there may have been some other slight mutilations. This is accounted for by another of the family traditions, which is, that the when the Protector's relations and admirers were occasionally admitted to the head they took the opportunity to pilfer such small parts as could be best come at., or were least likely to be missed.

It has been hinted that the title of some of Russell's predecessors to the property of this head was not quite *regular*. Notwithstanding that, it may not be impertinent to observe that one of the many circumstances of fact which have established the identity of the head exhibited is that of Cromwell's having been the only instance of a

Ch 13.2 Clerical Work

head being cut off sand spiked *that had before been embalmed* which is precisely the case with respect to the head in question.

It appears by papers delivered by Cox to the present proprietors with the head that in the year 1775 Dr. Southgate, late librarian to the British Museum, had been applied to for his opinion of its identity and that after attentive consideration of it for 20 minutes and comparing it with medals, coins etc he had delivered the opinion in these words:

"gentlemen you may be assured that this is the real head of Oliver Cromwell". The present proprietors have consulted others and all are satisfied that the head is indeed genuine.

Oliver Cromwell was the most intrepid and victorious general, the most sagacious statesman and the most powerful sovereign in Europe. A man on whose stupendous character and sections, all the history of research, all the energies of history, and all the splendours of eloquence have been exhausted. Who could inspire the most abstruse of all philosophers with poetry and the sublimest of all poets with politics – the most proud and warlike nations on earth with humility and dread, the whole world with respect and admiration and who at last, yielding only to death, left behind him a name which cannot be extinguished but in that oblivion which shall bury the e memory of all human actions

The rest of the pamphlet describes the medals and coins depicting Cromwell made by Thomas Simon, who was replaced at the mint when royalty was re-established.
The pamphlet is in the British Library

Tony Robinson narrated this story in a Radio 4 broadcast

In 1895 a great nephew of John living in London
"…….had a letter from a Mr Atkinson of Sevenoaks possessor of Cromwells' head ....asking if he wishes to purchase it".
From a letter written Dec 1895. by Hannah Cranch Wilcocks

References and Sources
- Axminster Heritage Centre
- Probate records
- FA Notebook 3
- 'History of the Town and Parish of Axminster' 1832 by James Davidson, unpublished, bound copy in Devon Heritage Centre (DHC ref Z19/21/1). Its table of contents shows it has a chapter of Biographical Notices, one of which is of John Cranch and his portrait.
- Letters at DHC 51/7/8/1-9

Footnote:
Numerous examples exist of his annotations in the margins of books on a variety of subjects as well as critiques of the books themselves in letters to friends.

Ch 13.3 *The Artist and his Paintings* 14

Assessments as a Painter, Man of Merit, Constable and the Edmonton circle, List of Paintings, Notebooks, Salcombe Castle Key and other Sketches

Assessments as a Painter
The Royal Collection Trust describes him as an **"Amateur Painter"**
The V and A , describes him as a **"genre painter"**. In discussing its ownership of "Playing with Baby" it reports that:
> "John Cranch …specialized in rural genre scenes that combine the lighting effects of Joseph Wright of Derby with the rustic figures and settings of George Moorland.
> Cranch introduces still lifes within the composition …… depicted in minute detail. While demonstrating the artist's skill at painting, these objects also conjure up the feeling of domesticity…. The workmen's tools bring the feeling of having just been left there….. Cranch's familiar observation of such domestic details reflects his own rural background."
>
> *Abridged from V and A website*

The art critic Arnold Wilson in Country Life 12 October 1972 refers to him as an **Eccentric Painter Of The Rustic Genre.**
It followed the Bristol City Art Gallery acquiring *Cottage Interior* in 1971:

"...a painting by John Cranch…… It is immediately apparent that although the work seems little more than an attractive small genre picture, …there is also an arrestingly distinct flavour epitomised in the grinning mouth of the young girl to the right. It is partly this grimace which prompts one to enquire whether the eccentricity of the picture reflects the character of the artist......*(note1)*

As an artist, Cranch is represented at several galleries …….*A Group of peasants around a Bonfire burning effigies of Guy Fawkes and the Pope..1793 ..*is not an undramatic little piece, with the bonfire giving a strong *contre – jour* effect. A larger Cranch …*Two Monks in a Landscape* is a more built-up work, with a gentle landscape and far less feeling of character........ the unexhibited *Death of Chatterton was* apparently well received.

The simple psychological play and expression in Cranch's paintings are very much his own manner, and in this respect his work is highly idiosyncratic. ….His interior scenes are, however, particularly fresh with first-hand observation of country life. …..there is no sense of second-hand repetition or the use of studio props in his wealth of detail.

Cranch enjoyed some fame with "poker pictures". , although this in itself possibly points to little success with oil paintings ....*(note 2)*

One can see from the evidence, both literary and visual, that Cranch was an enthusiastic amateur, with a bent for antiquarian pursuits and a distinct, if slightly eccentric, wit. He is an artist on a small scale and of small stature, but the savour of originality endows his painting with a sparkle to which the spectator can readily respond. "

Notes:
1. *Cottage Interior is signed and dated "Cranch 1793 Bath". It has also been described a Kitchen Interior*

2. He probably produced poker pictures to pass the time away as a break from paperwork whilst a clerk and before becoming a painter. It has been reported that his first painting "sale" was in 1791. Poker pictures only require a fire, a poker and some wood.
3. It has been claimed that he took up oil painting when he reached London. However there is at least one oil painting dated 1785, poorly executed so maybe "experimental".

A man of merit

John Thomas Smith in 1797 in a booklet entitled Remarks on Rural Scenery ... some observations and precepts relative to the picturesque wrote:
> "...I am indebted ...to my friend Mr Cranch who obligingly condescended to correct what he could not have descended to write"

In a chapter "On connecting objects and selecting those only which shall be suitable to their stations" Smith uses the *Death of Chatterton* as an example:
> "..painted by Mr Cranch under the very uncommon predicament of having taught himself the art of painting on oil after he was thirty six years of age. In this curious and interesting little piece, every object and incident is cautiously excluded which bears the least resemblance of ease or consolation while every image of misery is combined to awaken sympathy and point regret.
> .. the image of youthful genius ... could not have been more forcibly or feelingly repressed.
> I knew nothing of this artist till the merit and circumstances of his original essay induced me to seek a friendship which I shall ever hold it an honour to retain."

The **Death of Chatterton** was claimed at the time as being his best known work. It was acquired by Sir Winter Lake F.S.A . It should not be confused with a 1868 painting of the same by Henry Wallis which is now Tate Britain. The fate of the Cranch painting is unknown. It has not featured in any known sale. There are many theories as to its fate. The current Baron Lake has no knowledge of it. (*Private correspondence*)

Constable and The Edmonton Circle

The following is taken from articles about John Constable in:
> *The TATE Gallery & Suffolk Records Society 1975 XVIII pages 195 – 202*

In the summer of 1796 the young Constable was introduced to a loosely knit group of friends subsequently dubbed the "Edmonton Circle". They were
- Thomas Allen, Constable's uncle with whom he stayed at his country residence in Edmonton , Sussex
- Sir James Winter Lake Bt governor of the Hudson Bay Company who lived at Edmonton, London
- Charles Gower M.D. of "unsteady disposition, making medicine a play-thing"
- John Adams a diligent schoolmaster at Edmonton
- John T Smith
- John Cranch

Constable would have been very much the "junior" as all the others were in or over their 40's except for Gower who was in his early 30's

Antiquarianism, bibliophily and a taste for authorship seem to have characterised the group. This combination of interests which would have appealed to Cranch and his

Ch 13.3 The Artist and his Paintings

undoubted intellect. In 1791 for instance Lake, Adams, Samuel Ireland (the engraver) and Smith were a "party of pleasure" walking around the neighbourhood to discover and view antiquities *(note a)*

After returning home in the autumn of 1796 Constable he wrote a letter of thanks to Smith and Cranch "for the information and advice so generously bestowed". Cranch had produced a recommended reading list for Constable and it seems he had already bought at least two of the recommended books.

Cranch is mentioned in eight of Constable's subsequent letters to Smith. To begin with Constable is only too anxious to do something in return for the help he received from Cranch and to acknowledge his indebtedness. Later Constable appears to have adopted a cooler attitude towards Cranch, as in 1799 he writes (when he had just been admitted to the Royal Academy Schools)
> "Smith's friend (Cranch) has left off painting at least for the present. His whole time and thoughts are occupied in exhibiting an old, rusty, fusty head with a spike in it which he declared to be the real embalmed head of Oliver Cromwell!"

The evidence from the earlier letters, the reading list and from the fact that two of the earliest known oil-paintings by Constable *The Chymist* and *The Alchymist* are in Cranch's style, it is clear that Constable was indebted to Cranch for rather more than a few tips on the mechanics of the art of painting.

Constable also asks "I should like to know if Mr Cranch has sold his picture of the Alchymists. If he has not I think I should for him...".

The article's writer also describes Cranch's painting 1795 *Playing with Baby* as a painting typical of his "low life" genre "

Painter's Reading and a hint or two respecting study was written by John Cranch, dated 30 Sept 1796 for Constable. It is a typical Cranch document – not just a list of books to read but full of comment with numerous words underlined for emphasis.

In the Constable collection is a small oil-sketch on a wood panel. This is described on the back:
> "Last remains of an ancient convent –(nuns of the order of St Clare)- now part of a warehouse – belonging to Mr Mansfield, a broker, situate the south side of Church Street, in the Minories: see Stow's antiq.
> To my beloved friend John Thomas Smith, engraver of the Antiq. Of London, John Cranch A..D. 1796."

In his Ancient Topography of London (1815) Smith refers to this painting, but does not say whether he still had it.

His Paintings
Most of his paintings were "oil on panel" and the descriptions that follow assume this unless indicated otherwise. Where known, information is given about the painting's date, ownership or history, and approximate size in inches.
Images are available for these paintings. Those for which no image has been found are listed separately. Some examples:

Ch 13.3 The Artist and his Paintings

Ely cathedral

Mother and daughters

Tremeton Castle

British Institute
John Cranch exhibited in 1808 at the British Institute:

The Plaisterer [a]	9 x 9
A Snow Scene [b]	12 x 13
Cottage Interior with figures [c]	12 x 14
Cottage Door Conversation	17 x 15
Conversation, father and daughter	11 x 13
Haymakers Regaling	11 x 12
A Smith's Shop	10 x 10

Notes:
[a] The Plaisterer was also exhibited in 1807
[b] This could be the same as "A Snowy Landscape" and "Duck Shooting in the Snow"
[c] also known as Kitchen Interior

The first three are known to still exist. No information about the other four

Paintings currently in Galleries

Bristol Musem & A. G.	Cottage Interior (1793)	12 x 14 (purchased 1971)
Yale Center for Br.Art	The Plaisterer (1807)	9 x 9
Aberdeen Art G & M	View on the Shannon (1792)	13 x 8
RAMM (Exeter)	Village Cooper (1791)	6 x 6
	Village Baker	5 x 6
	Village Butcher	5 x 6
	The Miser (canvas)	7 x 10
	Carrier's Cart (1796)	12 x 17

The Carrier's Cart was described as "a fine piece of work" and donated to RAMM in 1937 by Sir H. Harmsworth, principle proprietor of the Western Morning News

Western Times 30.4.1937

V & A Gallery	(Farmer's) Cottage at Night (1795)	19 x 14
	Playing With Baby	11 x 15
Tate Britain - London	Monks Merrymaking (1804)	64 x 83
Musee de Louvre	Monks, lantern, Moonlit Landscape	24 x 28
In F.A. & Personal	Lady at Gate	7 x 6
	Fishing by river	
	Mother and Daughters (1803)	7 x 6
	Husband and Wife (1801)	6 x 8
	Windmill scene	6 x 6
	Trematon Castle (watercolour)	10 x 7
	Ely Cathedral	16 x 12

Ch 13.3 The Artist and his Paintings

Recently auctioned

Title	Year	Medium	Size
Two monkeys dressed as jockeys & racing pigs	2008	watercolour	
The Cellarer	1999		6 x 5
Interior of a Dovecote	2013		11 x 10
Tavern Scene with rustics by a fire	2001		14 x 17
Smuggler's coming ashore at night	2004		
Man with wife and babe	1997		7 x 6
Farmer's cottage at night	1997		19 x 14
Beggar by Gate	2011		4 x 6
Flower market	2012		24 x 36
Farmhouse (yard) Scene	2016	canvas	17 x 12
Wooded Landscape, figures outside a cottage	2003	canvas	20 x 26
Figure by a church in a winter landscape	2018		5 x 6
Pastoral Scene , wooded vale	2018		26 x 35
Penitents	2004		5 x 6
Duck Shooting in the Snow	2009	canvas	14 x 20
The Village Tavern			

No images Available

References have been found to the following, but as yet without an image.

- Blacksmith's Forge   auctioned   1998
- Figures by tree in river Landscape   auctioned   1997   15 x 11
- Penitents   auctioned   2004   5 x 6
- Pouring milk for mother & her kittens   auctioned   1994
- Landscape, figures on a road near the Crown Inn auc1996   11 x 8
- Last Remains of an Ancient Convent   auctioned   1996
- Two monkeys dressed as Jockeys & Racing pigs   watercolour   16 x 12
- Figures by tree in river Landscape (1795)   15 x 11
- Penitents   5 x 7
  (1813 painted at Bath for his friend, Abraham Crocker)
- Landscape with figures on a road near the Crown Inn   11 x 8
- Pouring milk for mother and her kittens   5 x 7
- Blacksmith's Forge (1795)   19 x 14
- Pastoral Scene With Figures & Cattle In A Wooded Vale   26 x 35
- Monks looking bored at a table.
- Fishing by a pond
- Two Monks in a Landscape
- Death of Chatterton

Acknowledgements
Information was sought and appreciated from the Galleries listed plus The Athenaeum, British Institute Catalogue, and the websites of Invaluable and Mutual Art (MA).

Notebooks

His notebooks are full of sketches of scenes and antiquities. They include a list of nearly 20 ideas for pictures probably drawn up when he was at Bath and found that he had to take up his paint brush again to earn some money.

They are mostly pen and ink. Some examples (not to size) follow.
Loose sketches in F.A. include his self-portrait and a sketch of Maria Bowring.

Ch 13.3 The Artist and his Paintings

The key of Fort Charles.
Original size of key in his drawing 16 inches x 3 inches (at its widest)

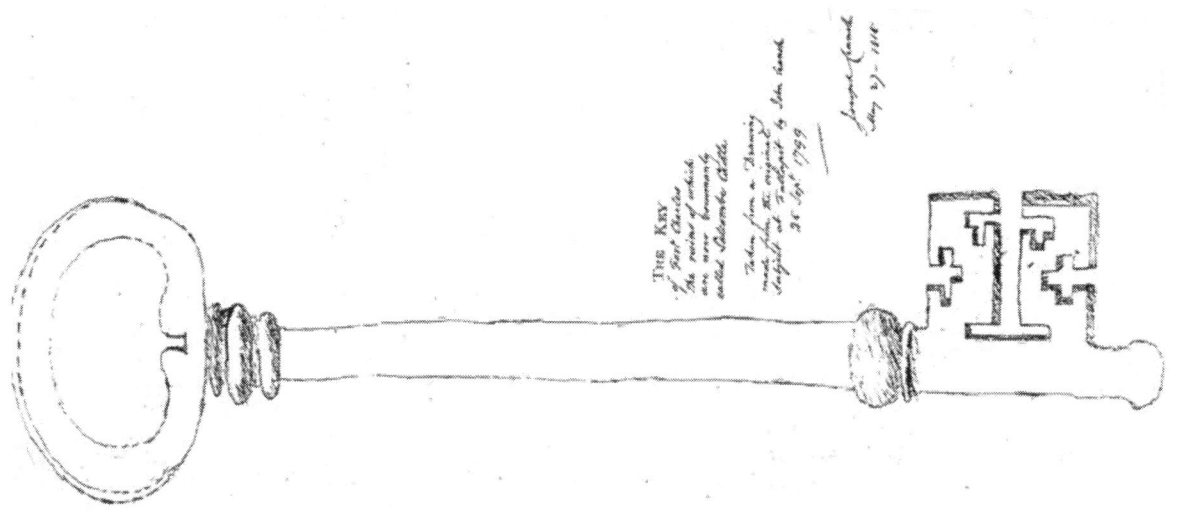

"Expeditions", Antiquity Smith, Johes Cranch, 1553, Mudie, Move to Bath, Bath and his Legacy

Expeditions

In family circles John is known as John the artist who dabbled in antiquities and finding "Druid remains".

His early observations in his surroundings and travels were developed when he went to London where he met like-souls. He embarked on numerous "expeditions" and visits to sites of interest as already indicated. When he returned to Kingsbridge in 1799 he led three "expeditions" with relatives, described in his notebooks.

At various times he trawled cementaries and recorded epitaphs of interest, often with commentary. An example:

> Faith was his wisdom
> Wisdom his virtue
> Virtue his truth
> And truth his pleasure

John commented:

> "too deep to be understood in any sense honourable to the defunct!"

Antiquity Smith (1766–1833)

A close friend and kindred spirit of John Cranch in the 1790's was John T Smith. He was an English painter, engraver and antiquarian.

During the 1790's John Cranch was moving in the same circles as Reynolds, Constable and Smith. Smith and Cranch were both fascinated by antiquities and painting. In 1795. Smith drew and engraved the portrait of John Cranch.

In 1796 Cranch supplied for "Antiquity" Smith a drawing of the Convent of St Clare in the Minories, for Smith's *Ancient Topography*

In 1797 he wrote "….arranging date to explore relics of St Faith's and chapel at Aldgate with Cox and James Ward"

In 1800 old wall paintings were found during extension work to the House of Parliament. Smith obtained permission to sketch them. He had to work early in the morning to avoid the workmen. It is said that they frequently demolished what he had just finished sketching and he kept this work up constantly for six weeks at the expense of his other work.

The result was his 1807 book *Antiquities of London and its Environs* which he regarded as his favourite work. It is a collection of prints of drawings he made about 1790-1805 of antiquities in Westminster that no longer existed. A copy is held at Birmingham Library, digitized by the Internet Archive and University of Pittsburgh. For readers with an interest in old buildings, it's a delight. The description of the book is:

> *Antiquities of London and Environs engrav'd and publish'd by J. T. Smith , dedicated to Sir James Winter lake Bt,Esq containing views of Houses, Momuments, statues and other curious remaoins of Antiquity engraved from the original subjects and from original drawings ……*

As a result of his work amongst the ruins of London he became known as "Antiquity Smith".

Johes Cranch

The Family Archives inherited several items of interest connecting John to Smith, such as a print of Eleven Churches in Kent and Middlesex *"drawn and sketched by J.T.Smith …1792 … "*. John Cranch wrote beneath it *"Given me by friend J.T.Smith 19 Feb 1795"*. There is also a print : Views of London No 2 1797 depicting a London Square and a print taken from Gentleman's magazine 1793 of Stepney Church.

The most interesting item is a drawing of a church window in which a Johes Cranch is depicted (probably Joseph). It is in a notebook of family historian E.M.Smith (unrelated to Antiquity Smith as we know), but the drawing and handwriting is by A.W. Cranch junr. Other copies by others of the original sketch exist.

There are a number of uncertainties about this sketch:
It is not clear which book in Mudie's Library[a] is being referred to, nor does looking at their lists help.
Smith must have seen the picture in a window pane in one of churches he saw being demolished and told John the Painter
The sketch implies that the window was originally in one of the churches depicted in the "Eleven Churches" print. This may not be so. Besides there are not 11 churches there – only 8 some with different perspectives.
It may be the window was in Chingford church Essex. That print is marked: "John Thomas Smith to John Cranch 1795".

The significance of finding that there was a picture and name of a Cranch in London in the 1500's is that it fits in with the theory that the South Devon Cranch family were woollen cloth merchants who would need to have a London agent. Such a person would be of some standing, quite wealthy and so able to contribute to his church. His relationship to the Devon Cranches is unknown.

[a] *Principle English Books In Circulation At Mudie's Select Library. January 1907.*

Ch. 13.4   Antiquities   23

Johes Cranch 1553
"Eleven Churches" drawn
& engraved by
John P. Smith
In Mudies Library

Charles Edward Mudie (1818 - 1890) was an English publisher and founder of Mudie's Lending Library and Mudie's Subscription Library. He started his circulating library in 1842 and by 1852 his "Select Library" operated from New Oxford Street, London
Book deliveries were carried out by vans, but the railway expansion allowed people to order books across the country.
Competitors of Mudie's in London in the 1870s included W.H. Smith & Sons. Mudie's library continued into the 1930s and came to an end as a result of the introduction of government-funded public libraries.

Ch. *13.4*   *Antiquities*   24

The Sudden Move to Bath
John posted the following letter to his brother William at Kingsbridge from Bath on Saturday 5 July 1810. The letter was actually written by a scribe as evidently John sent the same letter to at least three people.
> Dear Bill
> I have but a few moments to apprise you that a most extra-ordinary combination of circumstances has (almost suddenly) fixed me in this my favourite and delightful place, probably for life.

He then goes on to refer to a short note he has also written to his friend Crocker and one to "our dear bro Richard, Totnes" and will William please send this one onto his friend John Andrews (solicitor, Plympton).
William duly sent the letter onto John Andrews with this covering note
> Dear Sir
> I am at a loss to guess what this very extra-ordinary and sudden removal means. I am very anxious to know. I hope its something to his benefit and happiness. If you should have received from Mr Crocker the note my brother mentions I should be very much obliged to you to let me have sight of it
> I now flatter myself that I shall have the pleasure of seeing him once more at Kingsbridge as the distance is not so great.
> I remain sir your servant, Wm Cranch, Kingsbridge Saturday 6th 1810

The " extraordinary circumstances" remain unknown but it would seem John rapidly seized his chance to move out of London to Bath.

Bath and his Legacy
Bath had a number off attractions for John, not least an abundance of antiquities. He would have known about the work of people with similar interests such as the Rev. Warner. Warner practised in Bath 1794 – 1817 during which time he published "An Illustration of the Roman Antiquities discovered at Bath" and several satirical articles on Bath society.
In his later years (when John was in his sixties) he researched Bath's Roman history where his knowledge of Latin was invaluable and collected artefacts. His collections laid the foundation for the Roman Museum of Bath. John's work on the ancient history of Bath probably ranks as his most important and enduring legacy, though not so well known as his achievements as an artist.
As anyone involved with such research will know, there tends to be an apparent lack of recognition of the importance of such work by some sections of society. This can lead to frustration and John seems to have encountered this in his researches at Bath and in rescuing Bath's heritage. In a letter to his brother in 1816 he says:
> "Bath, a place which however beautiful in its nautical attributes and however fancied to be a seat of science and politeness ....is undoubtedly one of the most ignorant, vicious, ill-mannered and ill governed towns in Europe!"

DHC ref 51/7/8/9

In 1810, he recorded in a notebook fifteen "Cursory suggestions for the honor and improvement of this town". Many relate to a good water supply. Number 7 was;
> "All the hot springs to be ascertained and secured, not by partial, temporary jobs and driblets, but .....upon the best possible principles ......
> Compare [the Baths at Rome] with the miserable dark dirty awkward and inconvenient arrangements at the King's bath......"

13.5 Obituaries

Gentlemen's Magazine, Bath Papers, his Will, Davidson's Biography, Tributes by Hawkins and others.

Gentleman's magazine Vol XC1 1821 p 189
Somerset – at Bath, in his 70th year, Mr John Cranch, the artist, and painter of the unique picture of the "Death of Chatterton" now in the possession of Sir Jas. Winter Lake, bart.

Bath & Cheltenham Gazette Jan 1821
Jan 24, aged 70, Mr John Cranch, a native of Kingsbridge, Devon. In early life Mr. Cranch practised the law; but having a strong predilection for the Polite Arts, and a comfortable independence, he quitted the former pursuit, and settled in the Metropolis, where he studied painting; in which he attained no ordinary degree of excellence. His unbounded liberality at length materially injured his circumstances. Mr C next turned his attention to literature; and became the editor of a weekly paper; but here not being more successful, he became a resident in this his favourite city, where he long indulged in antiquarian researches, for which he was admirably qualified by the possession of a rich fund of literary information, and deep research into ancient and curious history ; and he contributed in no small degree to the development and collecting of those vestigia of Roman remains in which this place and its vicinity abound. His classic hours were chiefly employed in deciphering ancient records, abstruse passages and difficult writings; in which a few could equal and none excel him.

Mr Cranch was a fellow of the American Society of Arts and Sciences, and was the painter of a unique picture of the Death of Chatterton, now in the possession of Sir James Winter Lake, bart, F.S.A. But the subject of this sketch was not less estimable for his singular abilities and various acquirements; as a man, his character was marked by strict integrity, unimpeachable morals, great benevolence, engaging simplicity and unalterable friendship.

Bath Journal Jan 1821
(This repeats much of what is in the Gazette)
…..He was a man of the strictest integrity, morals and humanity, which he eminently displayed in every action of his life – and his words which seemed to flow from the instantaneous feelings of a correct heart, were delivered with the strongest sentiments of reason & profound judgment. The singular meekness or natural modesty which marked his whole conduct through life he retained with his latest breath, which secured the respect and admiration of all that knew him in life, and who now most deeply regret his death. Until within a few days of his demise his usual fortitude and vivacity of manners had not left him, when the great bulwark of his mind went down with his talents in the common convulsions of death. As the fatal hour approached, which he seemed to have as predestination of, his time had been spent in the general arrangement of his collections of antiquities, as if preparatory for a long tour.

Mr Cranch in the nobler sentiments of mental ornament was manly and vigorous although his manners possess the fascinating innocence of a child. As an artist many of his paintings are well known in this city, and particularly amongst his friends, by whom they are now held as most valuable trophies to his memory. Mr C. was in great repute as an antiquary of the first abilities, arising from a rich fund of literary information, and deep research into ancient and curious history, of which he was an unwearied pursuer – his classical hours were chiefly employed in deciphering ancient records, abstruse passages and difficult writings, in which few could equal and none excel him.

His Will
From a copy of the will (FA), dated Aug 16, 1819, valued at Bath 1821.
> "I give & bequeath all I have in the world to my new nephew John Cranch of Kingsbridge son of my beloved brother William Cranch."

The John referred to is John Roope Cranch of South Brent which accounts for there being many of John's items being there.

The Attenders at his funeral are listed in *MS Eng 152 with 7 transparent cartoons (Frome 1802)*, believed to be held at Boston Public Library.

The Biography by James Davidson
James Davidson was Axminster's leading chronicler. His extensive researches and writings were regarded as being both reliable and comprehensive. *(Axminster Heritage Centre)*

His overarching 'History of the Town and Parish of Axminster' (15 August 1832) was never published. However his original handwritten bound manuscript copy is in the Devon Heritage Centre *(DHC ref Z19/21/1)*. It represents a remarkable amount of work and Davidson treated it as the raw material for several of his later books.

Chapter XV111 contains Biographical Notices about notable people from Axminster, one of which was John Cranch.

It is the first known biography of John and provides an early assessment of him:

"John Cranch was born at Kingsbridge in the County of Devon on the 12th Oct 1751 and having when a youth evinced unusual quickness and understanding and great skill in writing was engaged by Mr John Knight, a land surveyor of Axminster, the steward of Lord Petre's estates, as a writer in his office at a salary of fifteen pounds a year. While there the Rev William Sutton, a Roman catholic priest, gave him instruction in Latin and other branches of learning, to which, as well as to his employment he attended with the greatest diligence. The beauty, rapidity and correctness of his writing were extraordinary, and in addition to his severer studies he made considerable progress in music and drawing. His particular talent for the last-mentioned art was manifested in a circumstance quite consonant with his decisive and original style of thought and action. During the absence of his employer from the office on a winter's day Cranch amused himself in front of the fireplace by executing a design of the panels of a large oaken chimney-piece with the pointed end of a red - hot poker, producing an effect by the boldness of style and execution which was greatly admired. At the end of five years Cranch engaged himself with Mr Simon Bunter, an attorney in Axminster, who gave him his clerkship and so highly esteemed his character that he left him by will more than two thousand pounds and appointed him his executor in trust.

With this prosperity he settled in London, where for a time, he followed his profession with a degree of assiduity which if it had been continued would have secured him a handsome independence. He published a work on the "Economy of Testaments which attracted attention, but prosperity became his ruin, and his taste for the fine arts led him to neglect his business and to desert the interests of his clients for the more agreeable occupations of music and painting. The latter he practiced under the instruction of Sir Joshua Reynolds, who used say that Cranch was the best critic and possessed the greatest judgment in paintings of any man he knew. His picture of the death of Chatterton, and others of less consequence attracted public notice and he was enrolled among the Fellows of the American Society of Arts and sciences. But stability of character was not one of his qualifications, and painting was in turn neglected for the still more hazardous profession of authorship. He projected a series of essays in the style of the Spectator, some few of which were published, but not even the title of them has survived. He was a diligent transcriber of remarkable epitaphs, of which he had a large manuscript collection, but which failed in teaching him the folly of a mis-spent life and the misery of its close.

The versatility of his genius and the variety of characters with whom his talents brought him into association led him into irregularity of habits, and a deficiency of right principle suffered him to become the slave of intemperance and its victim. He died at Bath unmarried in the year 1823 in almost extreme poverty and wretchedness, too indolent to exert himself for his own support and too proud to accept relief when proffered by the hands of those who had known him and esteemed his character in early life - a melancholy instance of the little value of natural genius and elegant acquirements, when not under the correction and control of Christian principle or even of sound judgement. A portrait of this talented but unhappy man was painted and engraved by J.R.T Smith in 1795 and a few of his pictures may be seen at Library House, Axminster, the residence of William Knight, Esq. "

Davidson adds some footnotes:
- The portrait of Cranch and his best picture the Death of Chatterton were formerly in the possession of Sir James Winter Lake Baronet.
- Note: these particulars were obtained principally from the Rev George Oliver of Exeter and W. Knight Esq of Axminster
- Sir Joshua Reynolds seems to have patronised Cranch in consequence of a family friendship, as it was the advice of the person of the same name, and probably a relation of Cranch, that young Reynolds was sent from Plympton to London in 1741 to study painting under Hudson.

Correction Note: John Cranch died in 1821, not 1823.

Comment on the Biography
The fact that Davidson obtained his information "principally" from people who knew him when he was still in his early 20's at Axminster may account for the rather soured opinions expressed. John's sense of humour may have been interpreted as irreverence and his "abandonment" of a sound occupation may have been regarded as irresponsible. And using a red hot poker on the house fireplace would hardly have endeared him to his host and employer. !

Subsequent Accounts
It is evident that for generations every subsequent account of John Cranch's life was based on Davidson's biography. frequently repeating his exact words such as "evinced unusual quickness ...etc", The other obituaries seem to be ignored.

The account by Jane Bowring Cranch in Devon Notes and Queries Vol 1 (1900), reproduces Davidson's account word for word with only some small additions and amendments. Her sponsor was her uncle Sir John Bowring, but neither publicly acknowledged the source of her version.

There is a reference in the F.A. to the Davidson (unpublished) book containing John Cranch's portrait.

The sum of *"more than £2000"* is probably mere conjecture by Davidson's sources and is often subsequently quoted as "being £2000" i.e. as exactly that amount.

Newspaper cutting stuck into Davidson's book at the end of his biography
To the memory of John Cranch, who was born at Kingsbridge in Devonshire, the 12th day of October 1751 and died at Bath (where he passed the last years of his life) the 22th day of January 1821 aged 69.

>Cranch! In thy varying course, through life's long stage
>Truth's path thy thoughts seemed wholly to engage.
>Each latent fact by thee with care was sought
>And ancient usage to attention brought
>
>Though law' awhile employed thy active powr's
>Though forced 'mid folly's feuds to pass thy hours
>Though doomed to wait the call in dullness's court
>Still Honour always gave thy cause support
>
>When competence at length allowed thy mind
>To quit the school for subtility designed
>The bounds of deep research thy genius burst
>And antiquities ranked thee 'mong the first
>
>The pen, the pencil – shade, light, verse, or prose
>Whate'er thy object – excellence arose
>Such charms were ever o'er the subject thrown
>The graces fondly claimed thee for their own
>
>When 60 years and nine had run
>And 70 had its full career begun
>Death on a sudden sped his dart's dreadful flight
>And sent thee hence to realms of glorious light
>
>Gone, honest Cranch! – yes gone - thy life closed now
>With confidence on virtuous deeds reposed
>And while succeeding ages glide away
>Remembrance of thy spotless worth shall stay

H
Devonshire, 8th March 1821

Note
H is Abraham Hawkins who evidently knew of John.

Tribute by S.F.
Bibliotheca Somersetensis (1902) refers to "A tribute of Affection and esteem sacred to the memory of John Cranch signed S.F published at Warminster in 1821"
SF could be Fryer, who wrote in John's notebooks. No trace of this tribute has yet been found.

13.6 Uncommon Genius

Some Notes on the Book

An appreciation and description of John Cranch's life is contained in the book "Uncommon Genius" by John Lamble, Wolborough press, Cambridge 2019

I contribute the following to a reader's understanding:

Family relationships
The relationship between the Cranches and their in-laws referred to in that book are set out in the charts in the following chapters in this book:

Ch 11.2   Tree Andrew 1720-1820   Joseph [2]
Ch 11.3   Descendants of Joseph [2]   Wilcocks, Smith, Moginie
Ch 12.6   Tree Andrew 1720–1820   The Bonds of America
Ch 17.2   Joseph [5] & Families   shows how the Lambles are related to the Cranches

Cromwell's Head
In the book, there is reference to a John [2]. This is John Roope Cranch, a direct ancestor of mine. If he had ever had the Cox-Russel contract document, the Family Archive would have some evidence of that. There is none, not even anecdotal. The most likely explanation is the one that Lamble gives: John the Painter gave the document to Selina's husband "for interest" as America would crave such information, whereas his English relatives probably were aware enough about Cromwell already (or simply not interested). It is also possible his American relatives retained more Puritan sympathies than his English relatives did at that time.

Reynolds
The Cranch benefactor was the Reverend Richard Cranch of Plympton (1682-1742), not his brother. See Chapter 6.7 of this book.

Sources
John Lamble makes reference to some local sources. In my research I started with the Family Archives and then found the same material in heritage centres. Which came first? I suspect that over the years a great deal of copying has taken place; in some cases it is known that material from the FA was borrowed by others. It may explain any unintentional duplication between Lamble's book and this one. As the reader will appreciate, the purposes of the two books are different.

CHAPTER 14
WILLIAM N CRANCH

Ch 14.1 William N. Cranch

William N, his Pocket book, Diary and Will, Mary's family (the Roopes), Aunt Sharland, Joseph [6] and his Trip to Bath.

This chapter continues the history of the family of Joseph [2] - see Charts 4.4 and 11.2 – with the son William N Cranch and his sister Mary in Kingsbridge.
It also covers Norden, the home of the Andrew branch for nearly 100 years. Also connected to Norden were the Wilcocks and the Roopes.
The chapters that follow cover his descendants. Unless indicated otherwise the information for these chapters comes from the Family Archives and personal knowledge.

William N. Cranch
William Nathaniel Cranch is referred to here as William N. to distinguish him from the many other Williams, although there is no reference to him being referred to in such a way. He was known as "Bill" in his lifetime.

Born	1754
Died	1820
Father	youngest son of Joseph [2] (one of the seven)
Mother	Elizabeth Lidstone
Married	Mary Roope
Brothers	John the Painter, Joseph[5]
Sisters	five, which led to relatives: Curtis, Lakeman, Wilcocks and Bond
Occupation	Sadler

He was born in Kingsbridge and lived there all his life, initially at Norden. He was a saddler working with his father and became a focus for the remaining Andrew tree branch of the Cranch family in Kingsbridge. He was close to his brother John the Painter and they shared many a day together. He was a Feoffee and belonged to the Ebenezer chapel there where all his children were baptised.

He married Mary Roope and had 8 surviving children:

Mary Roope C	second wife of W.C.Bond, America	see Ch 12
Ebbet	married Hugh Curtis	see below
Joseph [6]	married Margaret Lakeman	see below
William	went to America, died age 26	see Ch 12
Elizabeth Lidstone C	married John Wilcocks, her cousin	see Ch 11
Selina	first wife of W.C.Bond, America	see Ch 12
John Roope C	married Ann Stidston of South Brent	see below
Hannah	spinster	

Pocket Notebook
William made a pocket notebook dated 1779 in very small and controlled handwriting. The majority of the book is about the Surrender of Fort Charles and is almost identical to the entry in John the Painter's Notebook two. The rest of the notebook contains: "Exact copiers of [5] original letters written by [the poet Alexander] Pope to the Rt Hon William Fortescue" dated between 1720 and 1737. The significance of this is that William and his brother John probably copied out the notes on the Surrender of Fort Charles at the same time. John would be 28, and William 25.

The notebook also has lists of family members and a note about Kingsbridge Grammar school. His grandson William Cranch Stidston Cranch later also used up some of the spare pages.

The F.A. also have another example of William's mastery of the miniature. It is a reproduction of the Lord's prayer in black cotton on a round white cotton base measuring about one inch in diameter. Though so small, the clarity is amazing.

Diary

In his later years William N. lived in Dodbrooke where he had a garden and a barn. He made up his own little diary from an old hymn book with woollen thread binding. The entries reflect the interests of old age: gardening, bees, family. His family were particularly active at that time as his son William went to America in 1817

" 2 March 1818 Received a letter from son W^m dated Dorchester 1 Feb 1818. This is the first letter we have from him since his arrival in America"

Son W^m died in 1820 in Georgia, cause unknown.

There are also references to Selina's marriage to William Bond, letters to and from them, sister Wilcocks, Ebbett then in Kent, and her husband Curtis "on board H.M. Sloop Bustard" and 12 June 1820 "bought pig 1 cwt for 17/6d"

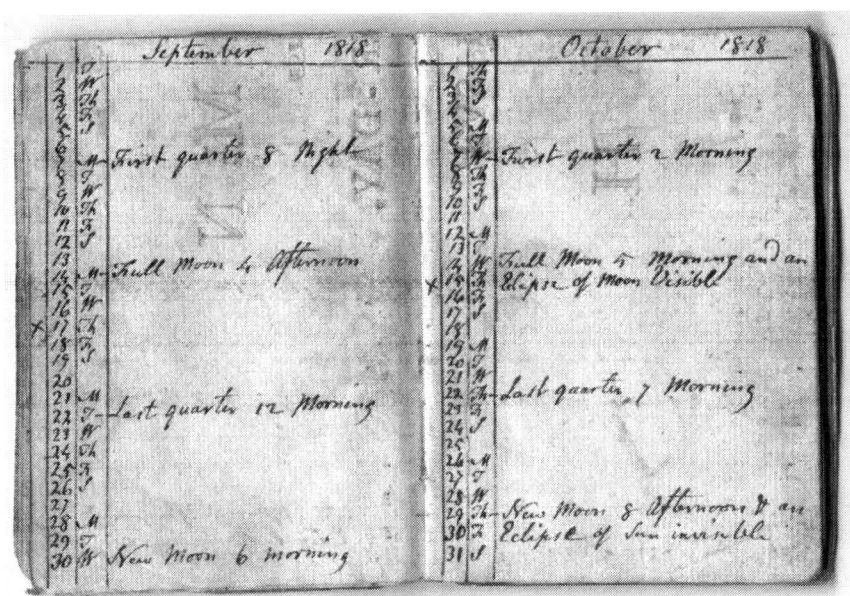

Will

He left all to his wife Mary, then to his son Joseph especially his saddler's equipment. He left a silver milk cup marked W.M.C. to his daughter Ebbett Curtis. His son John Roope C got his watch and a kitchen cabinet. By this time John Roope C was apprenticed to Stidston at South Brent.

Mary's family – the Roopes

In a rent book in the F.A is an account by Ann (William N.'s daughter-in-law) of the Roopes that she knew about. Apparently Mary's father should have inherited a fortune, but a "wicked Aunt" left him nothing. Her father was John Roope who was himself an orphan and had a hard upbringing by two miserly foster gentlemen until he found a good home with a third in Slapton. The will of the wicked aunt named James as her father, not John. The executors ruled that her father John and his four children were ineligible to receive anything.

Aunt Sharland

The account also refers to an Aunt Sharland, who seems to have been much favoured by Ann and probably was the source of the account. Aunt Sharland must have been a Roope, not a Cranch. It is possible that John and James Roope had a sister Elizabeth. It is known that an Elizabeth Roope married a John Nurse in 1794 and that an Eliz Nurse married a Thomas Sharland in 1817. This would mean that Elizabeth Sharland would have been born about 1774, making her about 70 in 1845 (when Ann's daughter Hannah died – see later). This fits.

Joseph [6] (1792-1874)

Joseph [6] was a saddler in Fore St, Kingsbridge in his 20's and 30's, continuing his father's and grandfather's business. His father died when he was nearly 18. He married a local girl Margaret Lakeman probably in the late 1830's. They moved to London (Brixton) probably because of poor local trade prospects and encouragement from Cranch relatives already in the London area. They had three sons (Chart 14.2)

Joseph [6] has contributed towards our knowledge of events: in particular evidence relating to the key of Salcombe Castle (see Chapter 8.2). His family (the Lakeman Cranches) kept in touch with the various Cranch branches and with the family of his brother John Roope C. His great grandson Graeme was interested in the family and he too kept in touch. He also was in contact with the Bond descendants in America.

As a young man Joseph [6] travelled from Kingsbridge to Bath in 1819 to visit his uncle John (the Painter). On Aug 8 he walked from Kingsbridge to the Seven Stars hotel in Totnes where he caught a coach, arriving at 5 in the afternoon at the White Lyon, Exeter:

"Met a great many country people going to & from their parish churches but those who travel in stage coaches seem almost to forget the day – at least the devotion that belongs to it,... an exceeding fine evening and I have just paid 14/- for a conveyance to Bath ..."   They had left Tiverton after nightfall
" Passing through some villages onto Wellington all is silent save where the ostler is waiting at the inns to exchange horses....Taunton...Bridgewater clock striking 2 morning Knocked up the folks at the inn and had some refreshment . Our fellow travellers greatly displeased with their breakfast. However it was Hobbs choice for they must have had that or nothing.....Brent Knoll.....Huntspill... arrived Bristol at 8 in the morning.. Set out for Bath arrived there in about 2 hours, put down at the Golden Lion ....went out in quest of my uncle. ......met each other at Dr. Wilson's door ....we dined at Wilson's and in the evening went out to see *Living of Bath*."
He spent two days at Bath: he describes his visit to Bath, including observing that at the Hot Bath the "waters heat was so great that I could not suffer my hand in it". He met Uncle John, Mr Montague, dined with Mr Chamberlain in Quinn Square, met Barret, bathed in the Avon "which as the weather was very hot I thought was most equable", met Mr Champernowne, Mr Friar, heard Miss Friar play the harp, dined at Wilson's on a joint of venison. "About 7 o'clock James Wilcocks arrived from London...poor fellow in a bad state of health he comes here for the change of air"

He then walked towards Wells and "being rather fatigued by walking 21 miles I went inside (the cathedral)", then proceeded on to Glastonbury (another 8 miles). He stopped there at the Abbey Inn, went to see the abbey and regretted he did not have more time as he had "engaged a sitting" on a coach to Taunton.

Ch 14.1 William N. Cranch 　　　　　　　　　　　　　　　　　　　　　　　　　　　*4*

It left at night and he got to Exeter by 4 a.m., then went on to S. Brent
　　"arriving by their dinner time".
He arrived back at Kingsbridge the next day (Sunday evening)

Notes
1. *Evidently "uncle John" did not accommodate the young man*
2. *Barret - publishers at Kingsbridge and well known to the family. Amongst the Cranch papers at DHC is the will of a Barret*
3. *James Wilcocks – born 1779, son of Mary who married James Wilcocks, James died in 1819 at Bath*
4. *Getting to S. Brent by their dinner time refers to being with his brother John Roope Cranch who was an apprenticed to and lived with Stidston. (see chapter 15.2)*

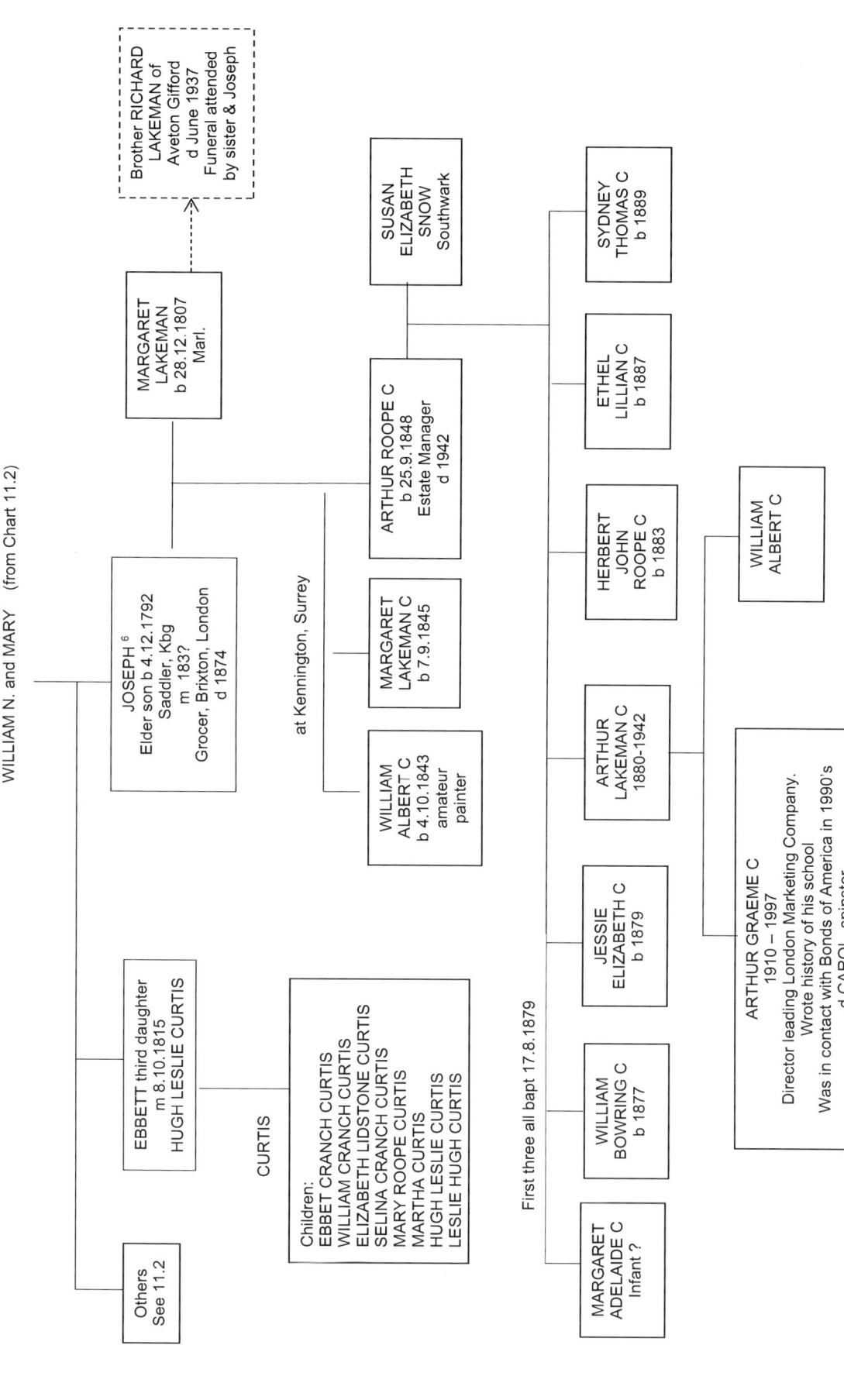

14.2 Chart   LAKEMAN CRANCH and CURTIS Families

Ch 14.3 Norden 6

History of the Cranch family home, Description by Hicks, The American Book, The Roopes at Norden, Mary ^{2} and Norden, Listing

Norden
Means the dene (valley) of Norton, the farm being at a higher level. Norden was a large manor house. There is a reference to Norden and its mill in the early 1100s. The Churchstow area was originally owned by the Abbot of Buckfastleigh. After the Dissolution of the monasteries, Lord Petre acquired land and property on the western side of Kingsbridge (the "manor" of Kingsbridge). He acquired Norton and Norden in 1558, and must have "upgraded" Norden to a state whereby it could be described as "probably C17".

Cranch involvement dates from about that time. According to various references in letters, Norden came to be regarded with affection by the family with their happy memories of living in it or visiting it. It was home to the Andrew branch of the family for nearly 100 years.

Andrew (d 1623) was using Norden whilst living at Batson. His grandson Andrew (1652 – 1728) moved from Batson into Norden as a tenant in the late 1600's. In 1712 he was prosecuted (with others) for not keeping clear a right of way. He took out 99 year leases in about 1715. His son John (who had been operating at first in Shaugh) returned to live at Norden with his family in about 1720, then retired to a house in Dodbrooke. Of his seven children, 6 were sons. The second son Joseph ^{2} stayed at Norden, another son Nathaniel lived close by (Mill St.), the others moving away.

Description by Rev Hicks in the 1660's :
> "As I went down the steep narrow bosky lane that leadeth to ….Norden, I remembered when in stiller times treading the same grassy path with the branches meeting overhead, a-thinking what sweet spot 'twas either to begin or end one's days in; and they ought count themselves favoured who are permitted to do both in such a peaceful hermitage…
> The farm house is long and low; there is a great stack of chimneys at one end and an iron vane …at the other. Divers little windows peer out like eyes upon a garden court with a row of bee-hives all along the south side and a dial to see what o'clock it is in the middle
> A single rich brown pear tree stands in a corner of the godly orchard. How pleasant seemed this vale of Norden as I gazed upon its sunny fields through which runs a brook of the clearest water ever while it goeth on its way singing the same soft ceaseless tune in the ear of man and to the greenwood above …
> A rose tree spreadeth over half the house, some of the gay roses were dangling about the casement (of a window) ……the bells of the nearest village church rang out a peel….
> *From Troublous times by Jane Bowring Cranch*

The American Book
We get much information from the descendants of William N. who would be a young boy in the 1760's. William N.'s elder brother (Joseph[5]), tells of a little booklet:

Ch 14.3 Norden

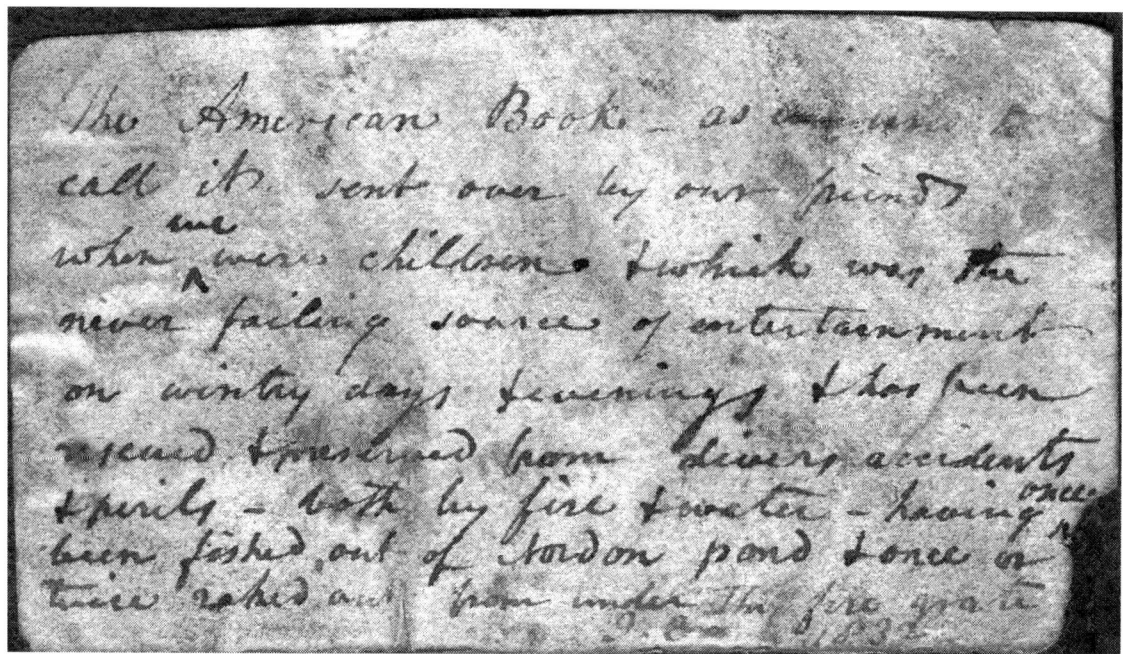

"The American Book – as is easier to call it - was sent over by our friends when we were children and which was the never failing source of entertainment on wintry days and evenings and has been rescued and preserved from divers accidents and perils – both by fire and water – having once been fished out of Norden pond and once or twice raked out from under the fire grate ."
Note attached to the booklet, F.A.

The American friends would be Joseph's uncle and aunt (Richard & Mary) who emigrated in 1764

Norden (continued)
In 1696 the Ilberts acquired the Norton farm (which included Norden) as well as Bowringsleigh. The lease on Norden would have expired in the early 1800's, but it seems the family moved out in the early 1760's. The Roopes were then known to be associated with it, then Joseph again and his daughter Mary.

From the lease granted by William Ilbert to James Roope in 1764 , "which is the house I now live in" is this clause:
> "Not to obstruct the lane leading from the street of Kingsbridge to the curtilage etc whereby the inheritance of William Ilbert may be affected"
> *Written by William N, undated in F.A*

This lease is in an Indenture signed by James Roope jun. between:
1. William Ilbert of Bowringsleigh
2. James Roope the younger, Kingsbridge shopkeeper
   "Ilbert, in consideration that the property is ruinous and in decay
   .... leases the property to J. Roope for 99 years .... The property was formerly occupied by Margaret Mill then by Andrew Cranch Senior or Joseph Cranch as tenant.
   The property consists of mansion, stable, linhay, curtilage etc herb garden, one little quillet of land; all within the parish of Kingsbridge "
   originally in F.A but donated to DHC in 1993

In 1780 James Roope was declared bankrupt. His wife had already died. The lease was bought out by Thomas Burnell (related to the Cranches). Joseph[2] moved back

Ch 14.3 Norden

into Norden with his daughter Mary and died shortly after. She moved out in 1808, thereby ending the direct involvement of Norden with the Cranch family.

The Roopes at Norden

"The traditional accounts of this family says that de Rupe or deRupa came over from Normandy with the Conqueror and shared honours and rewards which the Norman chief so liberally bestowed on his followers in that venture and who had distinguished themselves by their prowess at the Battle of Hastings when King Harold lost his crown, his kingdom and his life on that memorable day October 14th A.D. 1066."

Pedigree of Roope of Horswell, Devon, College of Arms London 1700

The Roope family were a very well-established family in the Kingsbridge area: in 1609 a John Roope donated fine brasses to St Petrock's Church, Dartmouth; in 1633 a John Roope is described as Gent; in 1700 a John Roope was a clothier and Gent; in 1727 Andrew C and Robert Bastard, clothiers, leased property from Susanna Roope, daughter of Mary Roope (this Mary Roope's father was George Kendall, Exeter, gentleman and heir); in 1758 a William Roope is described as a surgeon; and in 1798 a John Roope and Walter Prideau, lessees of the Town Mills converted them into woollen mills with workshops. (In 1845 they were converted back again). However as with any family, they had their moments as will be seen later.

The James Roope that leased Norden in 1764 after Joseph's family moved out was then aged about 40, his wife Jane 30 and daughter Mary 10. Jane died shortly afterwards. James and his brother John were involved with the building trade and probably leased Norden as it was cheap with a view to repairing it.

In 1766 James was described as a mercer and accused of assault and battery. The fine being paid by his brother John Roope.   *QS / 4 /1767*

Another indenture 14 July 1780 refers to previous indentures, that Jane Roope has since died and that James Roope (ironmonger dealer and chapman) was declared bankrupt 7 Nov 1780

The outcome of the creditors meeting was that Thomas Burnell bought the lease for £110, thereby clearing James Roope's debts.   *Among William's papers F.A.*

Burnell presumably asked the Cranches to move back in. (Thomas Burnell was very much associated with the Cranches and related - see chart for Nathaniel[1])

In 1786 Weymouth seat (a faculty of the C. of E.) was sold to Jeremiah Cranch. It was erected by the "late bankrupt John Roope and his brother the late bankrupt James Roope"   *DEX/9/a/1/Kingsbridge 2*

Mary [2] and Norden

In 1780 Thomas Burnell bought the lease back off the discredited Roopes to enable his relatives, Joseph[2] and his eldest daughter Mary [2] to move back into Norden.

Mary [2] had married James Wilcocks in 1778 and they had three children.

Mary's father Joseph [2] died in 1781. Her husband James died in 1788. Mary stayed at Norden, re-married in the early 1790's and looked after her father-in-law (not without comment from her brother John the Painter in some of his letters).

When her father-in-law died in 1808 she, with her second husband and children moved to London, thereby ending the direct association of the Cranches with Norden.

James Wilcocks was born at Bowringsleigh, son of the eminent Rev. John Wilcocks. He had attended Merton College Oxford, was minister at Churchstow and appointed headmaster of Crispin's Grammar School in 1779 and " quickly restored the seminary to credit".

The Wilcocks descendants (chart 11.3) took interest in family history and kept in contact with their Cranch relatives. (see chapter on Family Historians)

Listing
The Ilberts sold the property in the mid to late 1800's. It was again sold in the late 1900's, still in a poor state. The present owners have devoted much time to restoring and repairing it.

In October 1972 it was made a Grade II Listed Building, described as:
> Norden. Remains of Former Manor House to East of Norden
> Probably CI7 with alterations and additions, 2 storey …….. Local stone, old slate roof, massive shouldered chimney. Wide entrance door ……
> Probably medieval, ruined remains, lower half of massive walls, stone and part cob, rectangular on plan with cross-wall. No features apparent, some walls rising to 10 ft approximately. *English Heritage Legacy ID: 431553*

Norden today   Cookworthy P4166

CHAPTER 15
JOHN ROOPE CRANCH
AND SOUTH BRENT

15.1 South Brent

Brent Village, Fair, 3 Cranch Families, The Primrose Line, Beating the Bounds Poem

South Brent   DRA.IB.03181

The village of South Brent
South Brent is one of several villages lying beside rivers and streams on the southern edge of Dartmoor. It has historical links with neighbouring communities, the monastery at Buckfastleigh, farming and mills for corn and wool. Currently the Parish is the second largest in the South Hams and 6th largest in Devon. Originally the manor of Brent belonged to Buckfast Abbey from the time of its foundation in the early 11th century until the Dissolution when it was acquired by Sir William Petre,

It is one of the wettest areas with about 40 inches of rainfall annually. A popular saying (though not unique to Devon) is that:
"If you can't see Brent – it's raining
If you can see Brent, it's going to rain"
At times of heavy rain, the spate of the river Avon thundering down at Rock Bridge (Lydia Bridge) and along the Lawns in the village can be quite spectacular.

A notable feature is Brent Hill named after the old English word *brant* meaning steep. It is visible from villages many miles away to the south (the South Hams area). A relative once counted being able to identify 19 church spires from it.
The other dominant hill is Ugborough Beacon, shot at during WW2 by the army for target practice.

A feature of village life in South Brent was the active involvement of the community in entertainments and events in a Hall (Church or Village), and such activities as sports teams, bellringing, carnivals and strong support for the various Christian denominations. The village square was a notable meeting point and the (old) Anchor Hotel frequently pictured in the background. Until more recent times the village was host to a major event – the Brent Fair.

Brent Fair
Brent Fair is reputed to have been the second oldest fair in England. In 1350 a Royal Charter granted the Abbot of Buckfast Abbey an annual three-day fair to be held on Michaelmas Day at Brent Hill where a chapel once stood dedicated to St. Michael.

15.1 South Brent

By the 1700s the fair had been extended to one on May Day and the other on St. Michael's Day until the 1940s. Eventually the fairs moved away from Brent Hill down into the streets of South Brent itself where all the animals were auctioned in the streets. It could be a rather chaotic with people and livestock crowding in to the narrow streets. Windows could be smashed by the horns of cattle, but gardeners took advantage afterwards to collect dung!

The Fair was an event of real interest and importance to the surrounding countryside attended by everybody from parson to gravedigger. It was noted for Dartmoor ponies and geese. In its day was it equally as popular both for selling livestock and as a visitor attraction, particularly after the Kingsbridge – South Brent railway line opened.

After WW2 the Fairs had stopped but the effect of livestock in the village centre continued when the local hounds held their Boxing day meet there. Horses hooves were known to break house or shop windows and the gardeners were ready.
There are numerous publications available about South Brent. One which shows how cluttered and chaotic the streets were on Fair Days is in the *legendarydartmoor.co.uk*

This cutting is from a local paper (undated but probably in 1920's, author unknown)

One day I thought I would go and went
To the Cattle Fair at old South Brent
It seemed the same as in olden time
Except for once the day was fine
There were cattle there galore
With sheep and ponies from the Moor
And horses, Oh! so fat and smooth
That you would think they never move
There were many farmers from off the lands
That seemed to be always shaking hands
Their wives and daughters neat and fair
In all the fun they took their share

Then comes the dark and swarthy gipsy
I think one or two were tipsy.
And there was the noisy auctioneer –
Well, I suppose he must be there
Oh! I quite forgot the old cheap-jack
Was also there with his brother quack
And then there were those stalls of sweets
That are still to be found in all the streets
Where country swains did buy their share
To take home to sweethearts so dear
And when at last to come home I went
And left the Fair of old South Brent
In younger hands and far more gay
I felt I'd had a pleasant day   G.M.C.

The Three Branches of Cranch in South Brent
Three branches of the Cranch family have been known to live in South Brent. The first to arrive and settle was John Roope Cranch in about 1814. (this chapter)
The second to arrive and settle was William John Beck C in about 1895 (Chapter 17)
In the 1920s the family of John Partridge Cranch farmed at Avonwick but did not remain long (Chapter 6.10).

Just as Norden provoked fond memories of those that were associated with it, so did Brent, such as
"…. difficulties no longer deter me than a foot slip among the loose stones of Brent Hill would deter me from the ascent"

"… a fireside at Brent; the storm without; friends and good cheer within"
Letter from W.C Bond 1829 to Jespeph[5]

And:
"I often think …of a little cottage …… covered with roses on a road between Totnes and Berry Castle during our visit to Brent …"
George Phillip's Bond, Harvard Observatory 1852

The Primrose Line

The prospect of a rail link between Kingsbridge and South Brent interested nearly everyone in both areas. It was first mooted in the mid-1800s, eventually opening in 1893. It was a single track line branching off the main Exeter to Plymouth GWR line at South Brent. It had so many narrow cuttings and bends that the trains using it were restricted in the number of carriages (but not wagons) they could attach. Brent people referred to it as the "Kingsbridge" line, Kingsbridge people as the Brent line. More poetically it was called the Primrose Line and closed in 1963.

The John Roope Cranch family at Brent had a direct involvement in that some of their land at Avonwick was purchased so that the line could run alongside the river there.

Men and horses showing how busy the station could be   Cookworthy P04172

Truck marshalling, Brent
circa 1900   F.A.

Brent mainline station
circa 1900   F.A.

Kingsbridge station
         Cookworthy P4166

Beating the Bounds

As with many other villages, they performed a ceremony called "Beating the Bounds" to mark their parish legal boundaries. One such event is described in a poem written by Albert Elliot, an employee of A.W Cranch, builders, South Brent. The walk ended at a field containing assorted caravans, tents, stalls and games- and a ram roast!.

15.1 South Brent

Of all the age-old customs
That Brent Folks are so proud
The Beating of the Parish bounds
Is one that thrills the crowd
Twelves miles of good old Dartmoor
Over hill and dyke
From Corringdon to Dockwell
To claim our legal right

Its thirteen years since we last trekked
Across yon dreary moor
Most stalwarts of those good old days
Are - alas - with us no more
And as I pen these words of mine
My heart just missed a beat
That - Anno Domini - should cause
Me missing such a treat

The Council too deserve our thanks
For progress is their theme
To claim the rights Brentonians love
Is not an idle dream
Invitations were sent out
Their adverts made it clear
The menu was of "roasted ram"
Washed down with tea and beer

At 11.15 a.m. the starters "Flag"
Was hoisted to the mast
The chairman read the "Riot Act"
And Rules were duly passed
As I surveyed this mighty throng
You'll please excuse my laugh
Their "goal" was ram and draught

The Water board, I must admit
Made everything so clear
By leaving all the gates ajar
We had no trouble here
The only snag I must confess
Gave our yachtsmen quite a shock
They'd hoped to get some practice in
For the Tommy Lipton's Cup

The Morning News and Daily mirror
The B.B.C. and all
Despite the strikes and short of ink
Responded to the call
Rumours too, all proved quite false
About our dear old Ram
Some said he'd seen the "Dentist"
Or fallen in the dam

The Woman's Institute were there
You'll always find them willing
To pull their weight in times of stress
As the tea cups they were filling
The "Specials" too so neat in blue
Cleared every traffic jam
But to my surprise their longing eyes
Were focussed on that ram

At last the marchers drew in sight
To be greeted by a roar
Congratulations handed around
Speeches in galore
Red Cross workers set to work
But few casualties were seen
Some nice clean socks for aching feet
And for the riders Vaseline

The Council Stakes caused quite a thrill
Eight runners at the post
Timber Jack was favourite
With Body Snatcher close
Lever Puller looked quite fit
And so did Esso Boy
But a lady member won the race
To every punter's joy

So, we came to the end of a perfect day
And the end of a journey too
Our Chairman "A" and good old Jack
All kind thanks to you
If an O.B.E or K.C.B.
In honours come your way
There was no sham with beer and ram
The heroes of the day

A. H. Elliot
August 8th 1959

15.2 John Roope Cranch

John Roope Cranch, his Family, Location, Obituary, Hannah, the Stidstons, Gravestones

John Roope Cranch
Born   1800 in Kingsbridge
Baptised   in Ebenezer chapel, Kingsbridge
Father   youngest son of William N. Cranch.
Mother   Mary Roope
Married   Ann Stidson when he was aged 26
Children   Hannah Ann Cranch
            William Cranch Stidson Cranch (WCSC).
Died   1868 at South Brent

As a young man John Roope Cranch was apprenticed to Richard Stidson of South Brent, a glazier. With the Devon-wide decline in the woollen cloth trade, other employments for off-spring had to be found. The Cranch family in Kingsbridge had knowledge of South Brent as they were Feoffees for lands in the Brent area, so it is possible William N knew Richard Stidson was prepared to take on an apprentice to learn the glazing business.

John Roope C lived with the Stidson family and so became acquainted with the daughter Ann who was of the same age. In 1819 Joseph, an older brother of John Roope C, called in. He was on his way home from Bath where he had visited his uncle John the Painter. He arrived in time "for their dinner" and stayed overnight, before completing his return to Kingsbridge.

On 12 February 1820 John Roope C is referred to as a "glazier of Brent" when he was bound to William Cumming of S. Brent for £ 100 to be repaid 12 Aug next year plus £ 5 interest. John Roope C's father died on 1 October 1820, so the two events may be connected. Cumming is often featured as a witness in wills and deeds.

John Roope C married Ann Stidson ("at last" according to one correspondent) in 1926 in South Brent Church of England. Thereafter he worshipped there becoming a church warden. He was a Feoffee before 1849 and by 1866 he was Chairman of the trustees.

Upon the death of Ann's father in about 1828, John Roope C and Ann inherited property which was to feature in the family's affairs for generations to come. It would seem that John Roope C and Ann were quite frugal as the money they inherited was not spent. Indeed it probably increased through land sales offset by purchases.

John Roope C is mainly listed in trade directories of the time as a glazier, but that incorporated many other skills, such as painting, lead plumbing and brass work as these entries in trade directories show:
    Plumber (Whites 1850), Painter and Glazier (Billing 1857)
In the 1841 Census John Roope C is described a painter with two servants
In 1851 John Roope C and son WCSC are each described as "pauper and glazier", employing one man (John Hannaford).

Throughout his life John Roope C had significant income came from rents and property sales. In his later years John Roope C also had income from the farm at

15.2 John Roope Cranch

Binnacombe. In 1860 when aged 60 he needed the services of a surgeon (reason unknown). Evidently the need was so great as to have been recorded (it cost one shilling) and led to him handing over the running of his businesses to his son.

His Family
John Roope C and Ann had two children. Hannah Ann was the eldest.
The second was a son. At the baptism when it came to the point where the boy is to be named and anointed the following exchange took place:
Vicar "Name this child"
John Roope C "William Cranch"
Ann realising her husband had forgotten to include the source of their property said : "Stidson"
John Roope C realising the vicar would only baptise with the names given him and that the child could have Stidson as a surname, then said: "Cranch"
The vicar anointed the child and said: "I name thee William Cranch Stidson Cranch"
Thereafter William inherited the consequences of an apparent confusion at the font.

From the existence of letters (such as those listed received relating to his daughter Hannah (see later) it is evident that John and his family were in frequent contact with his relations, particularly those still in the Kingsbridge area and with branches such as the Wilcocks. Its due to him that he a number of items of family interest historically have survived. The basis of the F.A started with the material he inherited from his father who had also received had many items from John the Painter (uncle of John Roope C). This example from the F.A shows his handwriting:

Location
It is not absolutely clear where John Roope C and his family lived in S. Brent. The 1841 and 1851 Census gives their address as "Brent Town" which meant the village itself, not Brent Mills or outlying areas. They probably lived in the Andrew's tenement with its workshop on Hillside. This would be logical from a business point of view, being near the customers such as the Marley estate. In the 1839 Apportionment he is quoted as being a tenant in Binnamore. In the 1848 Land Tax assessment he owns and occupies a tenement in town and at Bennickknowle and rents out Longmeads tenement. By the late 1850's they were certainly living in the Binnamore farm which is located outside Brent towards Dartmoor.

15.2 John Roope Cranch

Obituary
John Roope C died on the last day of 1868, although 1869 is on his gravestone. Jane Bowring Cranch wrote a few days after his death (to John Roope C's son):
> "My Dear Cousin
> Your letter of this morning has given me great sorrow. Its communication was so entirely unexpected but truly in the midst of life we are in death. I need scarcely say that I had a most sincere regard and esteem for your excellent father. He was a holy dear and worthy man of the Lord now rare to meet with in this base world of show and pretence. ....
> The sad tidings of your dear father's death must have deeply affected Mr William Lavers for I know he had a very great regard for him. In one of his notes to myself I remember his saying "That choice man Mr J Cranch of Brent". Present my kindest remembrance to Mrs Cranch .... Tomorrow I shall write a few lines to your uncle Joseph and Mr Wilcocks.
> Believe me with sincerest sympathy your truly Jane B Cranch "
>
> *The Lavers were closely associated with the Cranches in Kingsbridge*

He is buried in South Brent churchyard in a grave prominently opposite the entrance to the church. He left his estate to his son William C.S.Cranch

Hannah Ann Cranch 1(827 – 1845)
John Roope C's eldest child was Hannah. She died at age 18, probably of "consumption". Her death at such an age clearly affected many people. The family received many messages of condolence. Letters kept were from:
- John Roope C's sister Ebbet Curtis, with references to their sister Mary and her family, and to Mrs Fifield. Ebbet's daughter Elizabeth and Hannah were good friends
- John Roope C's sister Elizabeth Wilcocks with reference to brother Joseph and that Mr Fifield lost his daughter at same age
- aunt Elizabeth Sharland who lost her only brother when he was about 16, and with reference to her cousin Charlotte
- niece Mary Roope Curtis with references to her family, Mary Wilcocks and her family and to her uncle Joseph
- G. Cranch (or C. Cranch?) of Kingsbridge with references to Sharland, sister Jane and to Ann Sandover of Exeter
- Charlotte Cranch with references to John's sister Mary (Wilcocks) and her family, Mrs Fifield, cousin Ann and that she lost her nephew in similar circumstances. "Denbow & Jane unite in kindest love".

There were also references in the letters to a newspaper notice (probably the Kingsbridge Gazette) and to Hannah's mother Ann sending likenesses of herself and John Roope C to the Curtis family.
All the letters express deep sorrow at the passing of one so young. The following is typical:
> "A painful trial awaits you this day my dearest friends. To part with the dear memories of those we love is a second death. May our heavenly Father strengthen and support you thro' the melancholy scene."

Among the letters was the following poem by Thomas Hood 1799 – 1845 described as a minor English poet and humorist. Judging by the comments in some of the letters, the poem seems to reflect the sickness suffered by Hannah.

15.2 John Roope Cranch

The Death Bed

> We watch'd her breathing through the night,
>   Her breathing soft and low,
> As in her breast the wave of life
>   Kept heaving to and fro.
>
> So silently we seem'd to speak,
>   So slowly moved about,
> As we had lent her half our powers
>   To eke her living out.
>
> Our very hopes belied our fears,
>   Our fears our hopes belied—
> We thought her dying when she slept,
>   And sleeping when she died.
>
> For when the morn came dim and sad.
>   And chill with early showers.
> Her quiet eyelids closed—she had
>   Another morn than ours.

John Roope C replied to the letter from his sister Elizabeth Lidstone Wilcocks as follows: (dated 19 sept 1845)

> "We have this moment read yours of the 17th. Dear me, what great ravage our enemy is making of our family circle and no earthly power can stay his hand. He is no respector of persons. All are alike his victims. His time of coming none can tell.
>
> I have now to say that the remains of our dear Hannah will be taken to her earthly resting place on Sunday tomorrow between 2 and 3, there to remain till the last great harvest. The hearts of our distant ones as will follow us to the grave. Oh, that sister Mary were here! You can have no idea of my feelings on her account the remorse of my conscience not having written a single word for years not even on the late mournful event. Slings now rend my poor heart in sunder but I must overcome my feelings! Have nought to fear for she is all forgiveness
>
> I can say no more "

Sister Mary would be the eldest of the 9 brothers and sisters. She was WC Bond's second wife and would be in America in 1845. Presumably John Roope C is referring to his sister Selina's death in America about 14 years previously.

The Stidsons

The Stidsons were of Stidson, South Brent, landowners of long standing, being listed in the Subsidy of 1581. In a document in the F.A. archives *(see below),* Richard Stidson inherited property from his grandfather Edward Stidston..

Richard married Ann Langworthy 13 May 1800 and had two children – Mary and Ann. His wife probably died before 1815 (when Richard made his first will). He probably died at S. Brent in about 1828.

Richard Stidson made a will in 1815 (which is when he inherited property) in which his daughter Mary was the main beneficiary. A new will in 1819 gave Mary (now apparently married with child) a legacy and house. Daughter Ann is now the main beneficiary and executrix. The will names the trustees as Thomas Sharland and

15.2 John Roope Cranch

Joseph Cranch of Kingsbridge. Elizabeth Sharland was a favoured aunt of his wife Ann (nee Stidston). Joseph was John Roope C's uncle.

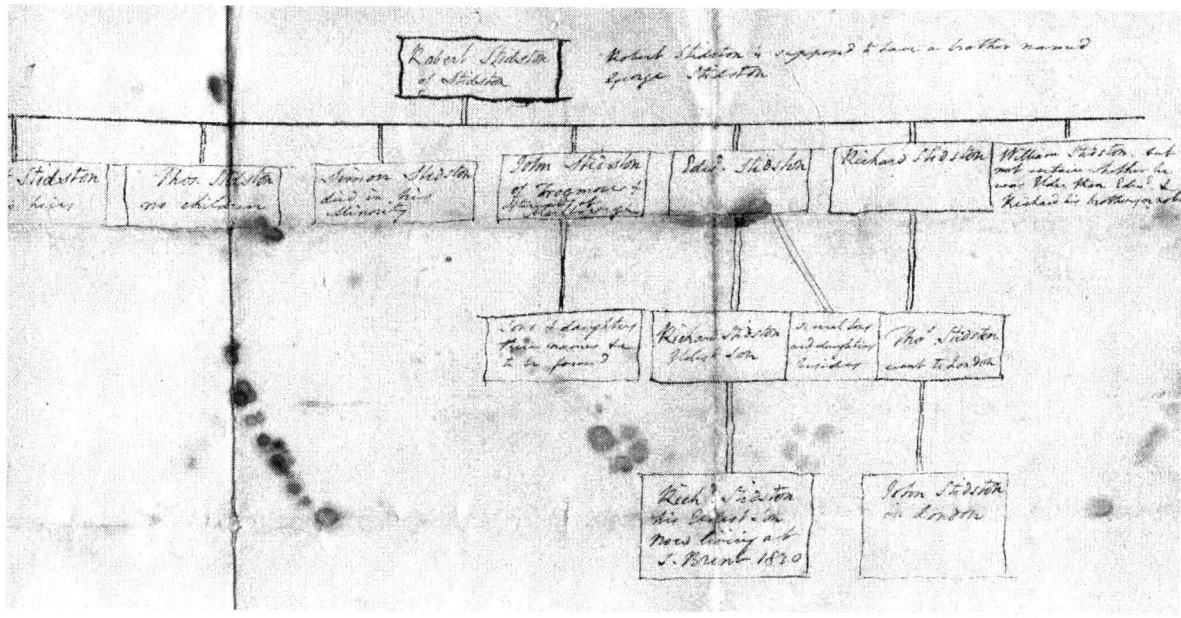

South Brent churchyard gravestones

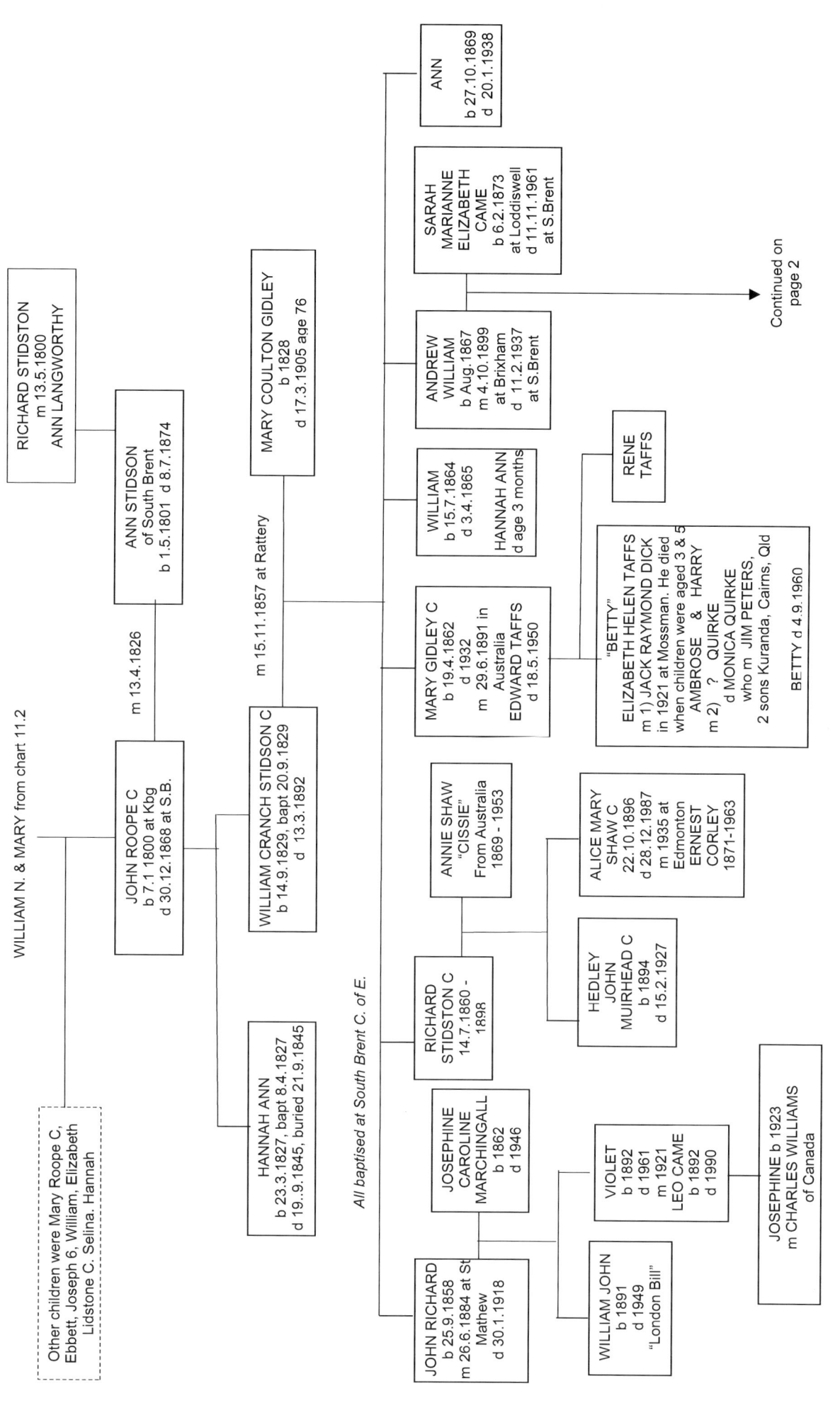

15.3 Chart   John Roope C and A. William C

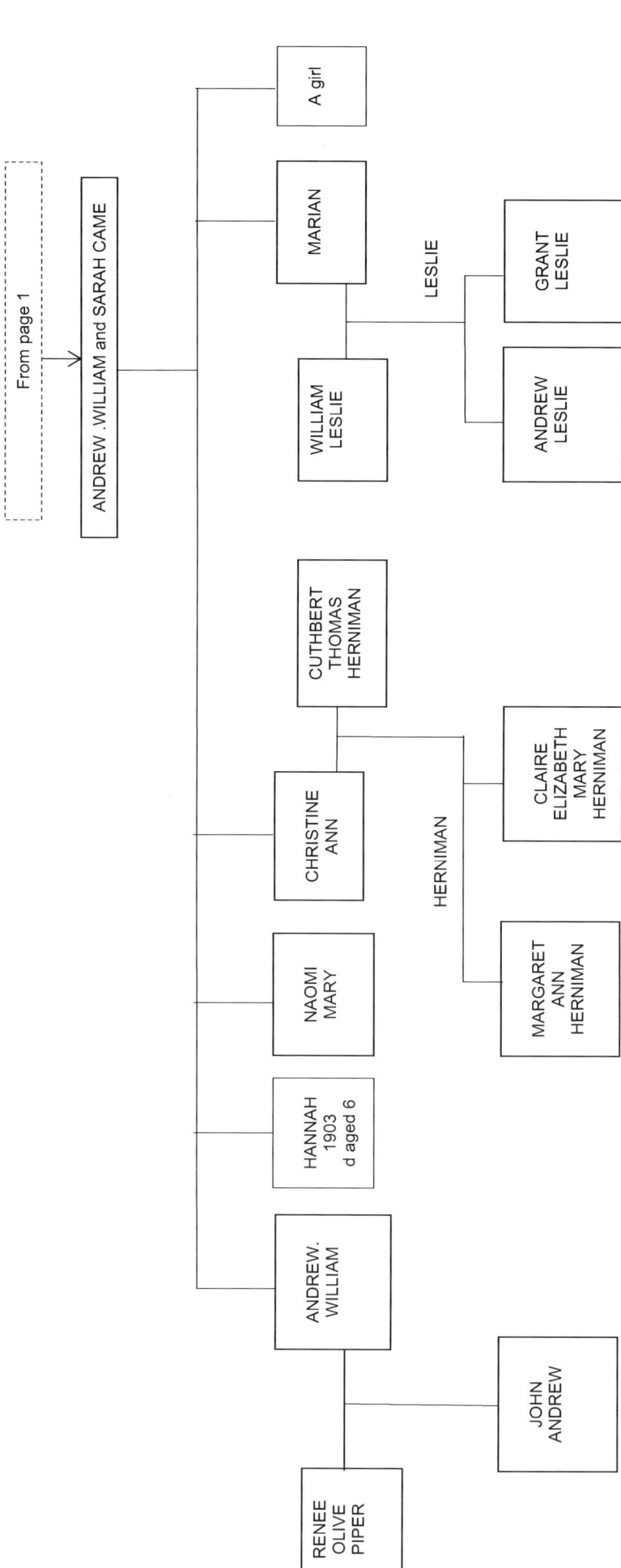

15.3 Chart   John Roope C and A. William C

CHAPTER 16
WILLIAM CRANCH STIDSTON CRANCH

Raft's Hole

Ch 16.1 William Cranch Stidston Cranch

His life, Vestry Meetings, Jubilee Day, Primrose Line, Tragic Death, His Wife Mary.

William C. S. Cranch

Born	1829 in South Brent
Father	only son of John Roope Cranch, glazier
Mother	Ann Stidston of South Brent
Married	Mary Coulton Gidley of Dean Prior
Surviving Children	sons John Richard C, Richard Stidston C, Andrew William C, daughters Mary Gidley C, Ann C
Died	aged 62 in South Brent

In his time he was known as Bill, but here he is referred to as WCSC as it is a convenient and unique label.
When he was only 16 his sister Hannah died.

He followed in his father's footsteps in trade and saw the business grow in his lifetime. In 1850 the business consisted of his father, him and a labourer (Hannaford). The 1881 census describes WCSC as painter and glazier employing two men with his son Richard a painter. Kelly's Directory 1883 gives him as Painter and Glazier. In 1889 when he was 60 he is merely referred to as "resident".

A significant customer was Sir W.P. Carew, (e.g father and son painting hot house), later "The Misses Carew" of Marley House who were extensive property owners. Work associated with funerals appears to have begun in the late 1860s "varnishing a coffin". Funereal work would gradually increase over the years.

He married Mary Gidley, a local person when he was 28 and raised five surviving children. The last one was born during the time of the building of the Main House. Mary probably had inherited property in Church St which became absorbed into the Cranch property holdings.

In the Volunteer Muster Roll Book for the 28th Devon Rifle Volunteer Corps, 1868, entry number 3 was for William Cranch, painter, 5ft 7" and signed by him. He was nearly 40. The next year he was a sergeant and involved in a day's field and drill exercise with the 4th Battalion which had to be curtailed because of the bad weather. In 1871 he obtained his Certificate of Proficiency. The unit was disbanded in 1873.

(Ref DHC 3250 / A2 / PF1)

He was put onto the List of Electors in 1869, the year after his father died. He then embarked on selling some properties and buying others. The result was the establishment of a Cranch family in the centre of South Brent.

Annual Easter Vestry Meetings

In 1876 he was proposed to become a Trustee of the church properties, but it was not until 1883 that he was appointed. In 1887 as vicar's warden
> "a cordial note of thanks be accorded to WCSC for kindly acting as
> Hon. Sec. to the Feofees for the past seven years".

The 1889 meeting had a great debate about the apparent autocracy of the vicar and lack of involvement by the churchwardens in deciding the distribution of alms.
The 1890 meeting debated the South Brent water supply "which at times was of a very animated character". Afterwards "a large company then adjourned to the Anchor

Hotel where an excellent dinner was provided under the new management of Mr Cranch".

In 1892 after his death the clerk was instructed "to write to Mrs Cranch and family conveying a note of condolence from the Feofees on the death of Mr Cranch"

Jubilee Day Celebrations

An event which illustrates village life at the time was the Jubilee Day Celebrations. At the initial meeting in March 1887 WCSC and his son Richard were included in the committee of 29 charged with organising the day. At the May meeting WCSC agreed to pay the train fare of one of the two people going to Plymouth to purchase more instruments for the band.

The committee's plan was to start the day (25 June 1886) with a Procession in the morning led by the South Brent Brass band to the Parish Church for a half hour's joint congregation service, then to the sports field for dinner (meat to be supplied by the village butchers) . Each person over 16 was to be given a pint of beer (supplied by the four pubs). Sports to follow (WCSC was to be a Steward). At 9.15 a torch-light procession up Brent hill where a bonfire was to be lit. Labourers were to be given the day off with pay. *(western Times 21.6.1887).*

The next day S.B bellringers were treated to a supper provided by the churchwardens.

In August for the annual treat for the Board Schools "tea was held in a field adjacent to the schools kindly lent by Mr Cranch"

The Primrose Line

His father had bought some shares in the proposed railway company. WCSC bought ten more @ £2 each. His son John spent another £50 on shares.

In the late 1880s land at Avonwick was compulsorily sold to the "Kingsbridge and Salcombe Railway" company so it could be put alongside the river there.

In March 1890 before the line was built, WCSC and son Richard subscribed to a fund for the widow and three young children of the late porter at the main line station "in recognition of the courteous and obliging manner in which he carried out his duties"

Death of WCSC

His death was tragic. He was bagging coal for the Feofees in the station yard when he was trapped between wagons. He died the next day. His bedside was surrounded by the doctor, a nurse, a solicitor and his scribe, his wife and possibly one or more sons and daughters.

His will is dated 1884 in which he described himself a "Painter". Although family tradition has it that his solicitor was present when he was on his deathbed, there is no evidence that any changes were made to it then. The will put his estate in trust for his wife who lived on for another 14 years. The execution of the will was not finally completed until 1911, nearly twenty years after his death.

Mary Cranch (nee Gidley) (1828-1905)

The wife of WCSC was a strict Victorian. Soon after his death the family home, once full, consisted only of her daughter Ann and son A. William (later to be joined by his wife Minnie). Son John was at sea. Although son Richard lived nearby, it was A. William and his mother who effectively ran the estate.

One day, on hearing that there was an unmarried young couple living in one of her Brent Mill cottages, she put on her black bonnet and was about to march down the street to evict them when A. William said "don't be so silly".

Mary had numerous Coulton relations. One frequented the Church House Inn at Rattery, fell down a bank on his way home and died. His wife was said to be a "gin widow" with many children.

In old age, Mary suffered and died aged 76. The South Brent Parish Magazine April 1905 recorded that:
> "On March 22nd the mortal remains of Mary Cranch were laid to rest in South Brent churchyard …. deceased who suffered from a painful and lingering illness, was the widow of a churchwarden who is still remembered as amongst the most faithful this parish as ever possessed. We unite with others in offering our heartfelt sympathy to the various members of the family in their great sorrow."

16.2 JOHN and his family

"Sailor John", Vi and Leo, Josephine, London Bill

John R. Cranch
Born   1858 in South Brent
Father   WCSC glazier of South Brent
Mother   Mary Coulton Gidley of Rattery
Died   1918 in Essex age 59
Married   1884 to Josephine Caroline Marchingall of Portsmouth
Children   Violet and William ("London Bill")

"Sailor John" Marine Engineer

John was apprenticed as an engineer at the Newton Abbot Railway Works. He then joined the Union Castle Shipping Line as a Marine Engineer especially on ships to South America. He would bring back to his home in Devon boxes of oranges. Later he had posts with the Royal Mail Steam Packet Company.

When first assigned ships he was based in London. After he married he lived in Portswood, Hampshire, his wife's birth area *(Census 1901)*. After he received his inheritance the family moved to Ilford, Essex (part of London as far as Devonfolk were concerned) *(Census 1911)*. It seems as if his wife was not enamoured of London life and there are some uncomplimentary family references to her generally.

John was not known to be safe with money. He frequently borrowed money from his youngest brother A. William, without the knowledge of his parents. He also borrowed from his other brothers and his aunt Ann. John's need for money soon complicated the winding up of their father's estate.

A postcard from his daughter Vi to his sister Ann (at the Main House) in 1917 says "Dad is home and ill, the same thing as last year". A year later she writes: "Dad thanks you for the butter and says he will write in a day or so, but I'm afraid he will not be able to do so"
John had suffered a stroke which left him speechless. He died at the end of WW1. His brother A. William attended the funeral in London and came straight home as soon as he could - the Zeppelins were dropping!

Soon after John died, his widow and daughter moved to Teignmouth and Violet married Leo at Newton Abbot in 1921. They had a daughter Josephine in 1923.

Vi and Leo.

Eustace Leopold Came, youngest brother of John's mother and about 20 years younger was a frequent visitor to South Brent where he would meet John and his family. He joined the Devonshire Regiment in 1914 and stayed with John's family shortly before being sent abroad for active service.
He was at Gallipoli when a bullet just grazed his leg but he could not be attended to for about three weeks by which time gangrene had set in. His leg was amputated at the knee. He was discharged 1918.
After the war Leo joined up with London Bill in various largely unsuccessful ventures such as the haulage of sand and gravel in Essex and working in garages.

Then Leo married Vi. Back in Devon, Leo returned to Woodhuish to work on the farm run by his brother Herbert until Herbert died in 1928. Leo became estranged from his family and moved around doing farm work in South Devon, lodging at his employer's

16.2 JOHN and his family

premises. He was known to have worked at Modbury, Liverton and in 1939 was at Sharpham Barton, Totnes living there as Farm Tractor Driver *(1939 Census)*.

Josephine (John's widow) died at the age of 84 in 1946. Violet (John's daughter) died of cancer in 1961 aged 68.

Josephine
Leo and Violet's daughter was a noted pianist. She toured America and married in Canada. Meanwhile she kept on the Teignmouth house. The top floor was a flat let out. The ground floor flat was Josephine's. Leo lived in the basement in the 1950's onwards when he was over 60. He had no responsibility for the house, but did keep an eye on his daughter's flat to which he had access.

His bedroom in the basement was at the front below pavement level. The living room at the back was at ground floor level facing south. This provided a degree of light and warmth to an other-wise dark and cold barely furnished bedsit.
He would walk about a mile up the hill of Exeter Road to his allotment (it is now a cemetery). He tended his allotment which also gave him some social contact and then walked back down the hill.

He was "a nice old boy", led a simple life, had a sort of stutter ("wuh wuh ray") and a dry sense of humour. In the mid-1960's he contracted shingles and was in hospital for some time. Josephine sold up her Teignmouth property and Leo moved to Canada to join her. She reported back to the family at Brent that Leo was reasonably happy there, much more so than in his earlier life. He died aged 91 in a nursing home. By co-incidence his brother Gerald Came died the same week.(Gerald's son Paul sent a message to Canada to say his father had died, only to be told Leo had also just died).

Leo

Leo's regiment just before setting out Leo is in middle chair first row of seats

"London" Bill (1891 – 1949)
William, son of John, went to Woodhuish Farm, Brixham after WW1 to work for his great grandfather John Mathew Came, expecting an easy life. He didn't get it. He persuaded Leo to put all his money into a joint grocery venture which was not a success.
He returned to London with Leo but kept in touch with his various Devon relatives.

Richard, Local involvement, Australia, Cissie, Hedley, Mary and her Will

Richard S. Cranch
Born   1860 in South Brent,
Father   second son of WCSC glazier of South Brent
Mother   Mary Coulton Gidley of Rattery
Died   1898
Married   1893 to Annie Shaw at Wallerawang, NSW.
Children   Hedley John Muirhead C and Alice Mary Shaw C

"Dick"

Richard was apprenticed to a paint firm in Bristol called Hall. He was listed with his father in Kelly's 1889 Directory as a Painter.

He was interested in art and painting and a few of his output survive. Known surviving paintings of his are three oil-on-glass: the Swan, Roses and Daisies; two copies of the Woodcutter oil-on-canvas, and some small watercolour sketches.

It was on account of his interest in painting that what was originally the front lounge room of the Main House in Brent was converted into a display showroom for his paintings. However this did not last for a number of reasons: his paintings did not sell, the death of his father in 1891 meant he had to work full time in the business (the Cranch Brothers) and he went abroad in late 1892. The shop was then converted into a general hardware shop and office.

He was an active member of the building firm Cranch Brothers and was involved in repairing properties in Brent such as the school house, building the cottages 10-13 Totnes Rd as well as The Pantry. His moulds for the plastering the ceilings at Marley House were kept for at least 100 years.

Local Involvement

Richard and his brother A. William took an active interest in local social and community matters, and Richard was involved in church affairs. He played cricket and attended their annual suppers. He attended a meeting of electors in 1888 held in support of Kingwell (J.P and churchwarden) to represent the Buckfastleigh ward in forthcoming County Council elections

Richard attended the South Brent **Lighting** Committee meeting in December 1889 (and others). No accounts had been submitted by the main collector (of funding for the oil) nor did the main collector hold any meetings in the last year. He had refused to accompany Mr Cranch (WCSC) the other collector on several occasions. WCSC said it was not his responsibility to produce the accounts. The main collector would do so at the meeting he had just called next week. The lighting was great improvement for South Brent.   *Totnes Weekly Times*

At the parish meeting of 26 3.1895 Richard spoke at some length on the question of the **Water Supply** at South Brent, referring to expenditures incurred and the fact that the District Council was making decisions instead of the Parish Council. There was an animated discussion, and the Chairman had to call order repeatedly. The meeting broke up in disorder.

Ch 16.3 Richard and his family

A typical building site, probably 1890s. Ugborough beacon is in the background

Australia
His sister Mary was engaged to marry the Rev Taffs who was posted to Australia before the marriage could take place. Richard chaperoned his sister Mary on her voyage out from Plymouth. They arrived in Melbourne Dec 1892.
The original intention was that Richard would return to Devon shortly after the wedding. However, he found life "holidaying" in Australia very much to his liking and so stayed on. He sent letters home asking for money to be sent out more than once and demurs at returning to assist in the Cranch Brothers building business.
Eventually it transpires he has met Annie Shaw ("Cissie")

Richard wrote from Wallerawang, March 18th 1893 to say:
> ….he had arrived at Wallerawang Jan 7th ….where he had visit from Mary and Edward………both quite well and happy … Mr Harris' charge for drawing up lease very moderate ………departure for UK intended to take place late April and if all goes well to sail on May 8th by the Orotalia, ….
> …trip up the Hawkesbury River ..onto Maitland the city that was flooded … going to bring home photos taken by Mr Crimp for Polly…I don't like Polly interfering …..I wish that I had brought my gun, as there is plenty of game a little distance around …..a great many parts of the colonies have suffered very much if not from "drought" and "bush fires" then Great floods. The Country was burnt for miles in Victoria which I saw on my way to see Mary …. …hope to see you about Midsummer ….three months after I intended.
>
> I remain Your Affectionate Brother Dick

Notes:
1. *it would seem as if Mary and Edward were based in Melbourne and Richard went to Wallerawang shortly after their wedding there and then travelled back again to see them (in February?).*
2. *Crimp – unknown*
3. *Polly – unknown but a S.Brent person*
4. *Lease – possibly in connection with his lease of Clarence House*
5. *Wallerawang is a small township near Lithgow in the Central Tablelands of New South Wales, north west of Sydney on the Main Western railway line. It was noted for its coal mines and Power Station. Charles Darwin stayed there in 1836. The church there is officially called St John the Evangelist, constructed in 1881 and used by both Presbyterians and Anglicans.*

Ch 16.3 Richard and his family

Richard and Cissie married on 26 April 1893 at St James' Church, Wallerawang, NSW in the presence of her mother Alice Shaw, her father being deceased. The marriage certificate from NSW describes Richard as builder.

Richard and Cissie came back to S. Brent and lived in Clarence House. Their son Hedley was born there. After Richard had finished building The Pantry, they moved into there. Daughter Mary was actually born in the family home.

Construction of (new) cottages in Totnes Road mainly carried out by Richard

Totnes Road circa 1900 (the new cottages are by the kink in pavement)   DRA.IB.000027

Death

He was fond of visiting the local inns towards the end of his life, probably as a consequence of contracting TB, as he was often heard singing late evening in the lane leading to his home. He made his will in May and died in November 1938. He left all to his wife in trust then to his children.

Cissie

"wife for 5, widow for 55" *(family saying)*

As a result of the wills of WCSC and Richard, Cissie was reliant on her brother-in-law A. William for the management of her husband's property and hence any income from it. This caused tensions between the two as A. William would not be in a position to hand over any net income until he knew the totals of income and expenditure incurred in maintaining the property (such as actual tenant income, repairs and taxes). On the other hand, Cissie could be tardy in paying for essential alterations to the properties.

After Richard died Cissie and her two children returned to Australia but came back to Devon after her mother-in-law died in 1905. Cissie and her two children then lived in "Waratah" in Springfield Terrace, South Brent, probably until her son Hedley died in 1927. Thereafter Cissie and her daughter Mary lived wherever convenient for Mary's work.

Cissie had numerous friends in England and returned to Australia from time to time. An Australian service man stayed with the family in 1918, clearly a contact of Cissie's. When she died in 1963 the family bought back Richard's property.

Hedley (1894 – 1927)

Hedley was always a "sickly child". He went to the grammar school near Plymouth Hoe. He joined a firm of architects, did well and was offered a junior partnership. As part of his architect's training he needed to demonstrate draughtsmanship. His two drawings (A3 size) of the Doric and Ionic orders and his discharge certificate at the end of WW1 were found buried under a pile of wallpaper offcuts in a trunk in the garden shed of his sister's house after she died.

Another set of drawings does not exist. He drew up architectural drawings of the family home in South Brent, but doing caused a problem. It seems Hedley's efforts were not appreciated. Hedley got angry and in a fit of pique destroyed them.

A year after being made a junior partner, he volunteered for WW1 service in the hope of joining Leo who was in the yeomanry. They never did meet. A week later the yeomanry merged to become the 5th Devons and went to the front. A month later Hedley was in France and was there for two years. He was often back in England to recuperate. He was in the Rouen and Ypres area after that carnage and sent postcards back showing the devastation. He seems not to have seen action at the front.

He was discharged in 1919 with sciatica and lung trouble, having caught pneumonia in the cold trenches. He developed T.B. The common consensus among the family was that he should never have joined up in the first place.

One of the many postcards sent home by Hedley

He returned to Brent. He does not seem to have had a regular job presumably being prevented from labouring because of his health, nor was he engaged in an office. He does not seem to have been employed in his uncle's building business but he did use the workshop and became an accomplished carpenter.

Two examples of his work survive. One is a replica, in oak, of the corner chair featured in many portraits of the family. The original chair still exists. It had a leather seat stuffed with hay. Unfortunately the seat was given a modern upholstery in the late 1900s.

A young Hedley on the original chair featured in many family photos.

He made a book case "to size". It was glass fronted and varnished, using whatever woods were available in the workshop. It was intended to sit on top of a bureau in a recess besides the fireplace in the house they lived in. Unfortunately too late he discovered the recess was not built true so bureau plus case would not fit. He made a base for the case and the bureau and case were sited instead on either side of the chimney breast. They remained separate items until an inheritor in Mary's will had a house big enough to put the two parts together. They fitted like a glove

He tried painting but was too frail and used the allotment known as Luce's where he kept bees. He too was interested in family history and was sure the Cranch family had a connection with Lucas Cranach the German painter. He wrote an extensive paper on him. This is from the front page:

The Painter of The Reformation.
This is the appellation usually bestowed

Mary (1896 – 1987)
Daughter of Ricard and Cissie attended the Richard Passmore Grammar School in Newton Abbot and then trained as a teacher. Her text books were full of pencilled notes. She had a sharp and knowledgeable mind and was a student of Devon.

Ch 16.3   Richard and his family

> Adam & Eve were dispossessed
> of a garden hard by heaven -
> They planted another one down in the west
> 'Twas Devon - glorious Devon -

So begins an essay in an exercise book about Devon. It contains several snippets about its history, festivals, places and their associations such as Brixham with the hymn "Abide with me" and the above ditty about the river Dart – "which every year claimeth a heart"

She married Ernest Frederic Corley, a widow, in Edmonton in 1935 after meeting him on a cruise. He was then 64 with two grown up sons. She was 40. He was a civil servant in the legal and tax departments. They lived in the Hinchley area. He died in 1963 age 82. It was not a happy marriage - "all he wanted was a housekeeper" she was heard to say. After he died Mary destroyed all evidence of his existence.
She moved out of their large house into a smaller bungalow nearby about ten years later.
She died at the end of December 1987 in hospital having had a stroke earlier.

Will
Some time prior to her death she transferred her ownership of her cottages in South Brent to her cousin Naomi, who then found she had to pay Capital Gains Tax. She sold them. Mary's will named three charities which inherited the bulk of the estate and numerous individuals. An executor in South Brent wrote:
> "Mary was a wonderful lady with a brain and handwriting as good at 91 as at 61 !"
> "…. we will be contacting a Funeral director …to open her brother's grave for the internment of her casket and the vicar for committal and will place an order for a granite stone with inscription to be placed on the grave after".

It was clear Mary was devoted to her mother and her brother as she had kept numerous relics of theirs including Hedley's drawings and his bookcase/bureau, her mother's wedding dinner set from Australia and scrapbooks and photo albums containing such items as Hedley's postcards from WW1.

She had also kept items which illustrated her meticulous nature. In a drawer was a small box contained bits of string. The box was labelled
>   "string too short to be useful"

Ch 16.4 Mary and Australia

Mary, Queensland

Mary Gidley Cranch
Born   1862 in South Brent
Father   WCSC glazier of South Brent
Mother   Mary Coulton Gidley of Rattery
Died   1932 in Mossman Queensland age 70
Married   probably 1892 in Australia (Sydney?)
Husband   Rev Edward Taffs, church minister
Children   Betty Taffs and Rene Taffs

Her future husband was first a painter, then a schoolmaster in Devon before becoming a minister. He was very religious. When he was in London (receiving religious instruction) Mary met him whist again visiting Lizzie Smith.

She returned to Devon. He was sent to Australia on missionary work.

The story is told that she drooped about the house with all imaginable ailments, unwilling to help anyone or anything until a letter arrived summoning her to Australia to marry Edward. Whereupon a miraculous recovery took place and suitable attire and arrangements for the journey were entered into with great gusto.
She was then aged 20. She was chaperoned on the trip out to Australia by her brother Richard (see Ch 16.3)

Queensland
She was married in Sydney (probably) and then they went on up to Mossman, Queensland where the Rev Edward Taffs had been posted.
She kept in contact with South Brent with letters especially at the time of the settlement of her father's will and with photographs of her children, her neighbourhood, and their church. In 1911 a storm destroyed "our lovely little church".

Ch 16.4 Mary and Australia

Mary taking tea with the archbishop and Edward

After she died, the Rev Taffs wrote in 1938 to "My Dear Annie" from "your loving brother" thanking for her Christmas letter. He says he is very well, attributed to being in hospital for 17 days with rest & no worries. He was lonely with no close friends but gave some information about his family.

Betty's family had been were living with him since before Christmas 1936. Her husband was a Roman catholic and they had three children. He was a labourer, out of work with a broken wrist. The eldest boy was 16 and had left school at Christmas with no work to go to.

He castigated England for "spending vast sums on preparations for another war" and in fomenting wars in various parts of the world", saying that Englishmen in Australia "feel terrible shame in causing defeat of Abyssinia", whereby England gained more than Italy, and referred to the Australian Nurses in Spain, for which he had printed a poster and organised a fund raising event.   The Rev died in 1950, aged over 80

After aunt Ann (Mary's young sister) died her niece Naomi corresponded with Mossman and in 1971 was in Sydney where she met Ambrose. In 1988 Monica (Mary's granddaughter) at Kuranda, Qld wrote in reply to one from Naomi.
She was sad to hear of death of A. William Jun. and Mary (Corley).
She described their house as a single story brick house with 3 beds in the mountains, with about 3 ½ acres mostly lawn. Her husband is Jim, youngest son is Steven, her daughter Donna has a baby Sarah 18 months old. They have Bull Terrier dogs for breeding. As far as is known, this family is still there.

Ch 16.5 - A. WILLIAM

Apprenticeship, Business, Interests, Family gatherings, Masonry and Church, Marriage, Hardship, the Great Fire, Death, Minnie

A. William Cranch
Born   1867 in South Brent,
Father   youngest son of WCSC glazier of South Brent
Mother   Mary Coulton Gidley of Rattery
Died   1937 in South Brent age 69
Married   1899 to Sarah Marianne Elizabeth Came ("Minnie")
                             of Woodhuish, Brixham
Children   A. William (jun), Naomi, Christine, Marian

Andrew William was known as "Bill" in his time but here is referred to as A. William.
His son was also called Andrew William Cranch and "Bill".
To distinguish between the two the son is referred to as A . William jun.

Apprenticeship
A . William was apprenticed as a carpenter and joiner to Geo L Style, builder, contractor, undertaker of Exeter from 19 Dec 1883 to 19 Dec 1887. He recommended that A. William join the classes at School of Art "as he will find it very useful to him & his business   *Letter 19 Jan 1884 to WCSC*
Evidently A. William continued at Style's after the end of his apprenticeship as Style offered him 12 month's work in the shop "for you to help me in the office whereby you would get an insight into that part of the business"   *Letter 30 June 1888 to "Cranch"*
This opportunity to study the administration and book keeping for a building business was to prove invaluable to him later. It might also reflect that WCSC saw A. William as being better able to run the business in the future than older son Richard.

After his father died in 1892 when A. William was 25 he and his brother Richard carried on the business as Cranch Bros. After Richard died and by 1900 it was just A.W. Cranch, builder, employing 8 men.

Business
A. William ran the building business in much the same way as any small village business traditionally did with much attention paid to his customers. Material costs were relatively high, so re-cycling and re-use was common. One day a customer came into the shop, wanting a certain type of brass hinge. A. William removed one from a knife box his family had – just what the customer wanted. The handle never was replaced. Another customer was unable to pay his bills – a mantle clock was taken instead.

After WW1 when it became clear what the general situation was in the aftermath of the war and the Spanish flu pandemic, A. William instructed his family what they had to do. His son A. William (jun) was to work with him in the business (dashing any hopes junior had of being a farmer), Naomi was to work in the shop ("I am not going to be a housemaid" she said), Chrissie to complete her schooling before being allowed to leave to do her nursing training. Marion was then still a child but was to follow her sisters to school at Plymouth.
A. William developed and expanded the business with his son to include house building, employing over 20 men until the advent of WW2.

Interests and activities

As a young man A. William was a "country sportsman": fishing in the river Avon, following the hounds and rifle shooting. Once a year he went with his second cousin "Walter" Smith to stay a weekend at the hotel at Torcross where they could both fish and shoot. Other expeditions were with his best man Wakeham and with his friend Hodder.

He was a founder member the S. Brent Rifle club which had its opening on 23 July 1902 at a site lent by the Misses Carew. Membership was about 40. By May 1903 he was Hon Sec. At the AGM next year he was congratulated on the efficient way he had kept the accounts and announced that after several years as Treasurer he stood down but remained on the committee.

He was involved in village affairs by attending meetings (e.g. about street lighting in 1893) and participated in concerts. In Oct 1893 he was granted a firework licence, presumably for an event. The S. Brent Institute held a series of monthly "at home" entertainments in 1890 and 1891, hosts including Mr & Mrs Stidston. In Feb 1890 "the musical parts gave universal satisfaction, especially the glees. Two capital comic songs "Do you know where Nowhere is?" and "Merry Young Knight" were sung by Mr. A. W Cranch. Miss Cranch *(Ann)* capitally gave "wishes and fishes"
In March 1891 they also participated   *(Western Times 14.2.1890 and 3.4.11891)*.

He was in demand at concerts for many years until one day whilst going to Dipford in a horse and buggy with his wife, he realised he had forgotten his song book. This distressed him, his performance was affected and he never accepted invitations to sing again. He was said to have had a good voice.

He played cricket for South Brent *(W.Times 1891)*, was on its committee then as Hon Sec and Treasurer and was still involved up to WW1.

Family Gatherings

Brent Fair was an occasion when various relatives (especially the Cames) and friends would descend upon the family home for dinner, often bed and breakfast, unannounced. The household would have to buckle to and cater for them. This started in WCSC's time and continued long into the next century. A. William's eldest daughter Naomi would often tell of stories about these fairs in the 1920s and her sudden guests. One such involved an old farming boy who was contorting his face at dinner. What's the matter? she asked
    "Kin't kitch'en, chile"
It transpired that the old boy had only one tooth and had difficulty in capturing a pickled union.

With so many relatives in the Cranch and Came families, there was always a need for meeting up. Hampers to be prepare, venues agreed and vehicles organised. A major one took place at Slapton in 1922 attended by about 40 people.

Masonry and Church

A. William was confirmed into the South Brent church on 24.10.1886 . He was appointed a South Brent Parish Trustee in 1893, resigned in 1894, elected a sidesman in 1895. He attended the annual Church Easter Vestry meetings and events such as the annual bellringers supper 1895. He participated in Feoffee activities such as their annual distributions of blankets, flannel, serge and sheets to the poor on Boxing Day 1904 *(Totnes Weekly Times 31.12 1904)*

In the early 1900s another churchwarden for a time was regarded a rake. A. William would not have anything to do with him. When the man soon left the district, he left several sires. One was later apprenticed to A. William as a carpenter.

He was appointed churchwarden again in 1909, but was not churchwarden from 1914 – 1925, a period in which the Veale Brothers had the contracts for church repair work. He was appointed churchwarden in 1925 and served until 1935, when his son took over.

He became a member of the freemasons shortly after his father died.
He remained committed to it for all his working life. He built the freemasons hall in Totnes Road in 1934. As a member he often attended events to represent them. One such was the funeral of a noted agriculturalist. Also there were the Rossiters (related to the Cames) and the distant relation Joseph Cranch of Kingsbridge played the organ. Joseph was a prominent musician in the mid-late 1800s. (see Chapter 17).
(meeting 17.1.1865 at Kbg, report in Western Times)

Marriage.
A. William was related to the Came family of Woodhuish Farm on the coast near Brixham (see footnote) so A. William had the opportunity to stay there as a young man, no doubt to partake in some shooting and fishing. There he met a daughter (his first cousin once removed). One day her father discovered that they had taken a walk unchaperoned and unauthorised by him. He was a strict Victorian. He banished the young man to bed without supper. The daughter wept, but her mother comforted her and managed to smuggle some apples to the young man.

Many years later they married.
> "In St. Mary's Church, Brixham, on Wednesday 4 October 1899, was solemnised the marriage of Minnie, eldest daughter of J. M. Came, and Mr A. W. Cranch, youngest son of the late Mr W. C. S. Cranch, of South Brent. The bride, who was given away by her father, wore a cream dress, trimmed with lace, tulle veil, with wreath of orange blossoms, and carried a shower bouquet of white flowers, the gift of the bridegroom. She was attended three bridesmaids, sisters of the bride, who were dressed in green with white fichus, and black velvet hats, trimmed with white ribbon and feathers, and wore gold brooches, gifts of the bridegroom. Mr T. Wakeham, Marley, acted as best man. The service was choral, the vicar, the Rev A. F. Carey, officiating, assisted by the Rev C. Ward. Later in the afternoon the happy pair left for Bournemouth. The bride's travelling dress was navy blue with hat to match. During the day the bells rang merrily. "
> *Totnes Times 7 Oct 1899*

Even that apparently was not without comment from her father – she was the eldest daughter, marrying after the second daughter had. Apparently not the done thing.

A. William and Minnie celebrated their silver wedding in 1924 and had their portraits taken.

Hardship

Money was always tight in his family, mainly because it was left to A. William to find the cash necessary to satisfy the requirements of his father's will whilst retaining as much of the estate as he could.

Such was the family hardship In WW1 that his son A. William jun attended Plymouth Grammar school in patched up trousers. The family home was sparsely furnished, so it was no surprise that when he and his son cleared his brother-in-law's farm (Woodhuish) in 1934, they acquired many items.

In the 1920s the house field was turned over to hay making to provide fodder for the horse and for sale to provide extra income.

The 1901 Fire at South Brent

This was a major conflagration and notable event at the time. The following is taken from reports in the *Totnes Times & Devon News (abbreviated to T.T.date)*

In Sept 1898 the parish Council noted that the "previous captaincy over the appliances of the Fire Brigade had resigned" and in a letter Mr. A. W. Cranch volunteered to accept the captaincy.
(T.T 24.9.1898)

At the Parish Council meeting in April it was reported that the newly acquired fire engine underwent testing Saturday evening last under the captain of the Fire Brigade (Mr A W Cranch). Leakages were found in the hose in places and the engine will apparently require some overhauling.
(T.T 24.4.1900)

"The inhabitants of South Brent just before 1 o'clock on Tuesday morning *(24th February 1901)* were aroused by the fire bell and cries that fire had broken out at the Vicarage house. The news spread rapidly and very soon people were carrying water upstairs. A small hydraulic pomp was used by which the whole building was saved. It was soon discovered that the flames had got hold of the beams and joists and reached the partitions of the rooms above. After about an hour the fire was got under control, considerable damage being done."
(T.T 27.2.1901)

The S.B Fire Relief Fund for those rendered homeless and lost property by fire was formed and appointed William JB Cranch of the Cornish Bank treasurer of Committee
(T.T 2.3.1901)

As it happened, in the week after the fire the Parish Council had its AGM and the election of the new committee. This was reported in the T.T covering nearly a full page under the headings:

> "The Brent Fire, Lively Council meeting, The Council's defence, History of the Fire Appliances, alleged Misleading Statements, Chairman under Examination, Heckling of Candidates ...... "

The report began:

> "South Brent was last week excited over the big fire and this week there was considerable excitement over the annual Parish meeting .... a certain degree of warmth pervaded the proceedings ...."

After the council had finished its annual report, the meeting developed into a public inquest about the fire. The water supply, siting of fire hydrants, their size, hoses, the fire engine performance, and responsibilities were all aired with the Council

attempting to correct alleged erroneous information and exaggerated claims which had been published in the "Herald" and the "Mercury".
Two facts emerged: 6 families had been rendered homeless; the Totnes Fire Brigade and their steam driven Fire Engine arrived about 4 a.m. and was there all day. There were two matters relating to A. William which the Council clarified:
The hose to be attached to the hydrants was placed in Mr Cranch's charge.
> "Why was this given to an outsider?" the council was asked.
> "Mr Cranch is a man everyone knows"

It was made clear he was not responsible for any repairs or maintenance of the Fire Brigade equipment, he merely let it be kept in his sheds.

The Council had endeavoured to form a Fire Brigade, but "no-one seemed willing to volunteer". Eventually Mr Cranch undertook to be Captain but up to the present:
> "it was a case of a Captain without any Fire Brigade"

This statement by the Chairman caused some mirth.   *(T.T.9.3.1901)*

Fire Aftermath
A more favourable press report appeared in the summer:
> "Brent as a health resort seems to be rapidly growing into favour, judging from the number visitors now in the place, and the number of buildings proposed to be erected. Four houses and shops are contracted for Church Street, on the scene of the fire of last year. Messrs Veale and Sons tender has been accepted."   *(T.T. 3.8.1901)*

A. William's tender was the highest by quite a margin.

Many improvements were made by the Parish Council, but not enough apparently as the Rev. H. S. Cole in his Parish Magazine of 18.3.1905 reported that
> "since the big fire the parish now has an excellent Fire Brigade, but the Fire Engine is inadequate. It cannot produce sufficient water pressure...... useless in the event of a large fire."

The old engine was kept in a shed of A. William's until sold for parts and scrap. Its side handles – about 3 yards long were kept. One was used by A. William jun as a handrail for the back stairs in the family home. The other was used by the author for various purposes until very recently.

Death
A. William suffered a major illness (most likely a heart attack, claimed to be result of plumbing overwork) in 1934/5 and was in poor health thereafter. On 11th February 1936 a cousins' party was being held at the family home when he died. His son A. William jun ensured the guests left quietly and prevented a distraught Naomi from seeing her beloved father.
The *Western times 16.2.1937* in reporting the death:
> "He was for many years a Trustee of the South Brent Charity Lands and a Churchwarden. The vicar spoke of Mr Cranch as being not only a neighbour, but a very good neighbour. Up to 2 years ago he was a very active member of the church and a regular communicant and he was one who for several sound reasons had their affection and regard "

The mourners at his funeral were his immediate family and a number of his Came in-laws. The congregation was over 100 consisting of employees, villagers, friends and masonic hall members. There were 30 floral tributes

Ch 16.5 - A. WILLIAM

Minnie i.e Sarah Marriane Elizabeth (Nee Came) (1873 – 1961)
Minnie was quite a talented woman, brought up to learn the skills of Victorian ladies. A few of her drawings survive as does her autograph book and some photographs.

Pencil and graphite drawing signed S M E Came 1889

She was tall and raised five children. She had more, unrecorded. One born after Marian was born with a cawl over its face. The midwife did not know what to do, so it suffocated. It would have been of companionship age for the youngest.

She was determined the family should survive after the hardships she and A. Wiiliam endured so as to preserve the family home.

The numbers of mourners at her funeral almost matched that of her husband's
report in western times

Footnote - connection between Came and Cranch
Two Gidley sisters:
- Elizabeth born 1822 married S.E Edmonds and had a daughter known as Pretty Bessie.
- Mary born 1828 married WCSC and had a son A. William, so A William and Bessie were first cousins
- Bessie had a daughter known as Minnie, so she was a first cousin once removed to A. William

ANN

Born	1869 in South Brent, the youngest surviving child
Father	WCSC glazier of South Brent
Mother	Mary Coulton Gidley of Rattery
Died	20.1.1938
Spinster	

In her younger days, Ann was involved with church and local affairs. She sang at the monthly "at home" series of concerts in 1890 and assisted with the Board School annual children's "treats".

The family home was a busy one, particularly after her brother A. William married, receiving numerous Cranch and Came relatives at the bi-annual Brent fairs. As the "maiden aunt", Ann was kept busy assisting.
She became the relative who developed contacts with the numerous relatives in both the Came and Cranch families and stayed with them all, often for long periods. A month with the Somerset Cames at Bridgewater for instance.

She was a collector of postcards, mainly of royalty, churches and family. They reveal the extent of her contacts. Many addressed to her at South Brent are forwarded onto a relative's address, such as Southdown, Brixham farmed by her uncle George Came. Among others are those from or sent to Lizzie Smith (a favoured cousin) at Harlesden and Hythe, Lizzie Taffs at Hastings (sister of the Rev Edward Taffs), Hedley in France or convalescing in UK, John & Agnes Came at Reading, brother John and Vi, London Bill in Tunis in 1916, Mary at Mossman Qld, and Beta (a Gidley related to her mother).

She also developed interest in the family tree and created with her nephew A. William (jun) the family tree known to them at the time. It was drawn on a large piece of wall paper which became the starting point for many a discussion by her great nephews and nieces in subsequent years. She got her niece Marian to type up some of her notes. All this was not always appreciated by her brother A. William: "put it away, Ann" he said more than once. Apparently he was content with keeping the archive matter but not with interpreting their significance.

She came back from another trip away with a heavy cold. This developed into pneumonia from which she died. At her funeral the mourners were the Cranch and Came families, the undertaker was her nephew A. William C (jun) and the bearers were his employees. A local paper undated reported.
    "she took a keen interest in church affairs".
The Western Morning News reported she was the
    "dearly beloved sister of the late A.W. Cranch"

Will
She had made a will in October 1937 which may have been prompted by her becoming ill. However before she died the family became aware of the will and was alarmed at the prospect of some of her property being sold away from the family. (Her brother had spent his whole life trying to keep the estate inherited from their father WCSC intact - an activity supported strongly by his wife Minnie). The solicitor was summoned to record a codicil which enabled her nephew A. William Jun to buy the property in question, if he so wished. Ann died the next day.

Ch 16.7 A Pictorial Record

WILLIAM N. CRANCH
1754 – 1820
of Kbg

MARY ROOPE
of Kbg
? - 1828

JOHN ROOPE CRANCH
1800 – 1868
of kbg
Started family business

ANN STIDSON
of South Brent
1801- 1874

WILLIAM C. S. CRANCH
Established the family in S. Brent

MARY C. GIDLEY
of Dean Prior
1828-1905

Their five children

JOHN
1858-1934
m
Josephine Marchingall

RICHARD
1860 – 1898
m
Annie Shaw

MARY
1862 - 1932
m
Edward Taffs

A .WILLIAM
1867 – 1937
m
S.M.E.Came

ANN
1869 - 1938

Ch 16.7 A Pictorial Record

The spouses

JOSEPHINE MARCHINGALL   ANNIE SHAW   EDWARD TAFFS   "MINNIE" CAME

Other family photos:

Ann late 1920s   A.WILLIAM 1934   A.WILLIAM 1924   Minnie 1924

CISSIE 1920s   HEDLEY C 1912   HEDLEY C 1920   MARY 1910   MARY 1970s

Cricket pre-WW1 photo : A. William prone front left

…….. a trout in the river Avon Mr A.W. Cranch succeeded in drawing one of 1lb 10ozs. Sport on the Avon is much improved and numbers are boosting Brent for moorland fishing
Western Times 16 June1902

CHAPTER 17

JOSEPH ^{5} AND HIS FAMILIES

Joseph [5] and the Josephs of Kingsbridge.

The full listing of the descendants of Joseph [5] is given in Chart 17.2 which follows. Joseph himself and part of his family remained in Kingsbridge. Others, often called John, migrated to South Brent and Tavistock.

Joseph [5] (1748 – 1814)
Born	1748 at Kingsbridge
Died	1814 at Totnes
Father	Joseph [2] (one of the seven)
Mother	Elizabeth Lidstone
Brothers	John the Painter, William N
Sisters	five
Married	Rebecca Elworthy
Occupation	Sadler

From information from Peabody, in a letter from his sister Hannah in 1771 and a note in the F.A family tree chart, Joseph [5] was a saddler. having learnt the trade from his father. He went to America in his late teens, came back and married. He set up in business first in Totnes, then Plymouth before returning to the Kingsbridge area.

He married Rebecca Elworthy in 1768. The name Rebecca frequently occurs in this branch of the family. She was probably a sister of James Elworthy who had married Joseph [5]'s sister Elizabeth.
They had several children. Of the two sons that survived Joseph remained in Kingsbridge and his descendants are still there as far as is known.

The Josephs (of Kingsbridge)
Little is known about the son (b 1770)
His grandson Joseph (b 1814) was a Painter & Glazier, and lived in Fore St with his wife and one of his sons Joseph (b 1849). He named his eldest son Henry Elworthy after his great aunt Elizabeth's husband Elworthy.

His second son, the "young" Joseph, was a prominent musician in the mid-late 1800s and local papers of the time contain numerous mentions of his involvement with local concerts. In common with many other local people, he was a supporter of the proposal to build a railway line from Kingsbridge to South Brent.

17.2 Chart Joseph⁵ and the Johns

JOSEPH⁵
b 29.2.1748 at W.Alvington
d 12.8.1814 at Totnes?

m 29.9.1768 at Marlborough

REBECCA ELWORTHY
b 22.1.1745 Stokenham
d 1803 at S.Milton

JOSEPH's father was JOSEPH² one of the seven see chart 11.2

All children b at Marl.

Children of Joseph⁵ and Rebecca:

MARY b 24.1.1745 m 2.1.1815 FRANCIS PEARCE

JOHN b 28 Jun 1778 at Salcombe d — m **MARY NORTON** b 1780 m 12.8.1804 St Edmunds Kbg

Infants: JOSEPH b 2.7.1770, d 21.9.1770; **JOSEPH** b 28.2.1772, d 27.6.1772

JOSEPH b 2.7.1770 m .... ?

ELIZABETH ? b 1813 W.Alvington m 1839

Children of Joseph b 2.7.1770:

REBECCA b 1806

JOSEPH b 1814 d 1898 ?

Children of Joseph b 1814:

EMMA JANE b 1840 m H BLAMEY at Exeter

HENRY ELWORTHY b 1841 d 16.6.1857

JOSEPH b 1849. Painter & decorator

CHARLES EDWIN b 1851 d 1854

Children of John b 1778 and Mary Norton:

JOHN b 18.8.1810 St Ed. Kbg d 1.10.1862

WILLIAM b 6.9.1813 d 1868 m 30.6.1834 SARAH EDGECOMBE b 1812 Stoke Damerel → *See p 2 right*

REBECCA b 1809 d 1875 m HENRY VEALE 13.7.1830 at Stoke Damerel

Also ? DRUSILLA 1814, **THOMAS E** 1812, **MARY A** 1816-1881

Infants REBECCA 1807, **DREWSELLA** —, **JOHN** 1805, **JOSEPH** 1818

John b 18.8.1810 m 18.8.1833 St Ed. Kbg **ELIZABETH HEAD OLDRIEVE** b 4.6.1811 Blackawton

All children born in Kbg. Lived in Fore St.

Children:

ELIZABETH b 1835 dress maker

JOHN b 19.1.1836 m 1867 at Tavistock d 1897 at Kbg → *p 2 left*

FREDERICK WILLIAM b 1840 d 1892 → *p 2 bottom right*

MARY JANE b 1843 drapers assistant d 30.11.1867 at Plymouth

CLARA b 1846 m **EDWIN LAMBLE** → *p 2 centre*

LEAH b 1847 drapers assistant d 18.3.1917

ALFRED b 1850

EDMUND b 1852

Continued on

3

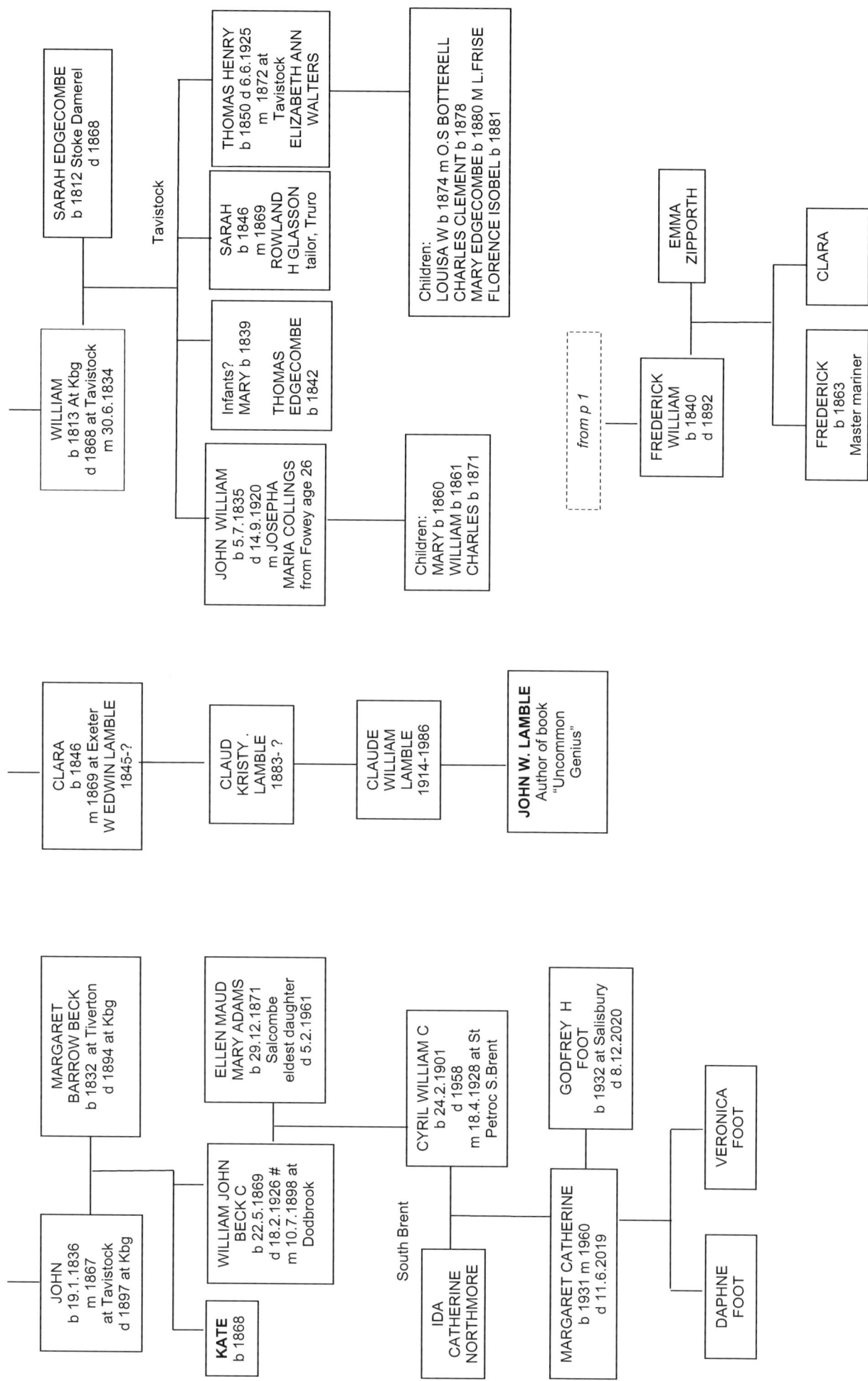

17.2 Chart Joseph 5 and the Johns

Johns of Kingsbridge, South Brent, Cyril, William of Tavistock

John of Kingsbridge, b 1788
Father   youngest son of Joseph [5], Kingsbridge
Mother   Rebecca
Married   Mary Norton of Kingsbridge
                 They had at least three surviving sons and three daughters.

The eldest son John (b 1810) was a tanner and currier (leather dealer) and a High Bailiff and deputy Parish Clerk.
He married Betsy Oldrieve and they had several children. They also lived in Fore St Kingsbridge. *(Census 1841, 1851, 1861)* They had several children. Their eldest son John (b 1836) also lived in Kingsbridge and followed his father's trades

The other son was William (b 1813) – see Tavistock

All the daughters seemed to be connected with the garment trade. Clara married a tailor and is the ancestor to John William Lamble who wrote the book about John the Painter. She lived at Newton Abbot and was joined by her sister Leah whose photograph is available from the archives in The Box at Plymouth.

Two other sisters Elizabeth and Mary had a shop in Totnes:

F.A.

John (1836 – 1897)
Eldest son of John (b 1788) and Betsey
He married Margaret Barrow Beck in Tavistock. Her parents were Master and Matron of the Tavistock Union Workhouse. (Margaret's sister Mary married Richard Skinner from Tavistock and their children were shown as staying with their aunt at Kingsbridge in the 1881 Census.)

Ch 17.3 The Johns of Kingsbridge and South Brent

His son **William John Beck Cranch** (William JBC) 1869 - 1926 trained to be a chemist with J.H. Adams, chemist at Salcombe. In the mid-1890's his father John was in contact with the Feofees of South Brent asking to reserve a shop for him in one of the developments taking place in Station Road, South Brent. This did not materialise.

South Brent

Instead in 1895 William JBC took over a Feoffee shop in Church Street in South Brent which the Cranch Brothers builders helped to fit out. This meant there were now two families living in Brent. The two families knew that they were related, but never sure how. The only clue they had was that they both had the portrait of John Cranch the Painter. In fact, the ancestors of both Cranch families were brothers of John the Painter

The shop still exists as a pharmacy, located next to the old toll house and is featured in a picture postcard in the W R Gay series 1916, believed to show William JBC standing in the shop doorway.

William JBC married his former employer's daughter Ellen Adams (Maud) in Kingsbridge in 1898 and moved to S Brent with his wife, Kate his sister and Ellen's sister Helen from Salcombe.

He became involved within the community and village life. He was on the Evening Continuation School committee in 1900 till least 1903. In March 1901 he is described as being "of the Cornish Bank" and was appointed treasurer of the S.B. Fire Relief committee.
(Totnes Weekly Times 2.3.1901)
It is not clear whether he had completely changed occupation by this time or whether he had two roles as chemist and banking.
Eventually he became the bank branch manager and was succeeded by his son Cyril (the Cornish Bank eventually became part of the Lloyds group)

Not to be outdone by the other Cranch in Brent at this time, William JBC "secured a fine trout from the River Avon by Brent Mill bridge of 1 lb 4½ oz". (Mr A W Cranch was reported a few years earlier as having caught a similar sized one)
(Totnes Weekly Times 1911)

Cyril

Cyril was born above his father's chemist shop during the night of the great fire in the lower part of Church St. He followed his father's footsteps as manager of the Cornish Bank. Initially his family lived at in Belmont Terrace. Later he had a bungalow built in 1930/34 by A.W. Cranch and son, builders of South Brent. As with his father, Cyril became part of the South Brent community. He audited the churchwarden accounts kept by his namesake A. William Cranch 1945-1967.
His daughter Margaret attended Plymouth High School.

William of Tavistock

William (b 1813) was rother of John, and grandson of Joseph [5] son of married and moved to Tavistock. His wife was an Edgecombe (recorded with various spellings). He was a tailor, then a Workhouse porter.

His son John William (b 1835) also lived and married at Tavistock. He retired after 47 years as a Rate collector and assistant overseer of Tavistock Urban Council

William also had a son called Thomas Henry, married with four children. Thomas was also a Collector of Taxes and worked for Tavistock U. C. and was an Insurance agent. He owned four houses which he let. He was involved in

> "A sad accident which occurred to a wedding party …. [the wedding couple] who had been married in the morning, …. the bride's brother and Mr T.H. Cranch the Registrar of Tavistock were being driven to Coryton Railway Station ……. Something caused one of the horses to bolt down a hill and all the occupants if the carriage were thrown out. The driver …is at present in a critical condition. Mr Cranch sustained a bad cut to the forehead and his legs and shoulders were bruised……the bridge and groom were cut and bruised."
>
> Western Times 31.122.1895

The family tradition of serving with the Tavistock council continued with Thomas's son Charles.

Acknowledgement
I am very grateful to the grand-daughters of Cyril for suppling much useful information and indeed encouraging the author to explore this branch of the family. Establishing their family tree was not straightforward. Any errors are mine.

CHAPTER 18
MISCELLANEOUS

Entrance of Berry Castle – Devon
Aug 31 – 1817

M1   Nathaniel of Exeter c 1800

References
1. *Sherborne newspaper April 17th 1797*
2. *Genealogical Notes and Family Trees in the notebooks of William Holmes DHC 426Z / Z/ 1*
3. *Lease records at DHC : 51/1/9/11 & 14*
4. *DRO 5423D / 8 / 7 / 2*

In Trinity Church Exeter, in 1771 Nathaniel was baptised, son of Richard and Mary (nee Cornish); daughter Elizabeth in 1774.
According to the newspaper the Town Clerk's Books were examined to show that
- Richard C was made free 1734
- his son Nathaniel 17 April 1797
- supported by William Holmes

On 19 August 1798, Nathaniel weighed 11 stone 10 lbs

He joined the Guild of Weavers, Tuckers and Shearmen in 1794 and was made master in 1797

John Holmes married Rebecca Hillman 8 Aug 1757. Rebecca was the daughter of David Hillman and Elizabeth Cranch who married in 1731 at Exeter St Leonards. She was an aunt of Nathaniel and sister to his father Richard.
Nathaniel served his apprenticeship with William Holmes, brother of John Holmes.
According to John Holmes, Elizabeth was
> "the aunt to the young man that served with me, namely Mr Nathaniel Cranch. By his marriage and by the death of his brother-in-law Mr David Hillman junior he had a fortune of more that £4000 and the best mother-in-law who was the widow with a son and daughter when my brother married"

Evidently Nathaniel inherited a substantial sum
In 1796 he ("gentleman") gave money for buying the old goal (i.e. County prison) premises to build the Castle street chapel by 1800. A Sunday school was planned – one of the first to do so .
(Later they built and moved into the Congregational Church in Southernhay)

In 1797 he ("gent" of Exon) leased off the Feoffees "a warehouse and lofts in a street leading from Southgate towards the Palace Gate"

On 1 July 1810 Nathaniel was declared bankrupt . The lease was re-assigned. The Feofees were involved as were four merchants who were the administrators of the estate of Nathaniel Cranch of Exon, merchant, and a bankrupt. Cited was the warehouse and lofts in Palace Street , earlier leases and a will.

(related matter reported in *Plymouth & West Devon newspaper* A Nathaniel , merchant of London, was involved in litigation)

A possible tree follows.

M1 Nathaniel of Exeter c 1800

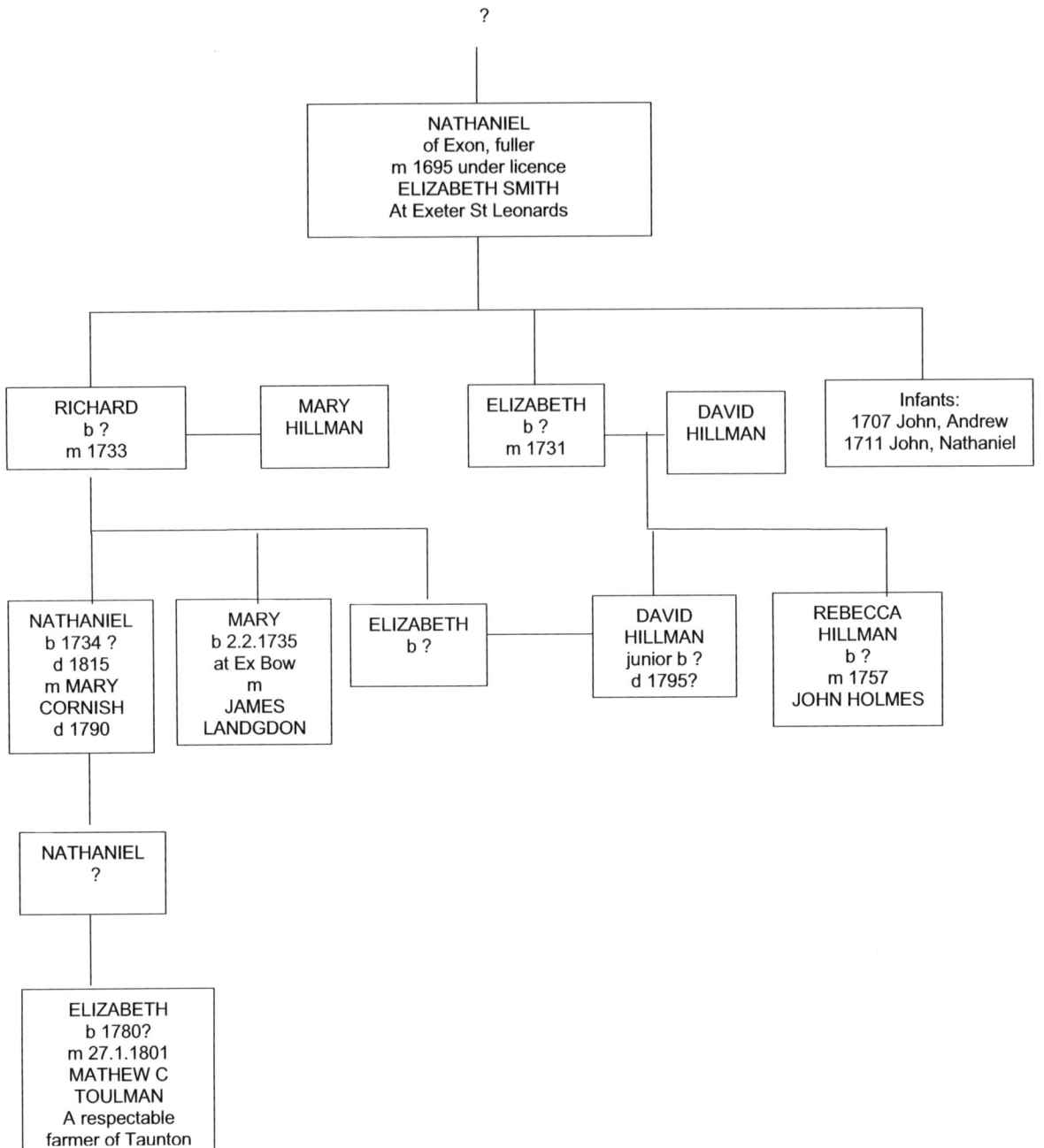

This was downloaded from Rootschat. Without checking, we can assume that all the information about Generations Two and Three are correct. The information of Generation one has been amplified and put in italics

GENERATION ONE
1. **William Cranch**, born 1796 in South Milton, Devon, (son of Joseph Cranch and Mary Quarm) baptized 8 Jan 1797 in South Milton, Devon, died Qtr 3 1871 in West Alvington, Devon, occupation Labourer & sexton.
   In fact Joseph and Mary had 6 children:
   - *Joseph b 1800, d 1850*
   - *William b 1796 as described here*
   - *Dorcas Seagar*
   - *3 others*

William married Maria Hodge, 4 June 1827 in Diptford, Devon.
   They had seven or eight children:
- *Samuel as described below*
- *Mary b 1830, William 1832, Elizabeth 1834, Caroline 1836, Dorcas 1839, Maria 1841*

Samuel Cranch born 1827, baptized 11 Nov 1827 in West Alvington, Devon. He married (1) Sarah Jane Gill, Qtr 4 1852 in South Huish, Devon. He married (2) Ann Elizabeth Gillard, 1877, born 1827 in East Portlemouth, Devon, died Qtr 1 1888.

GENERATION TWO

Samuel Cranch born 1827 married (1) Sarah Jane Gill. Children:
i. **William Gill Cranch** born Qtr 1 1853
ii. **Samuel Cranch** born Qtr 1 1855.
iii. Susan Gill Cranch, born Qtr 1 1855, baptized 1 Apl 1855 in South Huish,
iv. Mary Jane Cranch, born 1857, baptized 27 Sept 1857 in South Huish
v. John William Cranch, born Qtr 1 1860, baptized 27 May 1860 in South Huish.
vi. Sarah Elizabeth Cranch, born Qtr 1 1860, baptized 27 May 1860 in South Huish.
vii. George Wills Gill Cranch, born Qtr 2 1862, baptized 3 Aug 1862 in South Huish died Qtr 3 1883.
viii. Maria Cranch, born 1865, baptized 22 Jan 1865 in South Huish, Devon.

GENERATION THREE

William Gill Cranch, born Qtr 1 1853, baptized 3 Apl 1853 in South Huish, Devon, occupation Carter, Ag Lab, Coal worker. He married Sarah Ann Hales, married Qtr 3 1876, born 1855 in Kingswear, Devon. Children:
i. Sarah Maria Cranch, born Qtr 1 1877 in Dartmouth, occupation 1891 - Servant.
ii. William Henry Cranch, born Qtr 2 1880 in Kingsbridge or Dartmouth, Devon.

iii. **Frederick George Cranch** born Qtr 3 1881, died 16 Nov 1956 in NZ, occupation Sailmaker, then Machinist. He married Edith Anne James, married 1913 in New Zealand, died 25 March 1972 in NZ.
iv. Caroline Mabel Cranch, born Qtr 3 1883 in Dartmouth, Devon.
v. Mary Grace Cranch, born Qtr 2 1885 in Dartmouth, Devon
vi. Edward John Cranch born Qtr 3 1887.
vii. **Samuel Gill Cranch**, born Qtr 4 1889 in Dartmouth, Devon, buried 1 July 1962 in NZ, buried in Waikumete Cemetery, NZ, occupation Farmer.

viii. Bertha Florence Cranch, born Qtr 4 1891 in Dartmouth, Devon
ix. Minnie Maud Cranch, born Qtr 1 1895 in Dartmouth, Devon

Samuel Cranch, born Qtr 1 1855 in South Huish, Devon, baptized 1 Apl 1855 in South Huish, Devon, died 31 Jan 1919 in New Zealand, occupation 1871 - Ag Lab, buried in Hamilton East Cemetery, Hamilton.
He married Elizabeth Webb, 1 May 1880 in Wellington, New Zealand, died 8 Jan 1940 buried in Hamilton. Children:

i. Thomas Norman Cranch, born 23 Sept 1896 in Carterton, Wellington, NZ, died 1 Jan 1973.
ii. Elizabeth Ethel Cranch, born Sept 1881 in Wellington, NZ, died 1945.
    She married Frank Roland Harrison, 1904 in Wellington, NZ.
ii. William Samuel John Cranch born Mar 1884, died 13 Jan1959.
    He married Ada Florence Reynolds, 29 Oct 1910 in Te Aroha, Auckland, NZ
iv. Florence Beatrice Cranch, born Dec 1885 in Wellington, NZ.
    She married Alfred Dalton Fielder, 1916 in Hamilton, NZ.
v. Lily Myrtle Cranch, born Dec 1887 in Wellington, NZ.
    She married William Bowring, 1912 in Wellington, NZ.
vi. Ida Alma Cranch, born Sept 1890 in Carterton, Wellington, NZ.
    She married Vivian Hazeldean Knight, 1914 in Hamilton, NZ.
vii. Harold George Cranch born 1892, died 1976.
    He married Mary Gertrude Edge.
viii. Annie Muriel Cranch, born Jan 1891 in Carterton, Wellington, NZ, died 1991.
    She married William Robert Norman Warren, 1921 in Auckland, NZ.
ix. Vera Cranch, born 12 Oct 1904

Family Historians, Aunt Ann's Notes, Further Notes, Great Aunt Wilcocks, Wilcocks Letters

Family Historians
Many members of the Cranch and associated families have written accounts of the family. Among them:
- Jane Bowring-Cranch wrote the story of the rebel firebrand Rev Hicks "Troublous Times", based on his dairies. Jane also wrote with her uncle Sir John Bowring about John the Painter and John the Naturalist.
- Peabody in America wrote an exceedingly valuable reference to the family origins of the Richard Cranch that went to America in 1746
- Lizzie Smith (i.e. Elizabeth Mary Smith, E.M.Smith) researched family history and passed her records onto Graeme Cranch of London and some ended up at the Family Archives
- Renee Cranch did a lot of work in the 1990's especially on families associated with the Cames and Cranches. She became custodian of the Family Archives.
- Miss Michell from Loddiswell took a great interest in the Cranch family. Her father was a Methodist minister from Cornwall and had an original copy of Jane Bowring Cranch's book. She used the F.A. material to write articles about the visit of Abigail & John Adams to the West Country such as "One of our first American Tourists" *Western Morning News 13 Jan 1977.*
  She left notes which can be confusing
- Mrs Wilkinson who alleged regarding the origins:
    ….four brothers arrived in England in 1740 …. one went to London, another lived in Nottingham and his son was a friend of Jessie Boot and also of General Booth …buried in Beeston cemetery …another went to Kingsbridge.
  Clearly wrong but four brothers is an interesting concept

Aunt Ann's Notes
Typed up by Marian in 1933 under the direction of her aunt Ann Cranch and based on some papers sent to F.A by James J.C. Wilcocks 21 Sept 1906
> "in turning over some papers sent to me from Devonshire by my sister Hannah …I send you copies …"

Again these notes can be confusing.
Not reproduced here are the (mostly brief) notes on various family members about whom far more information is given elsewhere in this book. The letters are not refereed to either as they feature at the appropriate place in this book. The opening paragraph gives the source of the notes:

> Collected by Elizabeth Mary Smith from old letters in her possession …. (chiefly from an old book of collected letters in possession of John Cranch Roope Wilcocks of Stafford, to whose care they were left by his aunt Hannah Cranch Wilcocks, who died at Torquay 1 Feb 1915 ……with all her collection of family relics, portraits etc which she came to be in possession of her on the death of her mother Elizabeth Lidstone Wilcocks (nee Cranch) in January 1870 of Clapton, London. Much information was also gathered from letters ..written by James Cranch Wilcocks to his niece E.M.Smith between 1904 and 1910.

The old book of collected letters is explained as
> ".. some 200 pasted in a large book by some former member of the family and was in the possession of Hannah Cranch Wilcocks ….

So far this book has yet to be seen in the Family Archives

M 3 Family Historians

Other items of interest in the notes ;
- "My sister Hannah (*Cranch Wilcocks*) had a book published in U.S.A. containing a collection of letters of Mrs Abigail Adams which was sent to England by one of the Bonds and has in it a number of references to the Cranches of Devonshire."
- Letter from Hannah to J.C.Wilcocks recounting a stay at Kingsbridge with a Mrs Finch and meeting, but not speaking to, Professor Foude (the historian) who was researching there in 1799 and reference to Fairweather's book on Kingsbridge. *By co-incidence the present owner of Norden is called Froude*
- John Wilcocks (1785 – 1856) and his brother James Cranch Wilcocks (1779-1819) were born at Norden. Their parents being James (1742-1808) and Mary Wilcocks. Son James died at Bath buried in Walcot churchyard, John at London buried at Abney Park cemetery.

Further Notes
These further notes are suspected to be a continuation of the above notes. Verification of the items referred to has yet to be established.

A vellum bound diary of James Cranch Wilcock's [a] (uncle of James Cranch Wilcock's and of Elizabeth Lidstone Willocks (now Smith) and their brother and sister William Mary Ann (now Puttick) and Hannah Cranch Wilcock's who was born at Bowringsleigh Kingsbridge was in the possession of James Cranch Willocks [b] in 1906 (see letter to his niece, daughter of Elizabeth Lidstone Smith)

Notes a)1784-1856 b) 1835-1908

The book that Hannah Cranch Wilcocks had book published in America …. and all the old family letters containing interesting records of family history were in the possession of Hannah Cranch Wilcocks at the time of her death and were left by her will to her nephew John Cranch Wilcocks in order they might be preserved with care that future generations might refer to them if they were sufficiently interested in the old records, At the same time Hannah Cranch Wilcocks give verbal permission to her niece Elisabeth Mary Smith to borrow and read all these records in order to carry out her intention of making an orderly record of the history of the Cranch family for the benefit of the younger members of the family. So far she has been unable to obtain the opportunity of seeing see these old letters and records which would considerably add to and simplify theses notes concerning the history of the family which she is collecting from other sources within her reach – chiefly old letters in her possession and notes sent to her by her uncle James Cranch Wilcocks from time to time and which she always carefully preserved.

Jane Bowring Cranch …. lived at 3 South Place Kingsbridge and at 59 Fore Street …… wrote to Elizabeth Lidstone Smith …. mentioned various members of the family …. letters in possession of E. M. Smith

In reference to the visit by Abigail and John Adams, Jane writes:
Sir John & Lady Bowring & their daughter Miss Bowring visited herself at Bowringsleigh *(with the Adams)* "where they lunched with young Mr Ilbert who was most courteous" and "visited my dear uncle's grave which is in Alvington Churchyard with her" *(i.e. Roger Benbow Cranch).*
Sir John is still lively and vigorous at 73. His daughter is quite admired and is so pleasant and unaffected and talks well Lady Bowring appears very kind. They seem to admire whatever they saw of our lovely neighbourhood. Mrs Adams, Mrs Joseph Cranch's sister, lives near me *(presume this refers to the sister of Margaret Lakeman)*

The notes based on Jane's letters to Mrs Willocks continue
Oct 14 "a visit from uncle and his sons *William* appeared to admire our lovely neighbourhood much He promised to send me pictures of his father. I also begged him, if possible, to procure one of his Aunt Wilcocks. Theirs are faces associated with my earliest and dearest recollections "

> *From the context this is probably Joseph Cranch who married Margaret Lakeman. He did have a son called William.*

This entry continues;
"South Place, Dodbrooke, Kingsbridge announces the death of dear uncle of Jane Bowring Cranch buried in West Alvington churchyard, close beside his kinsman Roger Denbow Cranch after whom he was named"

This is a rather confusing entry – Roger Denbow C was an uncle to Jane. She had no other. Most likely she is referring to her great uncle. John Trathern. See chart 8.1

The Notebook of Lizzie Smith

Lizzie Smith, i.e. Elizabeth Mary Smith, was the great grand-daughter of James Wilcocks (1742-1788) and Mary Wilcocks (1742-1824), of Norden and was a niece of Hannah Cranch Wilcocks who inherited much Cranch material. Lizzie was very interested in Cranch family matters and was a regular correspondent with Aunt Ann, one-time custodian of the F.A.

In 1918 E.M.Smith said she had two miniature portraits on oil on pearl in her possession originally belonging to her mother and aunt Puttick. She assumes they were of Mary (Richard of America's wife) and their daughter Betsey, dated about 1784

Her brother Wallis wrote in July 1944 to F.A enclosing "some sheets I have come across" of his sister's and a notebook whose writing he "does not recognise". I now believe the notebook's origin was Joseph Cranch who married Margaret Lakeman. According to H.C. Wilcocks

> "My uncle Joseph Cranch ... was the chief genealogist ...."

The notebook has provided much of the information for this book and so it is not repeated here. Unfortunately the historian Miss Michell who accessed the F.A. in the 1970's to produce her version of "The Notebook of Lizzie Smith" included various other snippets of information. The result is a rather confusing set of notes which can only be resolved once the cataloguing of the F.A has been completed and access gained to the material in America. *(The English Civilisation Collection of the Biston Public Library has many letters from the Cranch and Wilcocks families)*

Great Aunt (Wilcocks)

According to the notebook, Walter Stephens Lethbridge painted the portraits of Mary Wilcocks and of a lady who presumably was a sister of James Wilcocks. The portrait is described :

> "Old lady in yellow shawl was in possession of Hannah Cranch Wilcocks who died at Torquay 1st Feb 1914. This picture with all the others of the Cranch family in her possession she left by her will to the care of her nephew John Cranch Roope Wilcocks then of Ealing, London". "

Copies of this picture photograph were made and distributed by the sister of H.C. Wilcocks and Mrs Elizabeth Lidstone Smith …. to the various members of her family". The picture is now in the F.A.

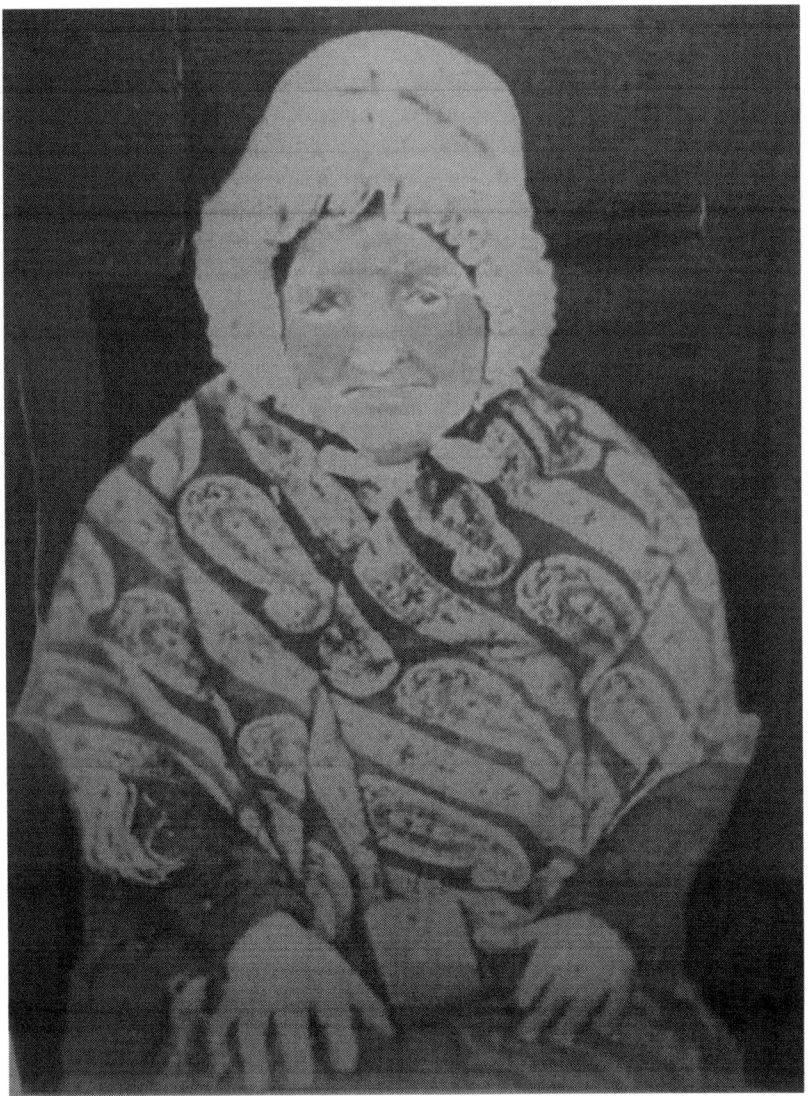

Great Aunt Wilcocks   F.A.

Wilcocks Letters
Many letters held in the F.A give clues about family history. For instance:
E.M.Smith said that "there were some 200 letters pasted in a large book by some former member of the family and possessed by Hannah Cranch Wilcocks at Torquay when it was passed onto John Cranch Roope Wilcocks of Stafford ……with all her collection of family relics, portraits etc which she came to be in possession of on the death of her mother Elizabeth Lidstone Wilcocks (nee Cranch) in January 1870.
The current location of the book of letters is unknown.

The author was raised and has lived most of his life in South Devon.

He was born in Plymouth while WW2 bombs were dropping.

His mother was a Cranch and had 32 first cousins. As a young boy he spent many holidays at the family home and heard many stories about them and his aunts and uncles. He grew up surrounded by these relatives and considered them an integral part of his life.

Later he became convinced the knowledge he gained about his relatives should be recorded for posterity, as it was very unlikely anyone else would do so. He little realised that over 50 years later the result would be a book covering centuries rather than a few generations or that it be only about one set of his relations – that of his mother.

He hopes that as the present generations disperse following the pattern of society over the centuries, his descendants will appreciate and be able to answer the questions "where did we come from"? and more particularly "who were the Cranches?".

The answers will surely surprise.

Central Kingsbridge

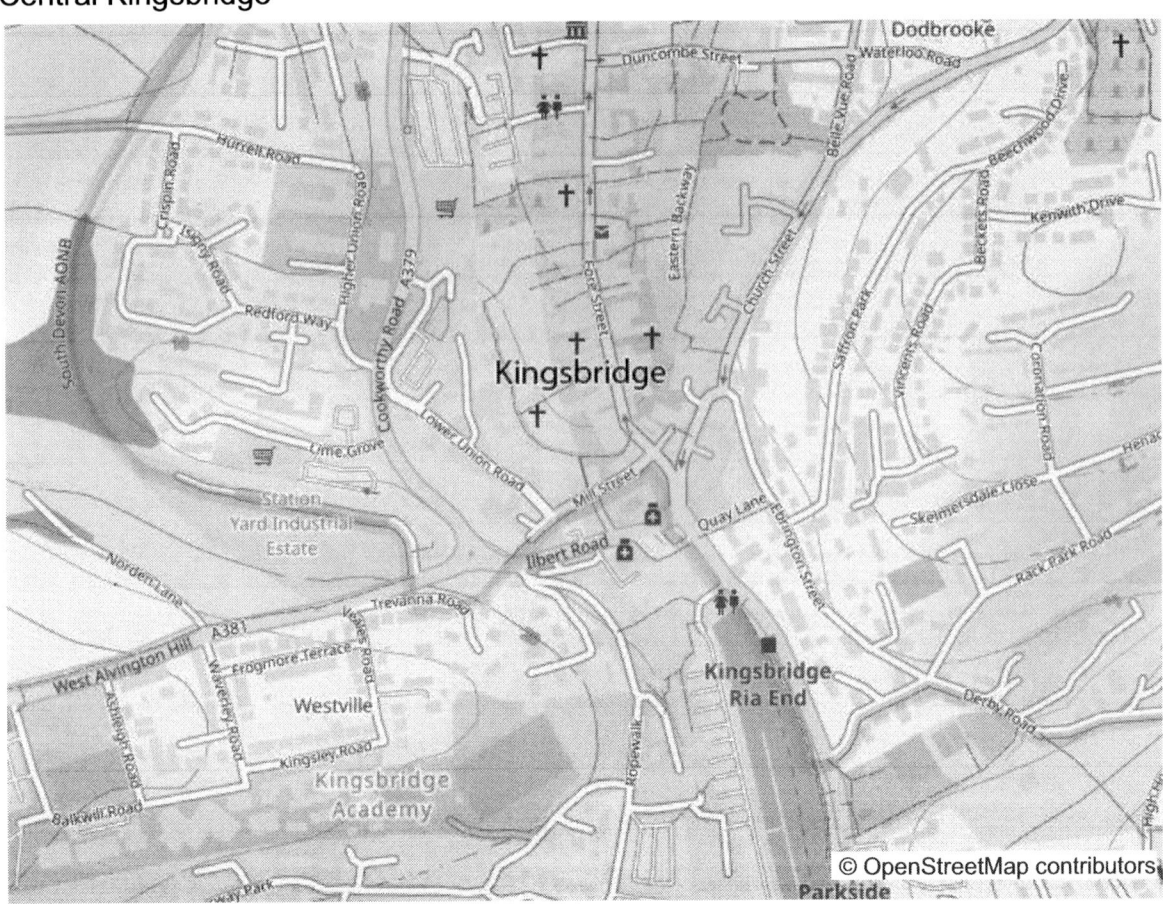

Salcombe area

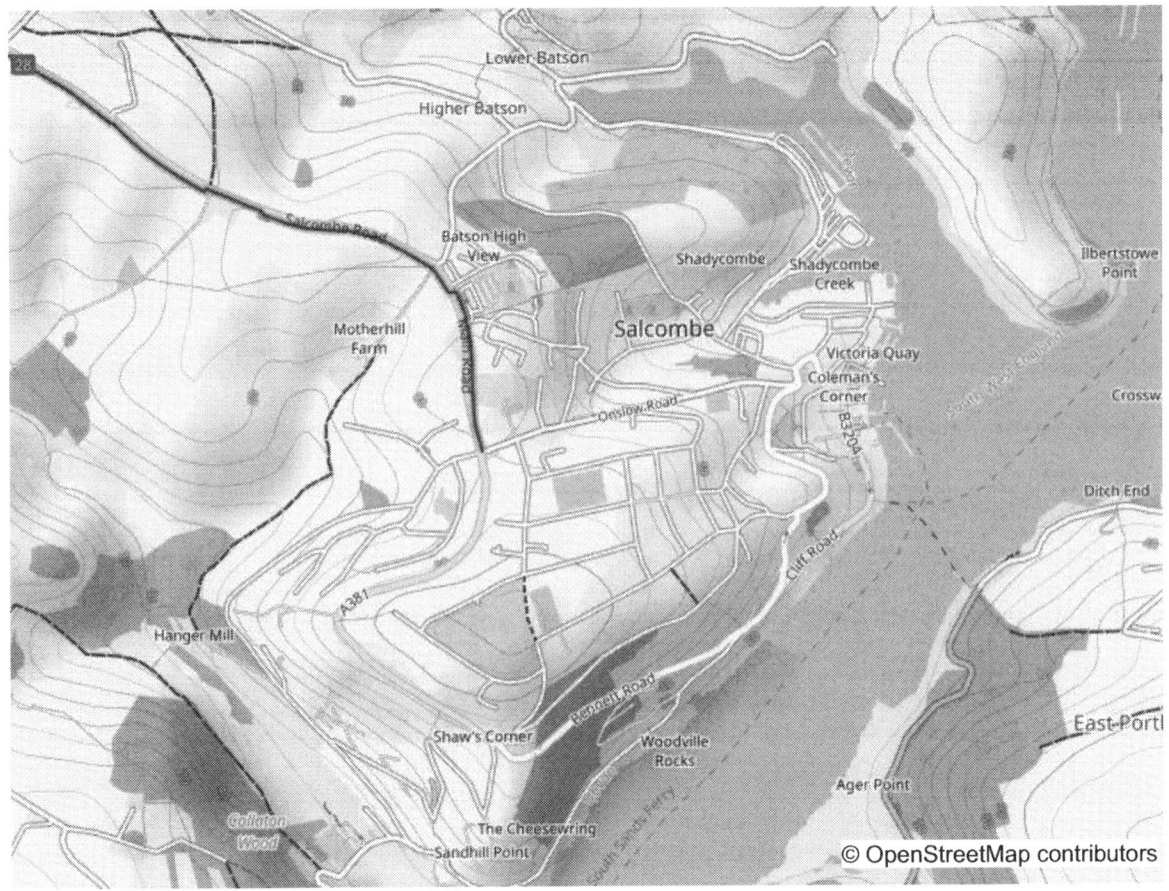

Printed in Great Britain
by Amazon